D0187509

ACTON SOCIETY STUDIES: 2

Constraints and Adjustments
in British Foreign Policy

ACTON SOCIETY STUDIES

Constraints and Adjustments in British Foreign Policy

edited by
MICHAEL LEIFER

LONDON·GEORGE ALLEN & UNWIN LTD
Ruskin House   Museum Street

ISBN 0 04 327039 5 hardback
     0 04 327040 9 paper

Printed in Great Britain
in 10 on 11 point Plantin type
by Alden & Mowbray Ltd
at the Alden Press, Oxford

CONTRIBUTORS

CORAL BELL
is Professor of International Relations in the University of
Sussex. She was until recently Reader in International
Relations at the London School of Economics.

DAVID COOMBES
has taught in the Universities of Hull, Reading and
Amsterdam. He is Professor of European Studies at
Loughborough University of Technology, and a Research
Fellow at Political and Economic Planning.

JOHN DAY
has held a Joseph Hodges Choate Fellowship at Harvard
University, and is currently Senior Lecturer in Politics in
the University of Leicester.

GEOFFREY GOODWIN
is Montague Burton Professor of International Relations
in the University of London, at the London School of
Economics.

ALAN JAMES
is a former Rockefeller Research Fellow in International
Organization at the Institute of War and Peace Studies,
Columbia University, New York, and currently is Reader
in International Relations at the London School of
Economics.

STEPHEN KIRBY
is Lecturer in Political Studies in the Universities of Hull

MICHAEL LEIFER
is a Lecturer in International Relations at the London
School of Economics, and recently was a visiting Professor
of Government at Cornell University, Ithaca, New York.

PETER LYON
is Secretary to the Institute of Commonwealth Studies
in the University of London, and Senior Lecturer in
Commonwealth Studies.

F. S. NORTHEDGE
has been on the staff of the International Relations
Department of the London School of Economics since
1949. He became Professor and Head of the Department
in 1968.

AVI SHLAIM
is a Lecturer in Politics in the University of Reading and
convenor of the post-graduate course on Political
Integration in Western Europe in the Graduate School
of Contemporary European Studies.

LOUIS TURNER
graduated from Trinity College Oxford in Psychology
and Philosophy, and has since held a Research Fellowship
in the Department of Sociology, University of
Salford.

JOHN WILLIAMSON
is Professor of Economics in the University of Warwick.
He has taught at Princeton University and the University
of York, and in 1967 was visiting Professor of Economics
at the Massachusetts Institute of Technology. From
1968–70 he was an economic consultant to H.M.
Treasury.

ACKNOWLEDGEMENTS

The idea of commissioning this volume originated with Trevor Smith, research adviser to the Acton Society Trust. Two members of the Trust's staff materially assisted its production: Miss Jackie Eames typed the final manuscript, and Mrs Susan Rayner prepared it for publication.

CONTENTS

Introduction

The imperatives of circumstance and the force of domestic demands place a heavy burden on national government in a time when its exercise is increasingly constrained by external factors. An awareness of such constraints and the interrelationship between international environment and domestic condition prompted the Trustees of the Acton Society to commission a series of studies into the changing nature of Britain's international position. These studies form the substance of this book.

The practice of British foreign policy since 1945 falls into two distinct periods. The first, spanning the decade following the end of the Second World War, was one in which great power standing was assumed, without much serious examination, and saw the transformation of Empire into Commonwealth and the creation of a Western European military alliance, albeit with substantial American involvement and underpinning. The second period began after the Suez adventure in 1956, which signalled abruptly a diminished capacity and demotion to lesser rank in the international order. Prestige was still cherished and sought after in the form of nuclear symbolism, but slogans about top tables, however relevant to the pursuit of domestic political advantage, hardly concealed a basic strategic dependence.

For a brief moment, the Labour administration of Mr Wilson indulged in a measure of romanticism and nostalgia, but the cold force of economic circumstances and notable diplomatic failures impelled a reappraisal. A succeeding Conservative government sustained a dedication to a European policy yet sought also the revival of international standing. In the light of a process of evident adjustment, these essays look at problem areas in British foreign policy and seek, in particular, to point to factors of constraint which have served and persist still to constrict its practice.

Alan James looks at the concept of national sovereignty and discusses its relevance to contemporary politics. He concludes that, despite nuclear weapons, the interdependence between countries in the fields of trade, monetary co-operation and aid, and the emergence of supranational institutions, sovereignty is real and meaningful to the modern State. He also points out that, logically, the ultimate goal of the European Economic Community implies loss of sovereignty for its constituent members.

Following this, Professor Goodwin considers British foreign

policy since 1945, the decline of British influence in world affairs, and the gradual realization that only within Europe can Britain hope to wield influence in the future. The changes that entry into Europe will necessitate for Britain are outlined by Professor Coombes and Avi Shlaim. They spell out the constitutional and administrative changes which will be needed and assess the prospects of common Community institutions replacing the authority of national governments.

The decline in Britain's status as a world power has shown itself most in defence planning and changing relationships with the other powers. One persistently recurring problem of defence planning has been the size and nature of British commitment to the North Atlantic Treaty Organization. Stephen Kirby explains the role that Britain has played in NATO, American influence on NATO's development, and the implications of the Strategic Arms Limitation Talks and Herr Brandt's *rapprochement* with his Eastern neighbours.

The retreat of British power from South-East Asia has posed another recurrent problem in defence planning. Britain's role in Asia was a legacy of the imperial past, and Dr Michael Leifer traces the development of events both in Asia and at home which have led to British withdrawal. He considers the present policy of limited presence east of Suez, and gives reasons for Britain's pursuance of this policy.

The themes of the next two chapters are the changes in relationships which have influenced British foreign policy. Professor Bell looks at the so-called 'special relationship' between Britain and the United States, its origins, and the constraints that this relationship has imposed on foreign policy because it has served as a framework for decisions, ruling out some of the theoretical options. Since 1946 the most visible common interest between the two countries has undoubtedly been strategic; British policy has assumed that American backing for Western European defence is essential. With Britain now looking towards Europe, the American–Soviet *détente* and the possible withdrawal of American forces from Europe, Professor Bell considers the future of the special relationship but concludes that it will probably persist for some time to come.

Britain's change in role from a colonial power to a position as head of a commonwealth of independent nations is discussed by Dr Peter Lyon. The problems which remain after decolonization, in terms of trade, financial aid and the need for Britain to consider not only her own interests but also those of the Commonwealth, all have implications for foreign policy. British relationships with Commonwealth countries have also complicated the issue of British entry into the Common Market, and Dr Lyon suggests some of the changes which EEC membership might make in terms of the aid and investment available for developing nations.

The case of Rhodesia provides an instance of failure for British foreign policy. John Day explains the motives of both the Rhodesian and British governments for taking the course of action they chose; the nationalist pride of the Rhodesian government which saw independence granted to black African countries whilst they were denied it, and the self-respect and care for prestige which obliged Britain to make constitutional demands in conformity with her principles. He chronicles the long drawn-out discussions both before and after Rhodesia's illegal declaration of independence, and the reasons why Britain has continued to try to bring Rhodesia back to constitutional legality.

Chapters IX and X look at the economic aspects of sovereignty and the extent to which policy is shaped by international factors in the business field. Professor Williamson deals with the obligations inherent in membership of international organizations and the rationale for international supervision of individual countries' economic policies. Louis Turner looks at the implications for the British economy of the growth of large multi-national business corporations. Various students have found that the activities of foreign corporations exert a neutral or beneficial effect on the economy, but objections to the multi-nationals have been raised on political grounds. Turner discusses the validity of these objections and the extent to which any country can afford to reject foreign investment.

In the final chapter in this collection, Professor Northedge considers Britain's place in the world now that she can no longer be regarded as a super-power, although British politicians of all colours are reluctant to relinquish the right to be consulted on world affairs. He analyses the grounds for Britain's claim to be included in the deliberations of the mighty, as he puts it, and argues that although these grounds may exist in theory, the hard unpalatable fact is that Britain has not the resources necessary to keep up the commitments involved in being a super-power. The conclusion to be drawn from this is that Britain's future must lie in Europe if she is to have any say in world affairs.

Naturally, a number of these chapters focus on policy towards Europe, but not to the exclusion or neglect of other significant areas of British interest and international economic factors which bear on this country's domestic difficulties. These chapters, in the range of their coverage and in the problems they discuss, will provide a perspective for assessing the future international position of a Britain whose adjustment to changing external circumstances is continuing year by year.

I The Contemporary Relevance of National Sovereignty

ALAN JAMES

The irrelevance of national sovereignty is a popular contemporary theme. But it is evident, even from a brief survey of some of its expressions, that those who espouse it are not agreed on what it is they all hold to be irrelevant. Someone speaking in these terms with reference to the danger of war, for example, might well mean by 'sovereignty' the right of individual States to possess armies and armaments; but a similar statement about sovereignty made in the context of a discussion regarding Britain and the Common Market probably employs the term to indicate the idea of economic autarky. These two instances, besides illustrating just part of the range of meanings given to the word 'sovereignty', also draw attention to the ambiguity which attaches to the word 'irrelevant'. Some use it to suggest the undesirability of an existing state of affairs; others to emphasize that the situation referred to no longer exists, or, if it does, is now unimportant. Correspondingly 'relevance' is used to mean either desirability or importance. This leads to a further point: claims regarding the relevance or otherwise of national sovereignty can by no means be assumed to be the result of disinterested enquiry; for sovereignty is an emotive word, and therefore valuable for tendentious purposes. The two assertions given above illustrate this, for it is clear that they introduce the concept of sovereignty in an endeavour to increase the attractiveness and force of the causes which they so obviously desire to advance.

It might be thought that one way of coping with the confusion which arises from sovereignty's semantic flexibility would be to ask how States use it of themselves and their behaviour. But this is not an immediately profitable line of enquiry. For it soon becomes clear that States, like others, sometimes try to take advantage of the term's almost reverential connotations by employing it as a support for a variety of policies. President de Gaulle, for example, complained in 1966 that the presence of North Atlantic Treaty Organization (NATO) forces in his country – albeit with permission – diminished the sovereignty of France. In reply, President Johnson professed to be puzzled by this point of view, saying that he had always seen the arrangement as a wise and far-seeing exercise of French sovereignty. Earlier in the decade, Rumania spoke on more than one occasion of how the taking of decisions on the principle of unanimity in both COMECON and the Warsaw Pact was a necessary consequence and bulwark of the members' sovereignty. After the Czechoslovakian crisis of 1968, the Soviet Union explained that it was nothing short of slanderous to suggest, as was being widely done in the West, that Socialist countries favoured the idea of limited sovereignty. Indeed, the movement of Soviet and some other East European troops into fraternal territory was designed above all to defend the full sovereignty of Socialist Czechoslovakia. And in the current debate on Britain's future *vis à vis* the Common Market, government spokesmen go to considerable pains to argue that entry would present no real threat to British sovereignty, properly conceived.

None the less, it is possible to enquire into what sovereignty means when States and analysts use it to refer, if only by implication, to the quality which distinguishes members of the international society from other notional entities. Manifestly, there is such a distinguishing quality for the right to participate in international life – to send and receive ambassadors, make treaties, join international organizations, and so on – is not open to everyone. Moreover, what entitles a State to do these things is widely summed up, in both general and official parlance, by the word 'sovereignty'. The United Nations' Charter, for example, proclaims the sovereignty of its members, meaning not that this condition is conferred on States by virtue of their membership in the UN, but that such membership is, in principle, open only to those who are already sovereign. Equally, the rights and duties of general international law apply only to those States who possess sovereignty: the States making up a federation, for example, do not enjoy such 'sovereign rights', nor are they subject to the duties which attach to sovereign States. In short, sovereignty is the criterion – the sole criterion – that must be satisfied before a state can join international society. It may be, and is, employed in a variety of other ways; but none of them, it is believed, is as fundamental as this – which is, therefore, the meaning it will be given in this essay.

So used, sovereignty has two sides, the first of which is supremacy. This aspect of the matter once reflected the existence within the State of a single superior, an ultimate fount of authority – the sovereign. Nowadays such monarchs as remain are far from absolute, and in most States it is very hard to identify, with any assurance, that person or body which is supreme. But the location of sovereignty is distinguishable from its possession by the State, seen as a whole, and an entity termed 'sovereign' is still supreme as a unit of government, as a distinct constitutional system. Within its territory, the sovereign State is the ultimate, and therefore the supreme, authority. It may be that other States enjoy legal rights in that territory, and may even be entitled to exercise a measure of jurisdiction there, but they do so on the basis, not of their own authority, but of a competence which has been granted them by the State concerned. Without a sovereign State's specific permission, no other State or institution may exercise governmental functions within its boundaries, or speak or act on its behalf in external matters. Being sovereign, a State is the sole guardian of its constitution and of the prerogatives which flow therefrom; it is, in constitutional terms, supreme. This does not mean that it is immune to pressure, and to the suggestions of some States it may be particularly susceptible. But this does not detract from its constitutional situation, and, for as long as supreme authority is to be found within a State, that State may be said to be sovereign – and no less so than in the days of absolute monarchy. Its internal arrangements may have altered, but not its position as an entity without a constitutional superior.

The second aspect of sovereignty – also the correlate of the first – is separateness. A sovereign State is one which, while almost certainly having many contacts and links with others of its kind, including a network of legal rights and duties, is none the less essentially distinct from them. It has its own governmental structure, which is not a part of any larger such arrangement; it exists alongside other sovereign 'persons', related to them, maybe, but constitutionally separate. This is a necessary consequence of the State's supremacy, for an ultimate authority, by definition, cannot be a part of or subordinate to another; it must be separate. Equally, a State which is separate from all others is, by virtue of that fact, in sole control of its domain: being on its own, it cannot but be supreme. Supremacy and separateness are therefore inextricably intertwined, each of them expressing, with a different emphasis, that constitutional self-containment which is the core and condition of sovereignty.[1]

From this it follows that sovereignty is an absolute and not a relative concept. There may be marginal cases and obscure situations, making it hard to say whether or not a State is constitutionally self-contained; but in principle it can only be one thing or the other. If it is not separate and supreme in constitutional terms, it lacks sovereignty. If it does enjoy these attributes, this is conclusive as to its sovereign status, no matter what its size or strength. It also follows that sovereignty cannot be divided into disconnected compartments, such as internal and external sovereignty. It is possible, as has been indicated, to look at sovereignty in rather different ways, emphasizing, as is appropriate, supremacy or separateness – its internal and external effects. But these effects flow from a single source: sovereignty, which is a status applicable to the State as a whole and only as a whole. If, therefore, events result in a State losing its separateness in international life, it has by the same token lost its supremacy inside its frontiers; there is no such thing as internal sovereignty independent of external sovereignty – not, that is, when 'sovereignty' refers to a State's constitutional status. In different contexts sovereignty will have different consequences, but sovereignty itself is indivisible.

It may be helpful to illustrate the argument hypothetically. A colony or a province which is part of a federal system is clearly distinguishable from its metropolitan power or federal State on the ground of its lack of sovereignty. It is a subordinate part of a wider constitutional structure and, accordingly, is not supreme in its territory. Putting it the other way around, the colony or province is not supreme, and hence it is not a separate unit. If, however, the metropolitan or federal State chooses, for whatever reason, to cut its constitutional ties with the area concerned (without any other such ties being established from a different direction), the process results in the creation of a new sovereign State. The former dependent territory is now a distinct constitutional entity, supreme in its sphere. It is subject to the obligations and enjoys the benefits of general international law, may endeavour to set up diplomatic links with other sovereign States, and is eligible to join appropriate international institutions. Unless it has given specific leave, no other State or body can lawfully issue it with directions regarding its internal or international behaviour, for these matters are henceforth within its exclusive competence. In the exercise of its freedom, however, the new State may possibly arrange to enter an existing federation or to merge with another sovereign State. Either action will extinguish its sovereignty, and therefore its status as a member of international society; for the territory in question will no longer be constitutionally separate and supreme.

To be sovereign is, therefore, in a double sense, a matter of considerable consequence, or so it would seem from the foregoing analysis. Nowadays, however, this conclusion comes under a good deal of fire, on the ground that it is outdated to speak in terms of supremacy and separateness. It is allowed that this may once have been the nature of social reality at the international level, and also that States still assert that their situation has not changed in any fundamental respect. But it is argued that, when States speak in this way, they are doing little more than the equivalent of whistling to keep their spirits up, trying to convince both themselves and others that their sovereignty is unimpaired, and yet at the same time and by the same token advertising their anxiety about it; for, it is said, the substantive facts of international life have changed greatly over the last fifty years, especially in the second half of this period, stripping States' claims to sovereignty of much of their earlier significance. Thus, while the student of international relations should note in passing that his subject still proceeds on the formal basis of State sovereignty, it is much more important for him to take account of the fact that, in practical terms, States are no longer separate and supreme, nor the only objects of interest in the international system. In this sense sovereignty has become irrelevant.

Three general points are often made in support of this argument. The first is that the constitutional supremacy of the State within its frontiers is now vastly less meaningful than formerly, on account of the ability of outside forces to subvert its authority or even destroy it completely. To use the phraseology popularized by Professor Herz,[2] the territorial State has lost its impermeability. The clearest evidence of this is to be found at the military level, where the development of nuclear weapons and delivery systems has brought all States within range of a degree of carnage which was unimaginable just a generation ago. Here, therefore, is an irresistible intruder, a huge destructive power which can definitely not be stopped at the gate. Of course, attention is being paid by the two super-States to means of defence against nuclear weapons, and a limited deployment of anti-ballistic missiles has already taken place. But even these technological giants have had to accept that, given their present knowledge and resources, they are unable to provide themselves with anything like an adequate protective screen against a nuclear assault; and, in the unlikely event of their being able to erect one, this would still leave all the other members of the international society as exposed as before.

But it is not just in military terms that the sovereign State has become permeable. Analysts who conclude that sovereignty is now irrelevant also point to the fact that outsiders relying largely on psychological means have a much better chance than formerly of harassing régimes they dislike and working for their replacement by ones more in accord with their own political complexion. This reflects both the great improvement in communications which has taken place in the present century and the dependence of governments, whether or not formally expressed in democratic procedures, on the support of their subjects. Moreover, the ideological polarization which has occurred in recent decades, together with the growing unpopularity and difficulty of straightforward annexation, has meant that considerable use is made of these upsetting opportunities. Thus there has been a steep decline in the practical importance of the theory that a country's choice of government is entirely its own affair. International politics can and often do impinge on the domestic scene in a far-reaching way, so contributing to the conclusion that the State can no longer be regarded as supreme. Not only is it the case that its ramparts can be scaled; they can also be undermined.

The second ground on which it is argued that sovereignty has lost much of its relevance draws attention to the extent to which States nowadays rely on one another for the satisfaction of their wants and needs. The suggestion is that they are interdependent to a degree which makes a mockery of their separateness. In diplomatic terms this finds expression in the efforts of all States, including the greatest, to secure support for their policies and, if at all possible, to avoid being in a small minority; the manoeuvring which goes on in the General Assembly of the United Nations prior to a vote is illustrative of this concern. At the economic level the interdependence of States provides material for elementary lessons about the importance of international trade and for observations such as the one which has it that when the American economy sneezes the British catches cold. The same condition is also reflected in the intricate web of agreements, both bilateral and multilateral, which channel economic aid and technical assistance to the numerous needy, and in the *ad hoc* and permanent arrangements for monetary co-operation which have been so notable a feature of the international scene since 1945. The comment that, in respect of economic matters, Britain has not been sovereign at any time during this period could equally well be applied to most other members of the international society, so sensitive have States become to economic developments outside their borders. It is also the case that many States lean heavily on foreign sources for their defence, obtaining weapons and training missions from abroad, and relying on outside help in their hour of peril.

The interdependence of States is clearly reflected in the institutions which have been established to facilitate their co-operation. And this leads to a third, and rather different, line of approach regarding the contemporary irrelevance of national sovereignty, one which emphasizes the devaluation or diminution of sovereignty by indirect rather than direct means. It does so by underlining the importance, as compared with States, of the new institutional actors on the international stage, of bodies such as NATO, the European Economic Community (the Common Market), the World Bank, and the UN. Attention is also paid to non-official agencies of trans-national significance, like some large business corporations. The argument is that it is in these notional entities that the really important decisions are now being made, and that he who wishes to understand what is going on in the world should therefore look in this direction instead of at the traditional components of international society. Sovereign States will continue to loom large in the life of individuals subject to them, just as the constituent parts of a federal State have a sizeable impact on the local inhabitants. But their sovereignty, while still of ceremonial and psychological significance, is inescapably losing its substance. The needs of the modern world are overtaking the State, depriving it, *de facto*, of its supremacy and separateness through the establishment of over-arching institutions.

So far as the last of these three arguments is concerned, it can readily be admitted that institutions of one kind or another now play a significant role on the international scene. A good part of the military capability of both East and West is deployed through multilateral agencies, and the economic life of Western Europe is increasingly affected by decisions taken at the headquarters of the Common Market in Brussels. The UN has little tangible strength, but its voice is by no means without diplomatic weight, and some of its specialized agencies, such as the World Bank and the International Monetary Fund, are able to exercise a real influence in the areas of their concern. It is also the case that multi-national corporations are becoming a factor to be reckoned with in a number of economies.

All this, however, is a far cry from a situation where sovereign States are more the passive than the prime elements in international life, more the pieces to be moved than the movers; for, although a wide range of important issues comes within the competence of international bodies, the questions remaining solely or essentially in national hands are far greater, in terms both of number and of moment. Moreover, even with regard to those matters which are affected by international decisions, it must be noted that the change is chiefly one of procedure. The manner in which international business is conducted has altered a good deal, but this has not also produced a different set of principals or transformed the outlook of the old ones. To all intents and purposes, States are in firm control of the bodies they have established, and, when acting as members, they interpret an organization's interest very much in the light of their own preoccupations and desires – which is only to be expected, in view of the fact that institutions are set up to serve the aims of their founders.

When, for example, the General Assembly or the Security Council speaks, the world is hearing, not simply from the UN, but also from that group of States which for the moment constitutes a sufficient majority in favour of the cause in question. Equally, those to whom the resolution is addressed will, in deciding what attention it deserves, pay heed, not just nor even chiefly to its institutional inscription, but also to the identity of those supporting it and the zeal with which they have done so. The UN is the formal actor, but its action is determined by essentially self-regarding States. Likewise, decisions made by NATO cannot go beyond the degree of agreement which exists among its members. The Common Market too, although it places a significant measure of influence in the hands of its independent commission, and may permit its Council of Ministers to act by majority vote on a number of important matters, is finding that in practice it is restricted to what its individual members will allow.

The hold of States on their perceived interests has not, therefore, been substantially loosened by the new arrangements; institutions are not yet consuming their creators. And, just as States are still clearly in command so far as inter-governmental bodies are concerned, the same is also true, generally speaking, of their relations with even the strongest commercial organizations. Accordingly, there seems little strength in the argument that, as a result of the appearance of new actors, States have lost, or are in the process of losing, their predominance on the world stage. They are still, not just in form but also in point of fact, overwhelmingly the most important members of the international cast. If sovereignty has been deprived of much of its value, it is not through subversion from above.

The second argument purporting to show the contemporary irrelevance of sovereignty bases itself on the interdependence of the units which make up the modern world. It does not deny their primacy when compared with other international actors, but claims that this primacy should be seen in collective terms, as to all intents and purposes States have lost their individuality. Affairs of all sorts are now so interlocked that it is unhelpful and unrealistic to conceive of international society as made up of separate entities.

As to the premise of this assertion there can be little dispute: States undoubtedly are interdependent, in the sense that they rely on each other for the alleviation of many of their anxieties and the meeting of many of their requirements. But the conclusion which is drawn from this is very questionable, for it does not follow that interconnectedness necessarily destroys the identity of those involved. The members of a family may be heavily dependent on each other, but that does not mean that they are thereby unable also to act as individuals; they continue to have minds and resources of their own, and may be expected to behave accordingly. Equally, at the international level, the mutual involvement of States must not be assumed to have eroded their essential separateness. And, in fact, this does not seem to have occurred. As the term 'interdependence' itself implies, the co-operation which has become increasingly imperative is between distinct units. Discrete decision-making structures are still easily identifiable, and it is upon their functioning that international intercourse depends. States continue to decide on what they can afford by way of concessions and on what their interests require that they insist. They may be, and often are, subject to considerable pressures and constraints, but this does not diminish their basic responsibility for their own conduct.

Britain's position is a good case in point. Her reliance on international trade and the role of sterling as a reserve currency produce a close connection between her affairs and those of others. In the past her economic strength prevented this from being a source of embarrassment, but since the First World War the situation has been altering – to Britain's disadvantage. Now she is much more vulnerable to economic forces and pressures; a particularly vivid illustration of this is the way in which, in 1956, she was induced by the United States to call off her assault on Suez. Similarly, in diplomacy she finds it prudent to pay much more attention than before to the views of her fellows, and in the military field she is very conscious of her reduced strength in relation to the super-powers. None the less, the fact remains that it is up to her to take her own decisions in international as in domestic matters – a right which has been underlined by the present Conservative administration. Undoubtedly, this is a much more confined and worrying process than formerly, but it is one where she alone is in charge. And in this she is typical: a sovereign State, however poor, and notwithstanding its connections with others on many important issues, is entitled to make its own choices. Thus a realistic analysis of international politics must take large account of the activities of individual States. Inter-dependence has not destroyed constitutional independence. The separate, sovereign State has by no means withered away.

The remaining argument about the irrelevance of national sovereignty places a big question mark against this claim, suggesting that it overlooks the significance of another new factor: the State's loss of impermeability. This is seen in its present exposure to external threats, both military and political, which is thought to undermine the importance which might otherwise be attached to a demonstration of the State's continued decision-making viability; now unable to maintain its supremacy, the State can no longer be regarded as sovereign. This approach, however, is suspect on several grounds. One of them concerns the impact of permeability. It cannot be denied that all States are now within reach of nuclear destruction, nor that today there are numerous opportunities for indirect aggression and no shortage of justifications for embarking on it. But this is a long way from saying that States are constantly subject to painful reminders of their lack of a hard shell. In practical terms it is generally true that the members of international society have little need to be preoccupied with their permeability; the vast majority of governmental changes take place as a result of internal political developments rather than of outsiders' plots. At the military level, the effect of being permeable is even less marked. The only States who have nuclear weapons pointing in their direction are those who also possess them or who are closely allied with a nuclear power, and the consequence of this mutual threat, at least in the existing technological context, is stalemate. Thus day-to-day international transactions show no sign of the theoretical alterations wrought by nuclear weapons, except that as between the nuclear powers there is greater caution at times of crisis.

None the less, it can plausibly be argued that possibilities and opportunities are not unimportant just because advantage is not taken of them; and that, in this particular case, the international society must be considered to have undergone a drastic and fundamental change on account of the equally drastic and fundamental threats to which its members are now open.

But this points to a further and more far-reaching criticism of the argument that sovereignty has been undermined by the State's loss of its hard shell. For this assumes that not long ago the hard shell was intact, that permeability is a mid-twentieth-century phenomenon. This is very questionable. Endeavours to upset a government by way of an externally controlled idcological and propaganda barrage, for example, are not at all new; they were a central aspect of the religious controversies and wars of the sixteenth and early seventeenth centuries. Following the French Revolution of the late eighteenth century, the fear of revolutionary doctrine played a key role in the international politics of at least the next fifty years, and the idea of national self-determination has found frequent and effective use throughout the present century. It may be allowed that psychological warfare has in recent years been raised to sophisticated heights, but as against this it can be noted that governments have also taken advantage of technological developments to improve their equipment for combating it. What has been seen, therefore, is not a new weapon, but the refinement of a very old one. States are not in this respect subject to a threat which they have never encountered before.

The same is true of military developments. The destructiveness of nuclear weapons and the range given them by modern rockets may seem to have introduced an entirely new dimension to international life, and in a sense they have clearly done so. But to suggest that they have cracked the foundations of the State's military impermeability is to imply that before the nuclear era invaders could always be stopped at the moat – a metaphor which indicates both the Anglo-Saxon character of the argument and its essential flaw; for, while it may have been valid for Britain up to the advent of the aeroplane, and for the United States until inter-continental missiles were developed, it has little relevance for most States. Neither surrounded by water nor set apart by the oceans, they have for long – since the birth of the modern State system – been within reach of their neighbours' armies, and also those of more distant powers, and from time to time have suffered indignities and depredations at their hands; a Pole would be unlikely to talk about the previous impermeability of his country, nor even the more geographically-advantaged Frenchman or Dane. What nuclear weapons have done, therefore, is not to undermine military impermeability but, for most States, to underline their existing permeability. An additional means of impinging on an enemy's territory is now available for some, in theory. It is a particularly dramatic and horrifying means, and there are those who feel that, in terms of a typology of armaments or the morality of war, the quantitative aspect is great enough to have produced a qualitative alteration; but, in terms of the susceptibility of States to the use of war as an instrument of policy, there has been no basic change for most.

If, therefore, impermeability is regarded as an essential attribute of sovereignty, it would seem that sovereignty has been irrelevant for a very long time – indeed, since the beginning of the modern international system. Yet this system has throughout its life professed to be based on the idea of sovereignty, in that this is the criterion which must be met before a State can become a member. From this it may be concluded, either that international life has always proceeded on a false premise, or that sovereignty does not involve impermeability – not, that is, when the term is used to convey that which distinguishes the States who participate in international society from those who are beyond the pale. There can be little doubt that the student of international politics, concerned to understand the way in which international life works and not to lay down the law about the proper uses of words, should prefer the latter conclusion. Sovereignty, it is evident, is not incompatible with permeability.

In general terms, therefore, national sovereignty would seem still to be a relevant concept. None of the three broad lines of criticism which have been considered will stand up to close examination. It cannot be said that all States have been subject, in roughly equal measure, to developments which have undermined their sovereignty. However, an important question which remains is whether some of them – the lesser brethren – can be said to be sovereign in anything other than name. The argument here is that a number of States are so weak, either absolutely or in relation to a larger neighbour, that it is unrealistic to speak of them as in supreme control of their own affairs, or effectively separate from all their fellow members of the international society. What, it might be (and sometimes is) asked, is the point of calling Iceland a sovereign State, when its population does not exceed that of a moderately sized British town; or Lesotho, which is not only small and poor, but is also wholly surrounded by South Africa? The same question can be put in respect of States of a different order of magnitude, but whose political freedom is severely restricted by reason of their geographical location – Czechoslovakia, for example, or Cuba.

There can be no doubt that it is not unusual for such States to find that their theoretical freedom of manoeuvre is virtually non-existent, in the sense that it would be highly imprudent and perhaps even physically impossible to take advantage of it. Cuba, in 1962, was the least of the cast in the drama which arose out of the presence of Soviet missiles on her soil. In 1968 Czechoslovakia discovered, at great cost, how limited was the control which she formally exercised over her internal affairs. Lesotho cannot but be aware of the need to step very warily in all matters of interest to the Republic of South Africa. And Iceland must know that she does well to lead a quiet international life. However, what is chiefly interesting about weak States is, not the more obvious concomitants of their weakness of the kind which have been mentioned, but the degree of freedom which they often enjoy, despite their clear lack of strength. Hence it is in a way remarkable that Cuba, but a comparatively short distance off the American coast, should have been able to defy and annoy the United States with such impunity since Castro's assumption of power in 1959. Czechoslovakia has not been so fortunate *vis à vis* the Soviet Union, but it can be very plausibly maintained that she is in a much more favourable position than any of the constituent republics of the Soviet federal State. Lesotho, too, gets very different treatment from her enveloping neighbour than does South-West Africa, the UN's interest in the latter notwithstanding. And ten years ago Iceland was able to carry her 'fisheries war' with no less a maritime power than Britain to what was, in all but name, a victorious conclusion.

This type of evidence suggests that the sovereignty of small States is by no means as nominal or irrelevant as is commonly supposed. It is not the case that the profitable use of sovereign privileges and attributes always requires considerable resources. Nor does relative strength provide larger States with a reliable guide to the political wisdom of strong action against a smaller neighbour. What a State does to a minority or a turbulent province within its own borders is usually regarded as entirely its own affair; but aggressive moves against a sovereign State, however troublesome it is and however clearly within the other State's sphere of influence, immediately become everybody's business. Thus the weak are far from helpless; indeed, many commentators have observed that in some circumstances a small State has more freedom of action than a super-power, and some have argued that such disorder as exists in the world is partly due to the political difficulties nowadays in the way of the great acting as international disciplinarians. Perhaps, therefore, the sovereignty of the small is not less but more meaningful than formerly; certainly, it would seem to be incorrect to conclude that discrepancies of power have gravely diminished the significance which should be attached to the sovereignty of the smaller members of international society.

In this connection it should be noted that small nations and territories have been not at all deterred from seeking sovereignty on account of their size. In the belt of new States established in Eastern Europe following the First World War, few could be regarded even as medium powers, and all of them lay in the shadows of Germany and the Soviet Union. That these two local colossi were both *hors de combat* at the time may have encouraged those between them to assume sovereign Statehood, but it is far from a complete explanation of their action; during the next twenty-five years many of them had very unhappy experiences, resulting in some fatalities and a number of serious disablements. None the less, this did not sour the appetite for sovereignty: of the seventy-six states who have been added to the UN's fifty-one original members since 1945, a large majority consists of entities which have only become sovereign since the Second World War. Nor can it be recorded that those of the lesser fry who now enjoy this condition show any sign of wanting to abandon it. Disappointments there have certainly been, and also some disillusion; but there is no desire whatsoever to return to the pre-sovereign womb.

Thus, while particular States may have to submit to awkward and perhaps painful limitations, this has no apparent effect on the attractiveness of sovereignty in their eyes. Nor does the possibly increased permeability of States cause them to think of throwing in the sovereign sponge; it is not so soaked as to be indistinguishable from its surrounding elements. Nor has the undoubted interdependence of States obscured their sovereignty. And while an important role is sometimes played by new international actors, they are still in the firm control of their sovereign creators. Sovereignty, therefore, has not been left behind by events, but remains full of meaning.

It would be surprising if it were otherwise. When any society goes to the trouble of establishing a status and setting out the conditions for its conferment, it generally does so, not just to pander to the pride or self-importance of those who will enjoy it, but also with the intention of effecting a real alteration or addition to the group's arrangement. Those on whom the status is bestowed will probably be entitled to do things which would not otherwise be open to them; someone raised to the peerage, for example, or in receipt of ecclesiastical preferment, will acquire new rights in consequence of his own status. And so it is with international society: traditionally, only those who are constitutionally self-contained are eligible to participate in international life, and, at least so far as full participation is concerned, this is still the position. A would-be member State must be able to demonstrate its sovereign status. In this basic respect international society, while developing in all sorts of other ways during the past fifty years, is unaltered, and apparently unaltering.

The widespread failure to recognize sovereignty's continuing practical importance is perhaps due in part to the fact that it is associated, correctly, with such terms as 'theory', 'concept', and 'status', which are often assumed to imply a lack of that down-to-earth significance which alone commands the notice of the 'realistic' student of affairs. But while it is true they have no immediate physical connotations, that does not mean they are without significance; for any society must proceed on the basis of a theory about who can belong, and may well employ a concept to sum up the requirements of membership; these requirements may amount to the enjoyment of a pre-existing status, and those who actually join will in any event by virtue of that act have a status conferred on them – that of membership in the society, in consequence of which they will acquire new rights and duties. In this regard, international society is like all others, and its key structural idea is that of sovereignty.

At this point, however, another source of misunderstanding often enters the scene, with the suggestion that sovereignty is 'only' (a revealing qualification) a 'legal' concept or status, and, worse still, one of international law. The last assertion is incorrect, for sovereignty, as used by States to describe their status, is not to be defined in terms of international law. Their relationship is the reverse of the one indicated, for international law applies to those who are already sovereign, in that they enjoy a particular constitutional position. The relevant law is therefore of the constitutional kind: one has to be separate and supreme in its terms to hold sovereign status, and hence to be eligible for the further status of membership in the international society.[3] And this, contrary to the implication of the pejorative 'only', is by no means unimportant just because it rests on a legal category.

Sovereign statehood is, in fact, widely sought and prized. Those who hold it, however weak and disadvantaged, evidently believe that, in one way or another, but not necessarily in economic terms, they are better off than they would be without it; and those who seek it do so in the expectation that it will lead, in this way or that, to an improvement, not necessarily material, in their lot. The vast colonial empires of 1945 virtually disintegrated in the short space of twenty years as their constituent parts, from India and Indonesia to Togo and Chad, assumed the mantle of sovereignty. This speedily became the done thing, but it also represented a genuine desire to run one's own affairs, come what may. The same impulse moves the Celtic nationalists in Britain, as it did, with a tragic degree of urgency, the Biafrans of Nigeria. Looking at the same phenomenon from a different angle, one can note that Canada, despite her close links with the United States, shows no greater keenness to become its fifty-first constituent member than does Poland to enter the Soviet constitutional fold, the rather different kind of bonds which already exist between the two notwithstanding. Numerous other examples could be given to show that geographical contiguity, even in the presence of other encouraging factors, generally fails to produce a desire for constitutional unity. This is because of the almost universal view that, in essence, sovereignty is the means whereby national identity can best be expressed or preserved, and on account of the accompanying judgement that this is the highest value, the cause which above all others must be served. In this light, national sovereignty is clearly of the utmost relevance.

There are, none the less, many who insist that, although sovereignty will not lie down it is already dead, it is an outmoded basis of social organization for the modern world. This is usually another way of saying that the observer in question does not like sovereignty, and would prefer something else, although it is often unclear whether he appreciates that there are only two real alternatives: chaos, arising from the internal disruption of all States, or a world government emerging from their amalgamation, whether voluntary or induced. In any event, such comments do nothing to destroy the validity of the assertion that, as far as the international society is concerned, sovereignty continues, in both objective and subjective terms, to be of fundamental and far-reaching significance, a concept of enormous practical import. However, the comment which has been referred to could also be making the point that sovereignty is not held in equal regard in all areas of the world, there being one in particular (Western Europe) where States are moving in the direction of its abandonment. This, of course, is not to say that sovereignty is being generally undermined; only that in one region there is alleged to be evidence of such a trend.

This argument is based on the correct claim that the Common Market, together with the European Coal and Steel Community and Euratom, are different, not just in degree, but also in kind from other institutional arrangements among sovereign States. Their theoretical character is summed up as 'supranational', the essence of which lies in an organization's capacity to treat the territory of members as a single whole, as an area without frontiers. Thus an organization of this sort may itself deal directly with natural and notional persons lying within its member States. Any binding decisions which it makes have an immediate impact on the rights and duties of the relevant individuals and concerns, and the officers of the organization may engage in face-to-face relations with such persons and employ legal remedies against them. It is as if the organization was a combined legislature and executive for all those matters within its competence, with its personnel in the position, and holding the authority, of civil servants. Governmental responsibility has been partly transferred from inside the several member States to the supranational organization, which is something in the nature of a federal agency for the function which has been placed under its control.[4]

The crucial difference between international and supranational institutions is well illustrated by the way in which they present their financial claims. The budget of the United Nations, for example, is passed by a two-thirds majority vote of the General Assembly, and each member thereby becomes liable for a predetermined proportion of the total sum. This is a legally binding obligation, but it does not mean that the UN can approach, say, the Treasury in London for Britain's debt or sue for it in the national courts; it must go to the governmental organ representing the State in external affairs, and can go no further. It is then up to the Foreign Office to raise the sum in accordance with the country's constitutional procedures, and, unless these procedures are complied with, it would be improper, in terms of domestic law, for Britain to honour her obligation under international law. This is because obligations arising from the decisions of international institutions do not take automatic effect within member States just by virtue of their source; the legal systems of international and any domestic society, like the political, are distinct, and for those within its territorial jurisdiction the State is the sole authority to which submission must be made. In asking for its money the UN has therefore to knock at the gate and wait outside for an answer. But a supranational institution such as the Common Market is in a fundamentally different position; it can pursue its claims directly with those concerned – with the national treasury for the financial obligation of a member State, and with individual enterprises and persons where they are indebted to the supranational body. In the event of difficulty, it may resort to judicial procedures, and, as supranational law is superior to national, the local courts are not entitled to reject a suit on the ground that it is contrary to the pre-existing law of the land. The supranational institution, in short, acts as would a government in relation to its subjects, treating frontiers as of no more account than internal administrative boundaries.

31

If a group of countries establishes several institutions of this kind, covering all important areas of national life, the end result of their effective operation will clearly be the existence of one sovereign unit in place of the many with which the process started. Each original member will have lost its constitutional supremacy and separateness, being at the close of the day but part of a wider governmental arrangement. It might be that this would be a *de facto* rather than a *de jure* development, perhaps with each of the entities still calling itself a sovereign State (as do the States of the American Union), and possibly even continuing its individual representation in some international activities. None the less, if it was evident that in effect all had merged into a single constitutional set-up, it could properly be said that each had lost its sovereignty. In such a case it would probably be difficult to pinpoint, with any confidence, the exact moment at which this had taken place. The edges of the process might be blurred. But this would not stand in the way of a firm judgement that, by a certain moment in time, a fundamental change had occurred in the relations of the States concerned, converting them from international to intranational. Each of these States would then have to be removed from the membership roster of the international society and replaced by the new sovereign structure which they now composed.

In principle, this is the goal of those who make up the West European communities. They have declared it to be so, and it is also the logical end of their present striving, for a full economic union which permitted its members to choose different diplomatic or strategic paths would be heading for disruption. If, therefore, things go according to plan – and it is a plan which will become increasingly difficult to reverse – the Common Market will lead to a situation where its members lack sovereignty. This may be spoken of as 'a pooling of sovereignty', or as 'preserving all that is good and true in the sovereign condition'; but, however skilful the exegesis, it will be impossible to deny the members' loss of that constitutional status which currently goes by the name of sovereignty, and all that accompanies it. Correspondingly, much may have been gained, and many disadvantages shed; there may be more to be said for the kind of relationship which exists between New York and Pennsylvania than that which now obtains between France and Italy. But it behoves intending passengers on the European bus, such as Britain, to be fully aware of all that might be involved in the journey. The route may be long and winding, and promise some most attractive scenery; but the vehicle has not been designed for the convenience of those who might wish to alight before reaching the advertised destination, and it is supposed to be proof against hijacking. In these circumstances, a long-term view is perhaps even more than usually advisable.

However, supranational arrangements in Western Europe do not yet extend beyond the economic sphere, and the handling of just one governmental function in this way is not enough to make a new sovereign State. Nor is there any sign that the members of the Common Market are hustling or being hustled towards that take-off point which would presage a loss of sovereignty. Community consciousness in economic matters is not so marked that in this respect the Market's headquarters in Brussels is becoming more important than the several national capitals. When that does take place, other strong supranational institutions will almost certainly be needed to co-ordinate and control a whole range of policy, both internal and external, and the outline of a fully fledged federal system will be in sight.

But at the moment six constitutionally self-contained entities remain clearly identifiable, and there is not so much as a whisper of doubt as to the continuing international capacity of each of them. The Common Market's interest is still interpreted in the light of individually perceived national interests rather than vice versa, and in recent years the integration process has lost some of its earlier momentum. Thus in 1966 the Market's independent executive, the Commission, was prevented from adding to its powers, and an understanding was reached which in effect gave members a veto in the Council of Ministers – its political body – so nullifying the Council's formal entitlement to reach most of its decisions by majority vote as from the beginning of that year.

These developments reflect the French desire to keep the Common Market firmly under national control, but this is not to say that its remaining members would otherwise be rushing towards a renunciation of their sovereignty. They may be very willing to go somewhat further along the supranational road, but they are not significantly less keen than France to maintain their status as members of the international society and their consequential right to protect their identity in the way which they think best. Nor are the four potential members weary of sovereignty, and it could be that Britain's presence, in particular, would reinforce the Common Market's current reluctance to progress in a rigorous supranational fashion.

What has happened in Western Europe is that some States have had a look at the possibility of an eventual merger, have indicated their acceptance of the idea, and have taken some steps towards it. But while those steps are of considerable size when compared with the previous situation, they are much less impressive when seen against the ultimate goal; sovereignty may have been called into question, but it is not obviously on the retreat. Elsewhere in the world even such limited developments as this are not to be found. Virtually every other possessor of sovereignty – and, in fact, no exceptions come to mind – regards it as a jewel of great price – indeed, as priceless – in the sense that it is most definitely not for sale; and, for as long as there is an international society, it is difficult to see how its organizing principle could be anything other than sovereignty, and very hard to envisage the sovereign State as holding a less than pre-eminent position.

In the absence of world government, therefore, sovereignty is almost inevitably a concept of the most fundamental importance; it sits four square at the very basis of international relations, and only those who satisfy its requirements may join in with a foreign policy of their own. In their mutual interactions, all States find themselves subject to constraints of one kind or another, which can be enormously frustrating. There is, however, no general, and hardly any particular disposition to abandon sovereignty. This may be accounted for, very plausibly, in terms of the even greater disadvantages which attach to its alternatives. But it is often the case, as may be so here, that those who adopt this line of reasoning to explain their lack of enthusiasm for change also have some private liking for their present condition. The continuing relevance of national sovereignty may thus be rooted in nothing more, and nothing less, than the fact that States like being sovereign.

NOTES

[1] Cf. C. A. W. Manning, *The Nature of International Society* (London, 1962), p. 166.

[2] See J. Herz, *International Politics in the Atomic Age* (New York, 1959), passim.

[3] If there is any argument at this level – as when a colony proclaims its unilateral independence – the traditional procedure is for the *de facto* constitutional position to be taken as decisive. But political factors may stand in the way of the application of this test, as in the case of Rhodesia.

[4] Cf. G. Schwarzenberger, 'Federalism and Supranationalism in the European Communities', in G. W. Keeton and G. Schwarzenberger (eds), *English Law and the Common Market* (London, 1963).

II British Foreign Policy Since 1945: the Long Odyssey to Europe

GEOFFREY GOODWIN

Great Britain entered the Second World War in 1939 as one of six – or at most seven – great powers and the centre of an Empire and Commonwealth of world-wide dimensions. However 'troubled' by the extent to which commitments outran capabilities, Britain was then still a world power, and one of the first magnitude.[1] Yet only thirty years later the authors of the Duncan Report on Britain's Overseas Representation recorded their belief that Britain could only claim to be 'a major power of the second order'.[2] Even that claim seemed to many good 'Europeans' to be pitched too high. Britain's future, they held, lay as a European power, not as a major world power; and, to become the former, she would have to eschew the latter. British foreign policy in the post-1945 period is, in large part, the story of how, reluctantly and painfully, she came to do so.

The disasters in the European theatre in 1940 and in the Asian theatre in 1941–2 mark the beginning of Britain's decline as a world power. By 1943 it was becoming increasingly doubtful whether in the post-war world she could match up to the newly emerging giants, the USA and the Soviet Union. A year later, in January 1944, Lord Halifax, then British Ambassador in Washington, expressed the view at Toronto, following a line of thought voiced by Field-Marshal Smuts the previous November, that in the post-war world, Britain, apart from the rest of the Commonwealth and Empire, could hardly claim equal partnership with what he termed 'the three Titans': the United States, the Soviet Union, and China. He appealed, therefore, for greater Commonwealth unity as 'a condition necessary to that working partnership with the United States, Russia and China to which we look'.[3] The response to his appeal was cool indeed. Yet this conception of Britain as the hub of a worldwide Commonwealth and Empire, enabled thereby to exercise a world role, was to colour British foreign policy for a decade or more after victory had been won and some would hold, well beyond the stage when it had any real justification.

Nevertheless, the immediate picture at the moment of victory in

Europe in May 1945 and in the Far East in the following August did partially conceal the inherent seeds of decline in Britain's standing as a world power. Britain's membership of the 'armed concert' of the victorious great powers, the Security Council of the United Nations, on which the future management of the international system was to rest, was a matter of right, and not, as in the case of France and China, of courtesy. Britain's military power stretched from Western Europe through North Africa and the Middle East to the Asian sub-continent and much of South-East Asia. Exhausted though they might be by the demands of the war, and battered though the British economy undoubtedly was, the achievement of victory and the experience of successfully 'standing alone' in 1940 and 1941 was a source of such pride to the British people that it made them – and their friends – disinclined to question Britain's continuing world status.

Yet the difficulties facing Britain were acute. In Western Europe Britain might be exhorted to 'take the lead' in its reconstruction and in shaping its political future, but Britain's economic capacities were taxed almost beyond endurance merely to furnish her occupation zone in Germany with the bare necessities of life, while Franco-British relations suffered first from de Gaulle's self-conscious assertion of France's newly restored independence, and then from France's punitive attitude towards a defeated Germany.

Confronted by these strains in a devastated Europe and by the westward advance of the Soviet Union into the vacuum of power left by the defeat and division of Germany, hopes that 'Left will look to Left with confidence and hope' had to be jettisoned, and Ernest Bevin, the new Labour government's Foreign Secretary, soon became convinced that American power had to be firmly anchored in Western Europe if the latter's economic health were to be restored, and if an effective counterweight to the Soviet Union were to be fashioned. The omens were not encouraging; at Yalta in February 1945 Roosevelt had indicated that he did not expect American troops to remain in Europe for more than two years after Hitler's overthrow, while Anglo-American relations were under considerable strain over differing occupation policies in Germany and as a result of the McMahon Act of August 1946. This Act effectively cut off Britain (and others) from access to American work in the atomic field, and was seen by Britain as a breach of earlier 'solemn undertakings' between Roosevelt and Churchill. In the Middle East American suspicions of British imperialism and of British oil interests were rife, while Britain's handling of Zionist claims to Palestine aroused vociferous criticism. Yet Soviet policies, especially in Germany, shattered the earlier American inclination to see British imperialism as a greater threat in the post-war world than

Soviet ambitions, and steadily brought American and British occupation policies in Germany into closer rapport. One of the decisive turning points of the immediate post-war years was the economic merger of the American and British occupation zones in Germany into a single bizonia in January 1947.

The offer of Marshall Aid later, in June that year, was seized upon with alacrity by Ernest Bevin, then British Foreign Secretary, who saw that aid as almost the last chance of propping up the toppling economies of Western Europe, not only to restore their economic life, but also to encourage their régimes to stand up to Communist pressures, both internal and external. The Soviet refusal to participate, or to allow her satellites to participate, in the European Recovery Programme deepened, and was to perpetuate, the growing division of Europe, but it was a source of some relief to Bevin himself. The energy shown by Bevin in mobilizing the West European response helped to cement Anglo-American relations. Yet his coolness towards the American European Co-operation Administration's calls for closer economic integration in Western Europe aroused a good deal of criticism in Congress, and was a source of friction also with France, who saw such integration as a means of building a Western Europe less dependent on the United States. Bevin was not unsympathetic to such hopes as long-term goals; indeed, according to Hugh Dalton (then Chancellor of the Exchequer) he 'hoped that the Commonwealth and Western Europe (with Britain as a bridge between both) might grow together. This would make a really great Third Power in the world. But this could only come slowly.'[4] The immediate need was to speed the economic restoration of Western Europe and to secure a more lasting American military commitment, so as to reduce the debilitating sense of insecurity.

This was the main intent behind his speech of 22 January 1948, a speech that led rapidly to the signature of the Brussels Pact on 17 March 1948 for the setting up of a Western Union consisting of Britain, France and the Benelux countries. The Organization for European Economic Co-operation (OEEC) to administer Marshall Aid bore witness to Britain's stake in the prosperity of Western Europe. The Brussels Pact committed her to the defence of Western Europe more firmly than ever before. But those intent on drawing Britain further into Europe found, to their dismay, that she set greater store either by her trans-Atlantic or by her Commonwealth and imperial connections. Close association on an inter-governmental basis was one thing, but full membership of a federated Europe – or of schemes which pointed in that direction – was another. The former might increasingly circumscribe Britain's exercise of her sovereignty, but, by comparison with federalist schemes, that sovereignty itself would remain intact. The vagueness of most federalist schemes also did little to commend them to Bevin, convinced as he was that their attempted realization might cause endless delays at a time when the resolve of Western Europe to resist what was seen as a calculated Communist campaign of subversion[5] might well evaporate unless underpinned by American military as well as economic power. Consequently, although the Western Union formed under the Brussels Pact could serve as a useful military planning prototype, its prime significance was a response to Marshall's plea that 'the countries of Western Europe must show what they were prepared to do for themselves and for each other before asking for further American assistance'.[6]

With the Brussels Pact the seed of the North Atlantic Treaty Organization (NATO) sprouted into life. Yet it was only with the *coup d'état* in Czechoslovakia in February 1948, and more especially the Berlin blockade from June 1948 to May 1949, that most Americans came to accept the need for a closer association of the Atlantic countries. The North Atlantic Treaty of April 1949, which also owed a great deal to Canadian initiatives, was seen as the crown of British foreign policy in the first post-war decade. In the first place, it was the means by which Britain was enabled to harmonize her interests and obligations in Europe with her ties with America and Canada. Secondly, it was from Britain's point of view in nearly every respect the ideal type of international organization. It was inter-governmental, with no federal overtones but with adequate opportunities for great power leadership, and it was of the size and consistency which made for effective collaboration. More important still, NATO was not simply an assurance of American help in the event of war, but the framework for building up an effective counterpoise to Soviet power.

This disposition to give primacy to Atlantic ties was a major factor then in Bevin's insistence, against French pressures, that the OEEC remain strictly an inter-governmental body, in his hostility towards the Council of Europe (and especially towards earlier Franco-Belgian proposals for an elected European Parliamentary Assembly), and in the Labour government's negative response to the Schuman proposals of May 1950 for the pooling of coal and steel resources in Western Europe under a supranational authority. The proposals were generally welcomed as a courageous attempt at Franco-German reconciliation, though privately they raised some anxiety as to the extent they might undermine Britain's 'leadership' in Europe. The crux of the matter, however, was that the Labour government were at that time intent on bringing these 'most vital economic forces' under national control, not on handing them over to a supranational authority which would be 'utterly undemocratic and . . . responsible to nobody'.[7] And, in so far as the proposals implied some loss of British sovereignty in favour of an incipiently federalist approach to West European unity, they were seen as 'not compatible either with our Commonwealth ties, our obligations as a member of the wider Atlantic community, or as a world power'.[8]

This same sense of aloofness characterized reactions in Britain towards the Pleven proposals of October 1950 for a European Defence Community (EDC). The Conservative government which came to power in October 1951, despite the earlier affirmations of commitment to 'Europe' by many of its leaders, declared that Britain was very ready to be associated, but not to join. The need for German rearmament was now accepted, though still intensely disliked; but it was held that only within an Atlantic system, underpinned by American power, could reliable restraints be placed on a rearmed Western Germany. Moreover, a European Defence Community, even if it were to prove acceptable (which was problematic), would distract attention from the building of NATO, which had been given urgency with the outbreak of the Korean War. Furthermore, if unexpectedly successful, it might even portend the creation of a closely knit and inward-looking European Community from which, as even such a committed 'European' as Harold Macmillan wrote in 1951: 'We should be excluded and which would effectively control Europe.' His hope that the Schuman Plan and, more important, the EDC would fail, so that Britain would be in a position to take the initiative in organizing an alternative system, was not shared by the majority of his colleagues in the newly elected Conservative government cabinet. But his belief that European unity might prove as much a threat to Britain as an attraction was frequently voiced privately, as was the fear that a more united Europe without Britain might tend to overshadow and undermine Britain's world stature. At the very least, although Franco-German reconciliation was to be warmly welcomed and the French insistence on effectively integrating – and so containing – West Germany within a West European framework could be understood, the emergence of a Franco-German axis as the basis for European unity was bound to be regarded askance by a Britain still intent on being 'with', but not 'of', Europe.[9]

This traditional ambivalence in Britain's attitudes towards Europe, the feeling that, as Winston Churchill put it in 1930: 'We are with Europe, but not of it. We are linked, but not comprised. We are interested and associated, but not absorbed', had been reinforced by the differing experience of Britain and of the countries of Western Europe during the Second World War. Britain did not suffer from quite that sense of insufficiency engendered by defeat or occupation, which for many Continentals deprived the concept of national sovereignty of much of its appeal and enabled national loyalties more easily to be transmuted into a new European loyalty. This disillusionment with the national State hardly existed in Britain; 'the British experience was of the unexpected solidity and endurance of their particular political community under a heavy battering and its ability to survive despite the loss of all Britain's traditional allies in Western Europe, and the unification of the Continent against her'.[10] In any case, although economic hardship at home and the contraction of Empire abroad made it quite evident that Britain was not of the same stature as the two giants, the USA and the Soviet Union, the image of Britain as a world power persisted; for what Britain lacked in material power could be more than offset, it was supposed, by the wisdom and skill she could still bring to bear, both in world affairs generally (through, for instance, the United Nations), and in influencing the policies of her more powerful ally, the USA, in favour of moderation and restraint.[11]

The traditional pragmatic approach of British foreign policy also told heavily against the more visionary proposals of the European 'federalists'. The suspicion of 'large conceptions and great schemes' and the conviction that 'the true line of progress is to proceed from the particular to the general' (Austen Chamberlain) were shared by Ernest Bevin and most of his advisers. The 'vague and puzzling idealism' of Briand's proposals in 1930 for European unity had provoked in the Foreign Office an attitude of 'caution, but cordial caution'; the reaction to 'woolly and imprecise notions' embodied in Schuman's initiative was very much the same. Once, when confronted by a plea for a five-year plan for Anglo-French collaboration, Bevin is said to have replied to Monsieur Alphand: 'We don't do things like that in our country; we don't have plans; we work things out practically.' His lack of sympathy for the Council of Europe reflected his belief that it lacked the prime purpose for which international bodies should be set up – namely, a precise and concrete body of work to do – or, as he is said to have exclaimed: 'I don't like it. I don't like it. When you open that Pandora's box, you will find it full of Trojan horses.'[12]

Moreover, from 1948 and in the short run at least, for Ernest Bevin 'the relationship with America was', as Coral Bell writes, 'the heart of the matter, however much the result might need to be disguised as an equalitarian multilateral treaty organization of the North Atlantic powers'.[13] Although much of Britain's 'special relationship' with the USA has been marked by 'the conscious resignation by Britain to America of her own place in the order of world power', nevertheless the Second World War had witnessed the most complete unification of military effort to be achieved by two allied nations and the establishment of a whole network of personal ties and friendships, born maybe of neces-sity, but sustained thereafter by a real measure of mutual cordiality. Moreover, although in the post-war world Britain might be no more than 'the most committed (though not the most docile) of America's lieutenants in the business of resisting the encroachment of Russian power'[14] and only a junior partner in the fashioning of a world economic order, the Anglo-American strategic relationship at the atomic, then at the thermo-nuclear, level inevitably gave a special quality to Anglo-American relations within NATO, while the whole Bretton Woods system of monetary co-operation reflected the notion of the dollar and the pound sterling as the two 'key currencies' in the world.

Not that the 'debatable alliance' was without friction. The assumption of the US under the Truman Doctrine of February 1947 of British responsibilities in Greece and Turkey did indeed bring in the New World to redress the balance of power of the Old, and greatly facilitated the process of British disengagement, but the increase of American influence in the Middle East generally and the often acute differences over Palestine and in the Anglo-Iranian oil dispute (1951-2) were a source of considerable mutual irritation. British attempts to build a collective defence system in the Middle East, which could both provide an effective substitute for Britain's previous military predominance[15] in the area and legitimize a continuing presence or right of re-entry, received little American support, even though the Baghdad Pact, to which Britain adhered in 1955, was modelled on Dulles's concept of a 'northern tier' system of Middle East defence (of Turkey, Iran and Pakistan); and possibly not without reason. By basing that Pact on an Arab State, Iraq, Britain's relations were embittered with much of the Arab world and especially those with Egypt, despite the Conservative government's decision in 1954 to give up the Suez Canal base.

Generally in the Middle East, Britain and France were distrusted by many Americans as 'uncertainly reformed burglars, who might stray back into their old ways',[16] while in Britain, not only was there some scepticism as to the potency of Arab nationalism, but American sensitivity to it was often regarded as either a form of hypocrisy (given their commitment to Israel) or an ill-disguised attempt to undermine British authority in the area.

In the Asian setting friction was particularly marked. In the first place, for most of the Labour government the new multi-racial Com-monwealth (created through the decisions of India, Pakistan and Ceylon in 1947 and 1948 – though not Burma – to remain within the Commonwealth on achieving independence) evoked both a pride in the peaceable dismantling of Empire[17] and a much more powerful emotional attachment than did either Atlantic or West European ties;

for many it provided a vision, even a model, of that peaceable co-operation between sovereign States upon which, it was hoped, a more stable and prosperous world order might be built. Labour leaders were particularly attentive to the views of these Asian members of the Commonwealth family (hence Bevin's decision in late 1949 to recognize the new Communist government in China), and were apt to regard relations with India as symbolizing hopes placed in the Commonwealth. Yet even for Conservatives who still tended to think of the Commonwealth mainly in terms of the old Dominions – and of their 'kith and kin' therein – the transformation of Empire into Commonwealth both helped to allay their resentment at the process and appeared to hold out the prospect of the retention of channels of influence which would enable Britain to retain her role as a world power more effectively. The controlled release of the wartime sterling balances to assist these countries in their economic development and the mounting of the Colombo Plan for technical co-operation in 1951 signified Britain's desire to do everything possible to make the new relationship a success.

Relationships between London and the Asian members of the Commonwealth, and particularly New Delhi, rose in importance with the outbreak of the Korean War in June 1950. British support for President Truman's decision to commit us forces in support of South Korea was immediate and backed by a modest military contingent (despite the heavy military commitment at that time in suppressing Communist guerrilla action in Malaya). But after the crossing of the Thirty-eighth Parallel, and particularly with the entry of Chinese forces into the war, American and British approaches to the handling of what had now become a direct threat to world peace began to diverge very substantially. In the British view, as Kenneth Younger, the Minister of State, expressed it, there was 'no alternative to a negotiated peace in the Far East, which would not be a disaster both for China and ourselves'.[18] Yet to many Americans China was unquestionably an aggressor, and had to be punished for her aggression. Anxiety lest United States policy for Europe might be adversely affected by any apparent backsliding on the part of her allies in Korea induced Britain – both then and in later instances in South-East Asia – to defer in the last resort to the American point of view. But to some at least there seemed for a time little to choose between Chinese truculence and American inflexibility. The recall of General McArthur on 11 April 1951 allayed the most acute British anxieties, but throughout the armistice negotiations Britain adopted a much more sympathetic attitude towards India's role as an 'honest broker' than did the United States, where the alleged ambivalence of India's attitudes was often construed as sympathy for the Communist cause, and so as downright immoral. The key role played by India in the Neutral Nations Repatriation Commission, the chairman and custodian force of which were provided by India, and at the Geneva Conference of Foreign Ministers on Korea and Indo-China between April and June 1954 seemed further to underline the importance of the London–New Delhi axis, for it was at that conference that Eden and Krishna Menon, despite the disapproval of Dulles, played an important role in helping to bring about a settlement of the French colonial war in Indo-China. Consequently, when Eden affirmed that Britain's Commonwealth ties were 'sacred', he was not only expressing the emotional attachment of most of the British people to those ties – he was underlining the extent to which they were thought to sustain Britain in her world role.

Clearly a prime source of Anglo-American difficulties was that outside Europe each had a very different scale of priorities; the Pacific and Far East being the high priority for the USA that the Middle East was for Britain. These differing priorities often clouded their perceptions of each other's interests. Certainly the British seemed to find difficulty in appreciating that Dulles regarded Asia as the main arena of Communist expansion, and that he was apt therefore to subordinate West European and Middle East desiderata to his containment objectives in Asia. Another source of strain was the eruption in the early 1950s of the McCarthy 'witch-hunt' against alleged Communists in 'high places' in the USA. The political élite in Britain for the most part saw great power tensions more in power than in ideological terms, and held that a tolerable *modus vivendi* with both the Soviet Union and China would eventually be reached; as early as October 1948, Ernest Bevin asserted, despite his disgust at the persecution of Social Democrats in Eastern Europe and the tension over Berlin, that 'we shan't reach any agreement, but we shall live together'.[19] 'Brinkmanship' had a part, it was granted, in a policy of 'negotiation from strength'. But what was really needed was what Macmillan later called 'firmness with flexibility'. Moreover, the horrifying potentialities of the new generation of thermo-nuclear weapons reinforced Churchill's and later Eden's determination to take advantage of the 'thaw' in Soviet attitudes (following the death of Stalin in March 1953) to reach some kind of *modus vivendi*, despite Dulles's oft-expressed scepticism of 'summitry'.

The rather rigid American insistence on imposing an embargo on what seemed an unnecessarily wide range of so-called strategic exports also not only threatened to cut off a potentially promising market for British exports, but it ran counter to the deep streak of Cobdenism in much of British thinking. Winston Churchill voiced this belief in trade as 'the great Mediator' in February 1954: 'The more the two great divisions of the world mingle in the healthier and fertile activities of commerce, the greater is the counterpoise to purely military calculations. Friendly infiltration can do nothing but good.'

In addition, there were personality difficulties between Dulles and Eden. Eden once referred bitterly to Dulles as 'a preacher in world politics'. Dulles, unlike Acheson, had few, if any, ties of sympathy with Britain; it was with Adenauer and Monnet that he felt most at home. Moreover, in the European context, although Eden tended to stand aloof from the movement for European unity, Dulles was apt to regard Britain as 'a necessary junior functionary in getting the Continentals, particularly the French, to ratify the EDC'.[20] Yet it was not Dulles who conducted the 'agonising reappraisal' when in August 1954 the French National Assembly failed to ratify the EDC Treaty. Rather it was Eden who, in committing Britain to the stationing of four divisions and tactical air force units on the Continent, was able to obtain agreement on the creation of Western European Union (of the Six plus Britain), and to the rearmament and entry of West Germany into NATO – which seemed both to sound the death-knell of European supranationalism and to knit Western Europe's defence firmly within a broader Atlantic framework.

By the end of 1955, then, the picture was of a contracting but still confident Britain, claiming a unique role in world affairs that stemmed from her special relationship, especially in defence matters, with the United States, from her position as the centre of a world-wide multiracial Commonwealth (and preferential trade and currency area), and from her leadership in organizing Western Europe along functional lines of inter-governmental co-operation in both the defence and economic fields. The post-war decade was one in which it had seemed perfectly feasible, if difficult, to reconcile these three main strands in British foreign policy objectives; the next decade was to belie such hopes. This was the decade in which the European *relance* left Britain first on the touchline and then as an unsuccessful suppliant, as her gaze shifted from across the oceans to the Continent. It was a decade marked by the second wave of decolonization (beginning with Ghana in March 1957), which inevitably accentuated the centrifugal forces within the Commonwealth, and by the 'special relationship' with the United States coming to look more and more like the Cheshire Cat whose grin had outlasted its material presence. These trends would have gradually eroded Britain's position as a world power in any case, but they were highlighted and possibly accelerated by the *débacle* of Suez in the fall of 1956. That *débacle* underlined the erosion of British authority in the whole Middle East. It was a revelation of British strategic and economic weakness; it disclosed the precariousness of Anglo-American ties; it sowed the disarray from which the Commonwealth has never really recovered; and it called into question the credibility of Britain's commitment to the concept of world order enshrined in the United Nations charter.

Despite Harold Macmillan's subsequent skill in restoring more than a modicum of friendliness to Anglo-American relations generally, in the Middle East and in 'defence matters' in particular (for example the McMahon Act was amended in the summer of 1958 to permit a sharing of nuclear information between the United States and the United Kingdom), the dwindling significance of the 'special relationship' in American eyes was increasingly evident. Nor did the success of the Commonwealth Conference in June 1957 and of Macmillan's tour in January and February 1958 blind him to the revolutionary change that the Commonwealth was undergoing. 'The addition of India, Pakistan and Ceylon had marked the end of the old all-white Commonwealth. It was now to be followed by the progressive dissolution of the colonial Empire, and by a rapid increase in the number of independent nations, great and small, which would, year by year, join as full members. . . . The old *pax Britannica*, which had for so many generations brought to about a quarter of the globe the inestimable advantage of order and good government . . . was now being replaced by a new and untried system. . . . The stream of gradual change was now to be augmented into a fast-flowing river, which might soon break its banks through its torrential force. Where in all this were we to find the unifying principle to make a reality of the Commonwealth in all the spheres of human endeavour ?'[21]

Meanwhile in Western Europe the stage was being set for taking up the path of economic integration first marked out in the Schuman proposals of May 1950. Following the Messina Conference (June 1955) and the Spaak Report, the Treaty of Rome for the constitution of the European Economic Community and for Euratom was signed on 25 March 1957, and these two treaties came into force on 1 January 1958. The initial reaction in Britain was one mainly of scepticism followed by a sense of alarm; scepticism because most doubted whether the Six would be able to agree on a course filled with so many un-certainties, and then alarm at the implications of that agreement for Britain. But the alarm was in most cases on mainly economic grounds at first. The Federation of British Industries European Integration Panel reported in September 1956 that the Six's plan of integration 'could have gravely injurious repercussions on British industry'.[22] Indeed, over the next four years 'business looked upon European developments not as an opportunity but as a threat'.[23] Moreover, however much Macmillan may have appreciated the speed at which Commonwealth relations were changing (witness his 'wind of change' speech of February 1960 in South Africa), the continued – if declining –

predominance of Commonwealth trade and finance in Britain's overseas
economic relationships was seen as a decisive reason for not participating
with the Six in the creation of a European Common Market. Yet
exclusion from that market was if at all possible to be avoided. Hence
the British interest in the Spaak Report's proposals for an arrangement
whereby other countries might join with the Six in a free trade area.
Partly because of pressure from the National Farmers' Union, Britain's
initial reaction was to work for the establishment of an industrial free
trade area, a proposal which did not endear itself to agricultural
exporters in France and the Six generally.

Britain's negotiations with the European Common Market powers
over the next decade and a half were, in fact, to be complicated by the
new dimension of 'collectivist politics', as Samuel Beer has called it,[24]
in which pressure groups through a system of functional representation
came to play a crucial role in the making of government policies towards
Europe. This role, it could be argued, was enhanced by the apparent
determination of successive British governments, Harold Wilson
possibly being an exception, to place the main emphasis in the negotiating rounds on the economic pros and cons for entry. There was,
indeed, amongst politicians a tendency in the late 1950s to 'perceive
Europe as in substance an economic matter – and a fairly low priority
one at that'.[25] Certainly, both at the pressure group and party level
there seemed little vision of the European idea and of its political
significance to the European negotiators. France's rejection in November
1958 of Britain's revised proposals for a free trade area may have been
inevitable in the light of de Gaulle's advent to the premiership in the
preceding June. But the inclination of the British negotiators to be
constantly looking over their shoulder at the demands of domestic
pressure groups, and to treat Commonwealth preferences as sacrosanct,
certainly gave the French every reason to suppose that they would
receive little benefit from such a free trade area.[26]

At first some satisfaction was taken in the creation of the mainly
industrial European Free Trade Area of the Seven[27] which had been
agreed in the Stockholm Convention of November 1959. But in the
course of 1960 governmental opinion moved fairly rapidly towards a
reassessment of Britain's relationship with the European Economic
Community.

From this assessment it was evident that the EEC was a going
concern with impressive rates of economic growth. Membership might
offer tangible economic benefits to a relatively stagnant, but techno-
logically advanced, British economy. Commonwealth trade was
declining, and looked like declining further relative to that with
Western Europe, Commonwealth preferences had lost much of their

significance, and the strain of preserving sterling as an international reserve currency was beginning to tell. Commonwealth political ties had also been severely strained by the withdrawal of South Africa; the 'special relationship' with the United States was in rapid erosion, and seemed to be in danger of being replaced by one of nuclear dependence with the cancellation of the Blue Streak missile programme; and the newly elected President Kennedy had indicated that America would welcome Britain's entry in the European Community.[28] Moreover, in June 1960 the Six had rejected the notion of 'bridge-building' between the EEC and EFTA.

The decision by Macmillan and the announcement which followed on 31 July 1961 that Britain would seek to gain entry to the Common Market was based more on political than on economic considerations, even though Macmillan operated 'by disguising his strategic choice as a commercial deal'[29] so as to edge a Common Market decision past domestic opposition. That decision was also almost certainly motivated less by the positive advantages that might accrue than by the reluctant awareness that the other two circles of Britain's influence and the basis of her world status were crumbling, and that serious damage might be done to Britain's political as well as economic standing if she were to continue to be excluded from an increasingly integrated and influential Europe. And there was always the hope that 'Britain could exert leadership within a united Europe, and that this offered a means for restoring the country to a place of world influence'.[30]

The rather dismal and tortuous tale of the 1961–3 negotiations need not be retold again here. 'The essence of the Prime Minister's problem was that, in order to gain domestic approval for the European course, he had pledged himself to obtain safeguards which, if not wholly incompatible with membership, were at least unlikely to be obtainable.'[31] Moreover, the continuing attachment to the Commonwealth, the deep divisions within both major political parties, and the mortgaging of Britain's nuclear independence for American nuclear hardware (in the shape of the Polaris) must have amply confirmed de Gaulle's suspicion both that Britain was 'not ready' for membership, and that in a crisis she would put her relations with the United States before her relations with Europe. In any case, de Gaulle saw British membership as a serious challenge to France's predominance within the EEC, and both he and Adenauer seem to have thought that, to avoid strain on the Paris–Bonn axis, it was much better to keep her out.

The implications of the collapse of the negotiations in January 1963 were slow to percolate into British thinking. Britain, it was supposed, could revert to her image of herself as a world power, even though not on the same level as the two super-powers. 'We are a world power and a world influence, or we are nothing', affirmed Harold Wilson, the new Labour government's Prime Minister, in 1964. Britain, besides the United States, was the only country to be a full member of all three of the major Western alliances: NATO, the Central Treaty Organization (CENTO) and the South-East Asia Treaty Organization (SEATO). Britain's nuclear capability, the assistance given by British forces to East African leaders in 1964 to quell mutinous troops, the British contribution to the UN force in Cyprus, and the effective support accorded to Malaysia in its confrontation with Indonesia appeared to confirm Britain's continued ability to conduct a global strategy, and to maintain in the Indian Ocean area a military presence, both as a support of her own interests there and as a contribution to a wider security system.

Yet disillusionment was rapid. Harold Wilson's attempts to mediate in the Vietnam War between the Johnson administration and North Vietnam were a dismal failure, and caused little but irritation on both sides of the Atlantic. His attempts also to mediate in the Indo-Pakistan War in September 1965 had to give second place to the successful Soviet mediation at Tashkent. In August 1965 the first Immigration Bill was passed, causing acrimony and acute criticism throughout much of the non-white Commonwealth, and in November 1965 the Smith régime in Rhodesia affirmed its unilateral declaration of independence. The British government's decision not to use force, but rather to rely on economic sanctions, brought bitter abuse from most African members of the Commonwealth, and in several instances led to a rupture of diplomatic relations. The Nigerian civil war with Biafra from 1967 and the deposition of Nkrumah the following year seemed but to underline the general state of disorder and disintegration within the Commonwealth; moreover, the importance of Commonwealth trade in Britain's external economic relations was rapidly diminishing relative to that of trade with EFTA and EEC; even relations with EFTA were bedevilled by the 15 per cent surcharge imposed on imports to meet the demands of the 1964 economic crisis. Despite the Labour leaders' initial lack of sympathy with Europe[32] all these developments told in favour of a reconsideration of the possibilities of renewed negotiations for entry into the Common Market.

In November 1966 the Prime Minister announced that discussions were being held to establish 'whether it appears likely that essential British and Commonwealth interests could be safeguarded if Britain were to accept the Treaty of Rome and join the EEC'. Britain's formal application was notified on 2 May 1967, after the Prime Minister and George Brown, his Foreign Secretary, had conducted a series of negotiations with Western European leaders. By now not only did the

Confederation of British Industries see a 'clear and progressive balance of advantage' for British industry in membership of the Common Market, but both the TUC Economic Committee supported, and the National Farmers' Union accepted, the application as being 'realistic and constructive'. Nevertheless, unlike the moves in 1961, Harold Wilson made it quite clear that the decision was basically a political decision. 'Europe is now faced with the opportunity for a great move forward in political unity, and we can, and indeed must, play our full part in it.' Yet President de Gaulle's reaction was immediately – and predictably[33] – unfavourable; for on 16 May he recited the obstacles and urged delay. The following November he notified his refusal to acquiesce in the initiation of negotiations. Nevertheless the Labour government refused to withdraw its application, and indeed revived it in 1969.

When negotiations were again set in train with the advent to power of Edward Heath's Conservative government, instead of following the Labour stress on the political significance of the application, the Prime Minister tended initially, as had Macmillan, to place the major emphasis on the economic issues and the economic advantages. This was misleading; although the negotiations focused on such issues as the British contribution to the financing of the Community's budget, the future of the Commonwealth sugar agreement, of butter imports from New Zealand, and of sterling as an international reserve currency,[34] the ultimate decision was not one that could be based on a 'computerized analysis of finely balanced economic calculations'. It was important to obtain the right economic terms, but underlying the economic issues were some major political questions. The crux of the matter was whether Britain, both politically and economically, could afford to be left in something of a backwater in the face of a Western Europe which was becoming economically much stronger than Britain, and was now more firmly set politically, in the light of the Hague Declaration of December 1969, on a course towards closer political unity. Outside the Community, Britain could hope to exercise little influence on either the economic or political future of the Community; inside, she would be a director, not a mere shareholder. Her influence in world affairs, not only in the commercial and economic, but also in the political and defence fields, could thereby be enhanced, and she could share with her partners the challenging task of creating a more self-reliant Western Europe with an aggregation of power which might enable it to play a major role in the world stage. Moreover, it was clear by now that the political aim was not the creation of a federated Western Europe, which would pose a real threat to Britain's sovereignty, but rather of a Western European community of sovereign States in some kind of

D

loose confederal relationship – with the Council of Ministers retaining firm control within the Community – which would enable it to speak with a more concerted voice on the world diplomatic stage, and to act in a more concerted manner in a wide range of economic, monetary and commercial matters.

Contrary to earlier expectations, this kind of relationship and the association and other types of agreements contemplated between the Community and developing Commonwealth countries might also allow many of Britain's existing Commonwealth ties, especially at the technical and professional levels, to survive, and even to flourish.

Conversely, as an earnest of Britain's willingness to think in European terms, her readiness to relinquish sterling's international role was particularly significant, while in the defence field, probably more important than earlier hints of an Anglo-French nuclear force was the confirmation, though with an important exception, of the Labour government's decision in January 1968 to end Britain's commitments 'East of Suez', the exception being to retain a modest British presence in Malaysia as a contribution to five-power Commonwealth military arrangements in that area. The prime objective outlined in the supplementary statement on defence policy of 28 October 1970[35] was to be the strengthening of the European contribution to the North Atlantic Alliance.

The successful outcome to the negotiations for British entry into the European Community was facilitated by the departure of de Gaulle and the longstanding and evident 'European' orientation of Edward Heath. The power structure within the Community had shifted, to France's loss and Germany's gain, and it became Bonn rather than Paris that was intent on an *Ostpolitik* of 'opening to the East', an *Ostpolitik* which was in many ways premised on the continued viability of the American-led Atlantic defence system. Britain's NATO ties were no longer therefore a disability but an asset to be shared. Within both Parliamentary parties in Britain, however, the picture has been more confused and at the level of public opinion at large there is still strong resistance, born out of a kind of retrospective nostalgia, to 'going continental'. A begrudging recognition of necessity is perhaps the most that can be expected. Whether an enlarged European Community can be induced to share Britain's still markedly world outlook or whether Britain as a consequence will be a more pleasant place to live in, remains to be seen.

NOTES

1 F. S. Northedge, *The Troubled Giant* (London, 1966).
2 *Report of the Review Committee on Overseas Representation, 1968–1969* (Cmnd 4107), p. 23.
3 For full text see Nicholas Mansergh (ed.), *Documents and Speeches on British Commonwealth Affairs, 1931–1952* (London, 1953), vol. I, pp. 575–9.
4 Hugh Dalton, *Diary* (British Library of Political and Economic Science), 17 November 1948; see also R. Manderson-Jones, *American Attitudes Towards Britain's Relations with Europe, 1946–1955* (unpublished thesis, University of London, 1968), p. 41.
5 The Cominform was set up in September 1947, one of its aims being to mobilize opposition to the European Recovery Programme.
6 Lord Ismay, *NATO: The First Five Years, 1949–1954*, Utrecht, 1955, p. 8.
7 Prime Minister Attlee, in *House of Commons Debates*, vol. 476, col. 36 (13 June 1950).
8 Sir Stafford Cripps (Chancellor of the Exchequer), in *House of Commons Debates*, vol. 476, col. 1948 (26 June 1950). Given the well-known opposition of the Labour government to the federalist approach Kenneth Younger, then Minister of State in the Foreign Office, is probably right in holding that 'all the evidence suggests that the object of the French government was to secure German acceptance of the plan in the form that suited France, and to run no risk of the British watering it down, while at the same time avoiding any accusation of having formally excluded Britain from participation'. He argues, therefore, that Britain did not miss 'this particular opportunity, for in the circumstances it was no opportunity', though she did perhaps fail 'over the whole period from 1945 to judge correctly how Europe was going to evolve'. (Comment by Kenneth Younger on Ulrich Sahm: 'Britain and Europe, 1959', in *International Affairs* (January 1967), p. 25.)
9 Prime Minister Churchill, in *House of Commons Debates*, vol. 515, cols. 891–2 (11 May 1953).
10 Coral Bell, *The Debatable Alliance* (London, 1964), p. 28. This experience was, of course, crucial in shaping the Atlanticist and Commonwealth (as against the Carolingian) orientation of British attitudes (ibid, p. 24).
11 Dalton, op. cit., 15 September 1948.
12 Lord Strang, *At Home and Abroad* (London, 1956), p. 290.
13 Bell, op. cit., p. 9.
14 Bell, op. cit., p. 8.
15 Based in large part on her ability to call upon her Indian Empire for men and resources; hence the significance of India's independence in removing one of the main props of Britain's authority in the Middle East.
16 Bell, op. cit., p. 51.
17 An achievement that was frequently contrasted favourably with the difficulties encountered by Holland and France, but was only rarely accompanied by any recognition of the blood-letting that accompanied the partition of India or the evasiveness of British policies over Palestine.
18 *House of Commons Debates*, vol. 484, col. 153 (12 February 1951).

[19] Dalton, op. cit., 15 October 1948.
[20] Manderson-Jones, op. cit., p. 250.
[21] Harold Macmillan, *Riding the Storm, 1956–1959* (London, 1971), pp. 378–80.
[22] Quoted in Robert J. Lieber, *British Politics and European Unity* (Berkeley, California, 1970), p. 92, n. 2.
[23] Ibid., p. 92.
[24] Samuel H. Beer, *British Politics in the Collectivist Age* (New York, 1965).
[25] Lieber, op. cit., pp. 150–1.
[26] Miriam Camps rightly remarks that: 'Too frequently the advantage of the particular arrangement proposed by the [British] government was praised as one which would enable the British to have the best of both worlds: free trade with the Continent and preferential trade with the Commonwealth.' Moreover, as she earlier points out, the British government's assumption that 'in agreeing to the OEEC examination of a free trade area it was making a move that was very much desired on the Continent' was sadly misplaced. *Britain and the European Community, 1955–63* (Princeton, 1964), pp. 104–5.
[27] Austria, Denmark, Norway, Portugal, Sweden, Switzerland and the United Kingdom.
[28] Camps, op. cit., p. 336.
[29] Richard Neustadt; quoted in Lieber, op. cit., p. 163.
[30] Lieber, op. cit., p. 163.
[31] Ibid., p. 236.
[32] Miriam Camps, *European Unification in the Sixties* (London, 1967), p. 142: 'The failure to foresee the impact of the 15 per cent surcharge on the EFTA illustrated just how far out of touch the new ministers were with contemporary European feelings.' See also: Cynthia W. Frey, 'Meaning Business: the British Application to Join the Common Market, November 1966–October 1967', *Journal of Common Market Studies* (March 1968).
[33] George Brown, then British Foreign Secretary, records that, at a meeting in January 1967, 'de Gaulle made his famous remark about the impossibility of two cocks living in one farmyard with ten hens. He said he had had a lot of trouble getting the five hens to do what France wanted, and he wasn't going to have Britain's (*sic*) coming and creating trouble all over again this time with ten' (*In My Way* (London, 1971), p. 220).
[34] A role which Susan Strange argues has 'been like a halter round Britain's neck' ('Sterling and British Policy: A Political View', *International Affairs*, April 1971).
[35] *Supplementary Statement on Defence Policy* (Cmnd 4521).

III The European Communities: Political Unity and British Interests

DAVID COOMBES and AVI SHLAIM

It is not a popular view today, perhaps, but the future historian might well have to admit that the most dramatic and decisive realignments of British policy since the Second World War were taken by Mr Macmillan's government between 1959 and 1963. It was Macmillan who led the Conservative Party away from what remained of its imperial posture to accept the notion of an independent Commonwealth and pointed it towards the movement for unity in Western Europe as a new base for its ambitions for Britain's security and prestige. That government also led a departure in economic policy towards conscious acceptance by government of responsibility for some sort of positive management of the economy as a means of maintaining domestic living standards. The changes were related, first, because the reassessment of economic policy which took place in the early 1960s borrowed freely from Continental European experience, and, secondly, because membership of the European Common Market was considered vital to national economic goals.

The reasoning which led to the application for membership of the three European Communities made in 1961 was accepted later by the Labour government of Harold Wilson providing a striking example of bi-partisanship in British foreign policy.

In view of this apparent consensus, based it seems on political and economic necessity, there has been a tendency to regard future British membership of a political and economic union founded on the present European Communities as more or less inevitable following the departure of General de Gaulle. Yet there would seem on the evidence available to be little positive support among the general public for the European policy of the party leaders, while there seems to be a good deal of ardent opposition to the supposed threat to British sovereignty represented by the European Communities. This could be explained away as a consequence of sheer boredom and irritation with an issue which has been presented in much the same way without any practical results over ten years. But one is bound to recall that political leaders of both main parties stoutly rejected for many years after the war the idea that Britain could join a political or economic union of Europe along the lines of the present Communities. It would indeed be rash to assume that the prevailing consensus of governments indicated a decisive change of attitude on the part of British political leaders or people on the question of sovereignty or supranational institutions. Therefore it is important at this stage of the debate to reach some balanced and realistic assessment of the likely effects on British sovereignty and political autonomy of membership of the Communities, and this is the task we have set ourselves here.

We do not intend, however, to present yet another set of arguments for and against British membership of the European Communities. Our task is to project the likely constitutional and political consequences for Britain of membership of the Communities as they are presently organized. We shall deal especially with the consequences for British sovereignty and for Britain's autonomy in conducting foreign policy. We intend to do this mainly by estimating what have been the constitutional and political consequences of membership so far for the existing members of the European Communities.

In the next three sections we shall deal successively with the constitutional consequences (the impact on national sovereignty implied by membership of the Communities); the administrative consequences (demands made on the machinery of government and representation); and, finally, the political consequences (the extent to which the scope of the present Communities includes the foreign policies of member states).

I

It is already quite well known that the procedures and rules for decision-making and law-making set up by the treaties of Paris and Rome are essentially dynamic, in that they are expected to promote more integration than the treaties themselves articulate or require. As one celebrated American student of the so-called 'system' of decision-making in the Communities has described it, 'though not federal in nature, its consequences are plainly federating in quality'.[1] The 'federating' qualities in the system do, however, need to be affirmed in practice by the member States in order to come into being, and they have not always been so affirmed or even admitted. For the time being, it will be as well if we confine ourselves to interpreting the constitutional requirements of membership of the Communities as they seem to have been up to the present.

The constitutional commitments which result from membership of the European Communities flow mainly from the obligation to accept the legitimacy of the common institutions provided by the treaties. This certainly means that – for the subjects included within the scope of the Communities – the British people would have to recognize new procedures of law-making and acknowledge the authority of new institutions, and in both cases to accept the participation of foreigners as equals. The Community institutions are empowered by the Treaty of Rome to make 'regulations' and 'decisions' (technical terms for two particular instruments of Community law) which are applicable directly in the member States and by which individual citizens and corporations can be bound, and ultimate redress in such cases lies with the Community Court of Justice.

In addition, the Treaty of Rome has no date of expiry and no withdrawal clause; ratification of the treaty by Parliament would require a formal departure from the constitutional convention that no Parliament can bind its successors. On the other hand, it is far from clear what sanctions exist to prevent a member State from acting in breach of the treaty, or from effectively withdrawing from it. Although the treaty binds its signatories to acceptance of the rules and procedures it lays down, if a signatory later decided to ignore those rules and procedures, there is presumably little the other member States or the Community institutions could do about it, short of imposing severe economic sanctions or using force. It is also worth remembering that, in signing the treaty, a member State does not in any way abrogate its own constitution as far as the working of its own political institutions is concerned. The practical innovations resulting from membership would almost certainly be confined to the intervention of Community institutions and the appearance of some important new laws.

The Treaty of Rome provides for a Council of Ministers, a Commission, an Assembly, an Economic and Social Committee, and a Court of Justice. In spite of their impressive titles, the Assembly (also known as the 'European Parliament') and Court of Justice are not, in fact, of much political importance, as the system functions now. The Assembly is not a legislative body, but it has the right to be consulted on most legislative proposals (as does the Economic and Social Committee), and to make recommendations on its own initiative. It may put written and oral questions to the Commission, receives an annual report from the Commission for debate, and can force the Commission to resign by passing a vote of no confidence by a two-thirds majority. This last power would seem to imply that it is the Assembly's function to lend or withhold support for the executive, but its powers have not been interpreted in that way in practice, partly because the

Commission is only part of the executive arm of the Communities (as we shall see), partly because the Assembly could not appoint a new Commission, and partly because the Assembly (given the way it is appointed) is not considered to carry real political weight. The Assembly's influence on the decision-making process therefore is marginal; it would not challenge the supremacy of the British Parliament.

In formal terms, the Court of Justice, as final arbiter in disputes arising from the Community treaties, would seem to be the nearest thing to a federal institution provided by them. As some British firms operating in the Communities have already found out, its jurisdiction extends to individuals and private corporations, and not just to common institutions and States. However, the Court is limited by the scope of its competence, which is restricted by the terms of the treaties. Except in so far as it decides disputes between member States on matters arising from the treaties and rules on breaches of them, its functions are best understood as those of a higher administrative tribunal or court of appeal, acting on defined administrative powers – an institution familiar in continental systems of government, but unknown in Britain. This change would, however, be specific and not general; it would apply to a particular set of decisions already taken and about to be taken; it would not require a fundamental change in British legal practice as a whole.

Britain would, however, need to adopt the whole body of existing Community law, and this would require Parliament to refrain from passing any legislation inconsistent with it. This in itself would not be a constitutional innovation, since many of Britain's existing treaty obligations (such as those arising from the United Nations Charter and from the European Convention on Human Rights) impose similar restraints. The novel feature of the Treaty of Rome lies in the power it confers on some Community institutions to impose obligations on member States and to make laws taking effect within them, as well as to administer and enforce some Community law directly; in particular, the Commission can make some statutory instruments of this kind without seeking the approval of any other body. However, this power is confined so far to a small and clearly defined set of subjects, and, in any case, these instruments like ordinary national delegated legislation would derive their force in the UK from a previous Parliamentary Act, which would have to be passed in the first place to make Community law of all kinds applicable in this country.[2]

For the most part, responsibility for making and executing Community law (including all the measures of any importance) is divided between two different institutions, one of which represents the member

States directly. These are the Commission – a college (at present of nine members) appointed by member States' governments, but required to act independently of them, and the Council of Ministers, a kind of permanent conference in which representatives of the national governments negotiate and vote. The Council is the supreme political organ of the Communities both in dry constitutional terms and in living day-by-day reality. Not only must all the most important legislative acts and decisions arising from the Treaty of Rome be ratified in the Council, but the Council also takes responsibility, where it is thought necessary, for co-ordinating the general policies of the member States and delegating tasks to the Commission on matters not specifically mentioned in the treaties.

Between 1951 and 1967 the institutional arrangements of the European Coal and Steel Community (ECSC) provided for a rather different balance of powers among institutions, but, since the merging of the executive institutions of the different Communities carried out by treaty in 1967, the constitutional provisions of the ECSC have conformed closely to those of the EEC and Euratom. It is also significant that the supranational role of the high authority of the ECSC (to which the British had objected so strongly in refusing to join that Community in the beginning) has declined substantially in practice over the years, so that the formal pattern established in the case of the EEC and Euratom in 1958 has followed closely what had already become actual convention in the earlier Community.

Although the Council of Ministers is an inter-governmental body, it is nevertheless said to be supranational. For one thing, it differs significantly from normal international executive organs in its corporate spirit and its conventional determination to reach agreement on common solutions, rather than to provide a platform for the unilateral defence of national positions; this is underpinned by the provision in the treaties of a variety of methods of voting, ranging from unanimity to qualified majority. After the end of the transitional period in 1969, most votes are meant to be taken by a qualified majority, but there is serious doubt about the prospects of adopting this rule in practice. However, the essence of decision-making in the Council is that decisions are 'negotiated' – i.e., taken by common agreement. The supranational aspect of decision-making in the Council is explained also by the role of the Commission, which is entrusted by the Treaty of Rome with an inviolable right of initiative and with the duty of acting as 'guardian of the Treaty' itself.

First of all, the Commission is given by the Treaty a virtual monopoly of initiating policy. It has the right to put forward what proposals it thinks fit on any matter covered by the treaties. With the exception of a few relatively unimportant examples, decisions envisaged by the Treaty of Rome can only be taken by the Council when it has a proposal of the Commission before it. This basic procedure, whereby 'the Commission proposes, and the Council of Ministers disposes', sets up a kind of dialogue between the two organs, and it is this procedure by which most decisions and laws have been made so far. In the dialogue the Council members express the views and represent the interests of the member States, while the Commission speaks for the Community 'as a whole' and promotes 'European' solutions to common problems. The Commission's authority rests, not only on its right to make proposals as just described, but also on its presence as an equal member at Council sessions (although it does not vote), on its privilege as the author of the first draft, on its right to modify its own proposals at any stage, and, above all, on the Treaty provision that, in most cases, the Council can amend a Commission proposal only if it votes unanimously. This last provision is especially important in enabling the Commission to play a mediating role, by ensuring that the common interest is taken into account in reaching decisions.

In promoting agreement in the Council, the Commission plays a vital role; but the Council always has the last word. Hence the Commission is obliged to discover the limits of the possible, and to submit proposals which have a reasonable chance of being accepted. Consequently representatives of the national governments have to be consulted at every stage of the process of forming and agreeing proposals. For this reason a body called the Committee of Permanent Representatives has assumed particular significance. This Committee, consisting of official representatives of the national governments normally with the rank of ambassador, has the official function of preparing the work of the Council of Ministers, and this means in practice that it hammers out preliminary agreements among the positions taken by the national governments and the Commission. On some less controversial issues, it has become a convention that, where unanimous agreement can be reached on this Committee, a decision can then be taken by the Council without discussion. As the work of the Council has expanded, this preliminary work of the Committee of Permanent Representatives has become indispensable as a means of relieving congestion and delay. The Committee has come to serve as a clearing house for myriad specialized committees (many of which are sub-committees of the Committee of Permanent Representatives itself), which serve as permanent channels of communication between the Commission and the Council.

However, the Commission has viewed jealously the expanding role of the Permanent Representatives, and it is certainly true that their role is not just the result of administrative convenience. The representatives of some national governments have been jealous of the Commission's position, and the rise of the Committee of Permanent Representatives owes something to this. Conflict between different interpretations of the treaties, institutional provisions and of the respective roles of Community and member States was mainly responsible for the most serious crisis within the EEC in the spring of 1965; a crisis which led to a French boycott of Community institutions for ten months.

In its early years the Commission of the EEC interpreted its role as being far more than that of a mediating international secretariat, even with the special rights given to it in the Treaty of Rome, and assumed in some ways functions of a political leadership. In doing so, it was considered justified by one interpretation of the Treaty, which saw the constitutional framework of the EEC as one stage in the evolution of a federal system of government in which the Commission would be the executive arm and the Council of Ministers a sort of second legislative chamber representing national interests. It is perhaps in its attempt to assert itself in this role that the Commission most acquired notoriety as a 'technocratic' body.

The Commission is, in fact, a strangely hybrid kind of institution combining political and administrative functions in an interesting way.[3] Although in practice its members are as often former civil servants or other professionals, as they are former ministers, in many ways they enjoy the status associated with the members of a political executive in a Western European State; it is they, and not the members of the Council, who appear before the Parliament to answer questions and defend Community policies (although increasingly the dominant role of the Council has been recognized by the frequent appearance of its members before the Parliament). The Commission has taken advantage of its need to consult the Parliament to seek support there for its proposals before sending them to the Council. More important has been the Commission's deliberate policy of making direct contact with representatives of Community-level interest groups, and using its information services to get general public support for its proposals. Another typical way of promoting legislation of which the Commission approves has been engaging national civil servants in the process of forming draft proposals at the initial stage; hundreds of working groups of national and Community officials meet regularly in Brussels, where the Commission's huge headquarters is situated. The purpose of this pre-legislative consultation is not simply to find proposals which are most likely to get the approval of all the member States, but also in the short term to champion the Commission's own position and, in the long term, to 'convert' national officials and other representatives to what is thought to be the common 'European' interest.

The treaties of Paris and Rome cover an area of government which, though limited in scope, is of the greatest political importance in modern conditions. However, although the Community institutions have a legitimate existence and will of their own over this area of government, it is only with the consent of representatives of the governments of member States that they can function effectively. Moreover, the scope of their competence can only be extended by unanimous agreement of the member States. It is certainly true that the power and scope of these institutions is intended, according to one interpretation, to increase over the years at the expense of that of the member States' governments. Indeed, especially if the Treaty provisions regarding majority voting in the Council are carried out in practice, the possibility of a national veto on most important subjects covered by the Treaty will diminish even further. It is clear also that the nature of collective decision-making at the present time already puts great limitations on the possibility of separate national action within the scope of the treaties. However, the diminution of national independence resulting from membership of the Communities takes place, not by a once and for all transfer of sovereignty, but rather by voluntary partici-pation in a process of joint decision-making.

There is certainly a sense in which the process of integration 'takes off' and acquires its own momentum independently of the will of member States. Yet the practice of the Gaullist régime in France has shown that the process can be held up, or even halted, by unilateral national action. So in a formal, legal sense the sovereignty of the British Parliament could be retained if Britain joined the Communities, in so far as the government of the day might still be held accountable to Parliament for its actions in the Community. If a government went too far for Parliament's taste in making concessions to its Community partners, then, although Parliament might not always be able to prevent the government's action in advance, it could always censure the government after the event. Indeed, it is difficult to see how any other conception of parliamentary sovereignty could be practised in relation to the participation of a British government in any inter-governmental organization. If governments are made less accountable to Parliament by concessions made as a result of participation in international organizations, then this is a general problem of parliamentary control of foreign policy, and not a special constitutional issue raised by member-ship of the European Communities.

In so far as sovereignty refers to the right of the British people, or their elected representatives in Parliament, to settle their own future or to hold their rulers accountable, then the real challenge of member-ship of the European Communities lies in the additional confidence it will be necessary to place in ministers and their officials to represent the interests of the British people. The present constitutional arrangements of the European Communities place vital responsibility on the national governments to act as representatives of their various countries. Just how far these arrangements provide for the right balance between people and their governments is a question to which we shall return.

However, the term 'sovereignty' usually refers less to the sovereignty of Parliament or the people than to the freedom of the national government itself to make and sustain its own interpretation of the national interest. In this sense British sovereignty would be protected in the European Communities by the ultimate right of the British government of the day to champion its view of British interests within the Community legislative and decision-making procedures, and even, for the time being at least, to veto proposals contrary to its view of British interests. It is true that the need to co-operate with other national governments and to respect the common interest as championed by the Commission would restrict the British government's ability to get its own views adopted. That ability is already restricted, however, not only by membership of a number of other international organizations requiring joint consultation and acceptance of common procedures of decision-making, but also by the political and economic reality of Britain's diminished influence in the world. In so far as the constitutional provisions of the Treaty of Rome would provide an additional restriction, the ability of British governments to overcome it would depend on their skill in sustaining their interpretation of the national interest in the various decision-making procedures of the Communities. At present this is largely a question of finding effective means of delegating authority to official representatives serving on the many committees of national ministers and civil servants in Brussels; and it is this practical, administrative aspect of membership of the Communities to which we shall turn next.

II

The decision-making process of the European Communities consists essentially therefore of an interaction between the Commission and the representatives of the governments of member states. Over this interaction the governments exercise control in Brussels, through the Committee of Permanent Representatives at the preparatory level, and through the Council of Ministers at the highest political level. In addition, the member governments have developed means of controlling their representatives to the Communities at the national level.

The means by which the governments maintain contact with the

Community institutions vary considerably from country to country.[4] In France, Community matters are dealt within a well co-ordinated manner at the political level by the Comité Interministeriel Pour les Questions de Cooperations Economiques Européenne which is headed by the Prime Minister and dominated by the Quai d'Orsai. It is served by the Secretariat General du Comité Interministeriel (SGCI), which canalizes the flow of information, closely controls the activities of the Permanent Representative, and issues detailed instructions to all French officials who go to Brussels. It is sometimes said that informal ties of a fairly strict kind are maintained with some French officials working in the Commission itself.

Germany is alone among the Six in not having an administrative body to co-ordinate the European work of the various Federal ministries; only special meetings of ministers or their delegates provide directives for the Permanent Representative. In practice, the Ministry of Economic Affairs and the Ministry of Foreign Affairs exercise dominant responsibility for European activities, and act as a bridgehead with the Community. If no agreement can be reached between the various ministries, the conflict is resolved by the Federal Chancellor, who also lays down the main guidelines of Germany's European policies.

Despite wide variations in the nature and effectiveness of national methods, two general trends can be discerned: first, the ministries of foreign affairs have on the whole succeeded in retaining a predominant role compared with the technical ministries; secondly, the extension of integration into politically sensitive areas has been accompanied by an attempt to tighten up ministerial control of the activities of officials.

Britain, joining the European game at an advanced stage, would be faced with special problems of reorganizing the machinery of government. British officials would have to play an active part in the plethora of Community institutions, committees and working groups. This would mean developing procedures for centralizing, directing and controlling contacts between the various branches of the central administration, as well as those between the Foreign Office and the Community institutions. The precise form which these changes would take are impossible to foresee, but Britain might benefit from the French example by adopting a two-tier system of co-ordination – one at the level of officials, and the other at Cabinet level.

This internal administrative adaptation would represent a great challenge to the British government, for the momentum of the decision-making process in the Communities always threatens to narrow the range and reduce the effectiveness of the national authorities. This trend is accelerated if, in the process, the government begins to lose control of the activities of its own civil service, and allows it to become enmeshed in the Community machinery of decision-making. One reaction to this is to subordinate the technical ministries, which might tend to be more 'European', to the Foreign Office, and to increase the safeguards and checks against *'copinage technocratique'*. It should be added, of course, that to do this would be to go against the whole spirit of the Communities, which are built on the notion of 'engaging' technical ministries and interest groups in the elaboration of Community policies above and beyond the national interest. But the tenacity of the national governments in retaining control has so far been remarkable. The general feeling is that the ability of parliaments and publics to keep a similar control has been far, far less.

A related problem arises from the accumulation of delegated administrative powers of decision by the Commission, which arise from the common agricultural policy, the policy for competition, State aids, the safeguard clauses of the Rome Treaty, and the regulation of coal and steel markets. However, national representatives are closely involved in controlling the Commission's exercise of these powers. To ensure the accountability of the Commission for the discharge of such powers, 'management committees' were set up for implementing aspects of the agricultural policy, consisting of representatives of member States and chaired by the Commission. These management committees have the same voting procedures as the Council, and they have to be consulted before certain decisions are taken. They serve as a model for administrative controls which might be exercised by member states in future in similar fields.

For, although the administrative powers of the Commission cover only a limited and clearly defined area now, they are likely to expand. This will entail a growth of bodies like the agricultural management committees, and put increasing pressure on the existing machinery, particularly if the Communities are enlarged. The overall effect will probably be to increase, rather than reduce, the volume of administrative activity of member governments in relation to the Communities, in spite of delegation to the Commission. Indeed, the difficulty of finding acceptable ways of delegating authority for the routine implementation of decisions to some common authority is going to be a major cause of inefficiency and delay, even though it results from a (possibly naive) desire to protect national interests.

III

The present scope of the Communities' competences may be limited, but there is a more substantial challenge to the power of national governments in the possibility that the scope might be extended by the momentum which the process of economic integration is said to possess. It is important to ask, therefore, what evidence exists that the tasks entrusted to the Community institutions have been expansive in nature: how far integration in one sector (say, price-fixing in agriculture) leads automatically to integration in others (say, monetary policy). The main conclusion of scholars on this subject seems to be that the Communities' tasks have proved to be expansive only in so far as the governments of the member States have had the necessary political will.

The Six governments have certainly made plenty of assurances that they intend to extend their customs and economic union to what they call a 'political union' by including foreign policy; indeed, the term 'political union' is generally used by them to mean extending their collaboration to foreign policy-making rather than strengthening the existing political institutions at a Community level. The concrete proposals for including foreign policy within the scope of the Communities (those which emerged from the ill-starred Fouchet Committee and those of the Davignon Committee which have now been adopted) have required institutional procedures which are far less supranational even than the present ones. The result of the Davignon Committee's work is that the six ministers of foreign affairs will meet twice a year to assemble, and, if possible, to reconcile their views on foreign policy, and that there will be a 'political committee' composed of national officials from foreign ministries meeting four times a year to prepare for the ministerial meetings.

The whole question of the effect on the foreign policies of member states of membership of the Communities is a fascinating but complicated one. The Communities were set up when great weight was given to a school of thought in international politics which held that achieving unity in social and economic co-operation of a functional sort was more useful than a direct confrontation of national interests. From this point of view it is almost as if the process of integration in the Communities were meant to take away the need for having a foreign policy at all. The more States co-operated with each other in carrying out common social and economic policies, thereby accepting the *de facto* authority of common institutions, the less it should have made sense to talk of them as having separate foreign policies.

If this process had worked, we would have expected to find that the role of the foreign offices of the member States of the Communities had already declined substantially and that the governments no longer treated their relations with each other as 'foreign'. However, as we have seen, the representatives of national governments, including a large proportion of conventional Foreign Office personnel, play a crucial part in the working of the Communities' institutions. Although there have been important changes in style, for the most part the relationships among the member States are still conducted according to traditional diplomatic methods. This in itself is evidence that the members of the Communities are a very long way from 'political union', in the sense of sharing common political institutions. It could be argued, indeed, that the two senses of 'political union' are closely related in that, until there are truly common political institutions (and thus a merging of sovereignties), there will still be need for separate foreign policies designed to protect the individual sovereign interests of the nation states.

At the same time, differences among the Six governments about their relations with third countries have played a vital part at important stages in the history of the Communities. British membership was probably blocked before (with disastrous results for the internal progress of the Communities) because at least one of the Six feared Britain's close relationship with the United States. British entry now will almost certainly raise acute questions about Europe's role in the world; this is so if only because one advantage British governments are said to expect from political unity is an increased voice in world affairs. It is certainly rather alarming that, in a world divided militarily and politically between East and West, in which there are urgent problems of social, racial and economic inequality and where localized violence of a most bitter and irresolute kind is rampant, the States of Western Europe have, as the overwhelming theme of their current 'foreign policies', the conduct of their relations with one another. That this situation cannot be tolerated has already been made clear by the attitude of French government under de Gaulle, by the *Ostpolitik* of Chancellor Brandt, and by general indifference, if not opposition, towards the European Communities expressed by a younger generation increasingly concerned with world problems rather than European ones.

In so far as the activities of the Communities up to now have led to the adoption of some common position towards the rest of the world (as they did, for example, in reaching the Yaounde agreements with the formerly dependent territories, in conducting the Kennedy Round negotiations in the General Agreement on Tariffs and Trade (GATT), and in dealing with applications for association and membership), the response has been pragmatic, not to say makeshift. Issues of principle and inarticulate assumptions have been disruptive whenever they have been admitted to exist, so for the most part they have been shelved. and there is still a powerful school of thought in the Communities which advocates that issues and assumptions of foreign policy should

E

not be raised, since they act simply to distract from the crucial matter of social and economic integration. It would seem, therefore, that the political ambitions of those who would seek through a united Western Europe to increase their influence in the world are likely to be frustrated – at least, that is, while the national governments concerned persist in clinging on to national foreign policies as essential bases of sovereignty.

A sector where progress is much more likely, and would emerge much more clearly from the Treaty of Rome, is that of economic policy. Here too, however, progress will probably be blocked by the reluctance of national governments to transfer competences to common institutions. The Treaty recognizes, and the member States themselves have become increasingly aware, that the creation of a common market without harmonized policies for unemployment, the balance of payments, inflation and economic growth may actually make it more difficult to maintain the economic welfare of those living in the countries concerned. For democratic governments, therefore, there is a strong temptation to find new means of intervention in the economy, even in the form of activity by common institutions. The member States pledged them-selves at The Hague summit to take immediate steps towards a monetary and economic union, and in consequence the group of national and Commission experts set up under M. Pierre Werner reported to the Council and Commission in 1970 on the realization by stages of an economic and monetary union. This report envisaged economic and monetary union in the course of the 1970s, meaning that 'the principal decisions of economic policy will be taken at a Community level, and therefore that the necessary powers will be transferred from the national plane to the Community plane'.[5] In spite of accepting the report 'in principle', the governments of the member States have in practice been unable to agree on more than a first stage of three years' initial progress towards monetary and economic union, involving mainly an intensification of the present procedures for voluntary co-ordination of national action. Here too, it seems, governments are unable to reconcile their view of the national interest with any substantial loss of their own powers, at least in the foreseeable future.

The expansion of the scope of the European Communities seems, therefore, to be very much dependent on the collective will of the governments concerned. The irony is that, while all the Six govern-ments as well as the governments of the present applicant countries see some expansion of scope, at least to economic and foreign policy, as highly desirable, if not essential, the sacrifice of national power which seems to be necessary cannot be obtained. The question of scope is inextricably tied to that of common institutions and national sovereignty. This suggests the conclusion that, although as a member of the European Communities a British government might successfully hold on to its right to speak for the British people in important sectors of government, its political and economic power in the world would not be increased in the way that is hoped.

IV

We should ask finally, therefore: 'What are the prospects of common institutions at a Community level replacing the authority of the national governments in important sectors of government?' We have already seen that the existing supranational institutions do not represent a substantial challenge to the national governments in this respect, and, even in so far as they might affect the freedom of action of governments in fields already covered by the Communities, it is significant that proposals for extending the scope of the Communities to more politically sensitive areas seem to call for institutions of an even more intergovernmental type (such as the proposals of the Davignon Committee). In so far as the months following General de Gaulle's resignation saw a second *relance* of the movement for European unity, it was the national governments which took the initiative at The Hague summit meeting. In so far as the governments have now pledged themselves to go beyond the Treaty of Rome, it is evident that they have decided to do so, not by a new Treaty of 'constitution' which might bind them in advance, but rather by co-operation among themselves on each specific question as it arises (as they have done on the subject of monetary and economic union). Supranationality itself may be a thing of the past.

In one respect, however, the renewed spirit of co-operation after de Gaulle had led to a strengthening of the Community institutions. In April 1970 the member States' governments signed a treaty providing for the progressive transfer to the Community of financial receipts from customs duties and agricultural levies and from a small percentage of the added-value tax, and at the same time increasing the powers of the European Parliament over the Community Budget. This means that by 1975 national contributions to the Community Budget (accounting in 1969 for £1,617 million, most of it spent on agriculture) will be replaced by the Communities' direct income (*ressources propres*).

Although it is felt that this is an important symbolic measure, it does not and will not represent a significant challenge to the power of national governments. In the first place the Communities do not have the power as yet to introduce new means of raising financial resources and the Community Budget is not permitted to go into deficit. In any event the Budget has to be approved by the governments of the member States in the Council of Ministers. The latter will in future be required to consult the European Parliament rather more than before, but the Parliament will have the ultimate right to amend only 4 per cent of the total Budget. Under arrangements now agreed, the national governments will be responsible for deciding all but a fraction of the Communities' expenditure, even though it will no longer be they who provide the money.

However, the role of national governments in the present Communities (which may even be increased as a result of membership) does raise the question of sovereignty in an acute form. This is because the decision-making procedures of the present Communities provide a disturbing threat to the sovereignty of the people living in the countries concerned and to their representative institutions; for it should be remembered, as we mentioned before, that the power and authority of a government is not the same thing as the power and authority of the people it claims to represent. In discussing the challenge to British political institutions of membership of the Communities we should perhaps be more concerned with its effects on the accountability nd responsiveness of the institutions responsible for government (whether at a national or Community level) than with its effects on the influence of the national government as such.

Thus it should be recalled that it is governments, and not oppositions, which are represented in the Council of Ministers; that it is far from clear how far the Commission takes account of views and interests other than those of governments in the member States; and that at present the European Parliament has no real means of influencing decisions. At the same time, as more and more decisions are taken in Brussels or Luxemburg the more remote and the less responsive the whole business of government becomes. Not only does the Community system require individual governments to come to the Council with a consensus already worked out (and thus with the backing of Parliament and public opinion assured in advance); it is also difficult for a government to be accountable effectively, even after the event, for its actions in the difficult and shifting negotiations which take place in the Council.

It is largely from awareness of these disadvantages of inter-governmental decision-making that federal institutions have been proposed, requiring not just a transfer of certain competences to the centre, but also new forms of representation, alongside the existing states. However, although the European Communities have often been described as federal, there is only one truly federalist clause in the Treaty, and this requires the approval of the member States before adoption. We refer of course to Article 138, which requires the Assembly to draw up proposals for its own election by direct universal suffrage according to a uniform procedure in each of the member States.[6] Despite a great deal of work on drawing up proposals for direct elections, little progress has been made towards getting any accepted and, although discussions have recently been renewed, there is little prospect of success in the foreseeable future.

Membership of the European Communities does, therefore, threaten the sovereignty of the British people, but only because satisfactory representative institutions have not been developed at a Community level. This is why it is so absurd to treat the question of sovereignty, as in the current national debate, purely in terms of the rights and competences of governments. An additional reason is the fact that, in order to realize the advantages they seek from entry to the Communities, governments would need to surrender to common institutions far more of their existing competences than they seem willing to forego at present. Meanwhile they have already largely admitted that, without membership, they cannot provide the protection and welfare which their citizens expect. The prospect of membership of the European Communities should have led to a serious discussion of the whole question of the future usefulness and viability of the national State in this part of the world. For, while the national State is certain to be with us in Western Europe for some time to come, there seems to be no alternative to the creation alongside it of new forms of political representation and authority. The trouble with the Common Market and the current debate in Britain about it is that this challenge has not yet been faced.

NOTES

[1] E. B. Haas, *The Uniting of Europe* (Stanford, California, 1968), p. 527.

[2] The views expressed here on the legal consequences are based on *Legal and Constitutional Implications of United Kingdom Membership of the European Communities* (Cmnd 3301, May 1967).

[3] See D. Coombes, *Politics and Bureaucracy in the European Community* (London, 1970).

[4] For further details see Université Libre de Bruxelles, Institute d'Études Européenes, *La Decision dans les Communautés Européenes* (Bruxelles, 1969).

[5] *Report to the Council and the Commission on the realization by stages of Economic and Monetary Union in the Community* (supplement to Bulletin 11 (1970) of the European Communities), p. 26.

[6] In addition, of course, the powers of the Parliament to hold the Commission accountable may be taken as federalist, if considered together with the clause on direct elections.

IV Britain's Defence Policy and NATO

STEPHEN KIRBY

One of the most persistent problems of post-war defence planning in Britain has been to determine the size and the nature of the military contribution to the North Atlantic Treaty Organization. The difficulty arises in the main because Britain's involvement in NATO and her military commitments in other parts of the world have been very different and often incompatible. In NATO, Britain is bound by treaty to provide and maintain certain specified and substantial military forces, and also to relinquish some independence over their control. The interests her troops help to defend and the strategy they employ are decided by a collective process, in which Britain has by no means a controlling voice; nor is Britain's military contribution the most vital for the defence of NATO's interests. Outside Europe, Britain has retained – if decreasingly so – military commitments that have been highly valued because they have been linked with Britain's imperial past, and because they have demonstrated an independent British world role. These commitments – in South-East Asia, the Persian Gulf, and elsewhere – have been more flexible than those towards NATO, but in the past have involved British troops in combat situations which have often demanded substantial reinforcement. Successive British governments have had to weigh the importance of a vital, but shared and interdependent, security interest in Europe against her more independent interests elsewhere, and they have had to decide how best to meet the constant and substantial military demands of the NATO commitment and the widely variable and more open-ended demands of her military commitments outside Europe. This essay seeks to examine the way in which involvement in NATO has affected formulation and the execution of British defence policy, and in particular to assess the extent to which the NATO commitment has come to dominate British defence thinking to the detriment of her traditional world role.

The two Labour governments under Harold Wilson are celebrated for presiding over what has been described as Britain's 'retreat into Europe',[1] and for attempting to abandon British military commitments east of Suez. But the decisions to concentrate Britain's defence effort in Europe were not made until more than half-way through the Labour government's six years in office. Indeed such a 'retreat' became discernible only after a series of policy contortions had been devised in an attempt to retain the global outlines of the defence inheritance. In 1965 Labour government leaders were extolling the value of Britain's world role,[2] despite an awareness that this placed a heavy burden on the nation's resources. Even though there were continued pressures for economic restraint, the Defence Review of 1966 was an attempt to prevent a lessening of Britain's military role overseas by devising a new and cheaper strategy. It was not until July 1967 that substantial reductions in commitment 'east of Suez' were announced, reflecting what the Government described as 'the evolution of (its) policy towards Europe'.[3] But the most dramatic changes of policy followed the devaluation of the pound in November 1967. The decision 'that British defence forces, apart from those needed to meet certain residual obligations to dependent territories, particularly Hong Kong, should by the end of 1971 be concentrated in Europe'[4] was announced on 16 January 1968, and was accompanied by proposals to make sweeping reductions in service manpower and military expenditure. These were radical and major changes of policy, but the precipitate manner in which they were introduced and the embarrassment they caused indicates that they were patently not a planned or deliberate run-down, designed according to some preconceived notion of what Britain's defence role should be.

This major revision of Britain's military role was a clear political choice that reflected the Labour government's priorities for public spending, but it might not have felt constrained to make it were it not for the persistent effects of domestic restraints upon defence planning. One of the most prominent was the belief that, unless the burden of the defence budget upon the nation's resources was substantially reduced, the United Kingdom had little chance of avoiding recurrent economic crisis and of achieving long-term economic health and growth; in particular, it was argued that the foreign exchange costs incurred in the maintenance of overseas defence commitments were especially damaging, because they directly and adversely affected the nation's balance-of-payments. Another restraint was the notion of 'overstretch' or the assessment that Britain's armed services were not large enough to cover all the commitments left by the Conservatives, and also that in some respects the services were dangerously under-equipped for the military role they were expected to play. Economic restraints made the rectification of the equipment problem impossible, and the recurrent short-falls in voluntary recruitment threatened further unplanned reductions in the armed services, already under strength.

The Labour government argued that these restraints made it imperative to revise Britain's defence policy. They tried first in the 1966 Defence Review to find a cheaper strategic formulation which would allow them to cover the existing range of overseas commitments within the confines of a smaller budget. This having failed it was emphasized that only major foreign policy decisions could open the way to economies in defence expenditure. Denis Healey outlined this problem when Secretary of State for Defence, as one of planning 'an orderly reduction of the defence expenditure then programmed, and to *insist* that the political departments made the reductions in our defence commitments required by this reduction in our capabilities'.[5] The short-falls in service manpower remained a pressing problem, particularly since its own poor record of recruiting offered the Labour government little hope of improvement, but domestic monetary restraints were the main determinants of the decision to emphasize Britain's commitment to NATO.

The strength of this argument is supported by the fact that there were no conspicuous international incentives for Britain to begin a concentration of her defence efforts in Europe early in 1968. The United States did not disguise its disappointment at Britain's decision to pull out of South-East Asia at a time when American troops were heavily involved there, and Australia, New Zealand, Malaysia and Singapore were attempting to delay the speed and moderate the effects of Britain's withdrawal. In Europe also, there was a lack of evident attractions for Britain's increase of interest. In January 1968 Britain had only just experienced a rejection of her second attempt to join the Common Market, and General de Gaulle, still to experience the blow of May 1968, appeared firmly in power and no more likely to compromise on co-operation *vis à vis* NATO than he had been with Britain over entry into the European Economic Community. Britain's decision also came before the invasion of Czechoslovakia, when the prevailing attitude among the European allies was that European security was stable, and that even a considerable imbalance between the conventional capability of NATO and that of the Warsaw Pact countries would not invite the sort of direct aggression that the alliance was first set up to deter. Britain and her West European allies had been withdrawing troops from the alliance, even though the United States and Canada were demanding that Europe accept a larger part of NATO's defence burden. The fact that Britain's decision was preceded only three weeks earlier by the withdrawal from Germany of one battalion of the British Army of the Rhine and one squadron of RAF Germany indicates that initially the substance of Britain's 'concentration' of defence effort in Europe was rather hollow. For the Labour government in 1968, NATO was a fall-back position, retained because it was deemed to be irreducible and it was conspicuous among Britain's overseas commitments only because it was to bear the smallest proportion of her defence retrenchment.

In opposition, the Conservative party had been highly critical of these changes in defence policy and of the reasoning that lay behind them; in particular, they criticized those arguments that suggested that defence spending has a special responsibility for Britain's economic ills and those arguments which described defence cuts as an 'economic necessity'.[6] It was also made clear that, in their opinion, the manpower problem arose only because the Labour government's inept handling of defence policy had led to a decline in rates of recruitment. However, even though the present Conservative government has inherited a Defence establishment drastically pruned of commitments and of capabilities, monetary and manpower restraints continue to weigh heavily on its defence planning.

Edward Heath's government has not shown itself willing to devote a significantly larger proportion of public funds to defence, and plans for a more ambitious military role in the world have been made conditional on the establishment of a sound and prosperous economy.[7] The Foreign Secretary has said that economic viability and reconstruction are the pre-conditions of authority for our foreign policy, and that without them Britain cannot fulfil existing obligations or pursue any new commitments, however desirable in the context of political strategy and British interests.[8] A recently published report by the Organization for European Co-operation and Development, however, describes Britain's inflation problem as 'probably among the most acute faced by any major country',[9] suggesting that a sound economy is still some way off, and the government itself has emphasized that public spending, including that on defence, must be cut if Britain is to avoid recession.[10] Budgetary cuts already announced for defence have only been nominal, but it has not been possible politically for the government to increase the defence budget in a way that has allowed them to provide a much greater range of strategic options than existed when they came into power.

Nor was the government able to ignore what it acknowledged as 'serious deficiencies in manpower'.[11] It had been unable to prevent all the major unit disbandments planned by the previous administration, and had committed itself not to reintroduce any form of selective or conscript service,[12] despite forecasts[13] that suggested that rates of recruitment, although much improved, were not sufficient to make up the deficiency of 12,000 men that already existed in the armed services, or to provide the long-term requirement for 40,000 other ranks per annum. The three-year engagement introduced in 1968 and the large pay increases of 1970 eased the problem, but demographic factors and the increasing demand for higher education means that there will be a diminishing pool of men available for recruitment despite an economic climate which has encouraged applications.

These restraints have intensified for the government the problems of allocating resources to defence priorities, but even so the Conservative party leaders have on a number of occasions announced their intention to revitalize Britain's overseas military role. At the Conservative Party Conference in 1970 Mr Heath emphasized the importance of both Britain's independent interests and the role she could continue to play outside Europe. Under his government 'a new era of British diplomacy'[14] was to open up, and a new freedom of manoeuvre was to be achieved which would enable the government to seize whatever opportunities events might offer Britain not only in Europe but in the Middle East, Africa and South-East Asia as well. The revival of Britain's role in the world was also an aspect of the supplementary statement on defence of October 1970. Whilst accepting NATO as Britain's first strategic priority, it declared the Conservative government's first objective to be the resumption, within Britain's resources, of 'a proper share of responsibility for the preservation of peace and stability in the world'.[15] This objective was underlined by Mr Heath when he asserted in his Guildhall speech that 'the voice of Britain in the councils of the world is going to be louder and clearer than it has been, and it will be an unmistakably British voice'.[16]

The Conservative government has so far retained a small military presence in South-East Asia and has postponed the laying-up of the aircraft carrier *Ark Royal*. The facilities offered by the Simonstown Agreement with South Africa have been maintained, and negotiations continue to seek terms upon which the United Kingdom can retain forces in the Persian Gulf. These measures do offset the predominance of Europe that was evident in the defence planning of the previous administration, but only at a cost.

The extra expense of implementing these plans has necessitated the cancellation of equipment like the C5 jet transport for the RAF, and the abandonment of conversion projects like that of H.M.S. *Lion* to a helicopter carrier,[17] precisely the sort of equipment that will be essential if the government wishes to retain the strategic mobility necessary to operate effectively outside Europe in the future. Also, to retain commitments that were previously excluded from assessment of the service requirement of manpower is to risk compounding the problem of 'overstretch', already made quite serious by deployments in Northern Ireland.[18] Indeed, even the modest extra-European role envisaged by the Conservative government may be difficult to support, for recent political and military developments in Europe have made more attractive and compelling the defence policy orientations of January 1968.

The invasion of Czechoslovakia by the Soviet Union and four of its Warsaw Pact allies on the night of 20/1 August 1968 was the foundation of the rekindling of interest in a militarily viable and a politically unified NATO for all its members. Initially concern arose from the stationing of twenty Warsaw Pact divisions, mainly Soviet, in a position close to the East–West frontier that was particularly sensitive and vulnerable. On balance this increased the military options open to the Warsaw Pact and, against a background of steadily increasing Pact military capability and the development of an impressive Soviet naval presence in the Mediterranean, the efficient and swift conventional occupation of Czechoslovakia highlighted the deficiencies and vulnerabilities of NATO's own conventional force levels and military options. This prospect was particularly worrying for the European members of the alliance since, even after the invasion, pressure continued in the United States for a severe reduction in numbers of its conventional forces stationed in Europe. One of NATO's first reactions was that its Defence Planning Committee issued a statement in early September announcing the halt of further reductions of Western forces. The NATO ministerial meeting planned for December was brought forward by several weeks to discuss the implications of the crisis. Its final communiqué was above all an affirmation of renewed political solidarity amongst allies who agreed that the continued existence of the Organization was more than ever necessary and that they would work towards the improvement of NATO forces 'in order to provide a better capability for defence as far forward as possible'.[19] This decision inevitably committed NATO's members to a substantial development of conventional forces which, until then, and despite NATO's flexible response formulation of November 1967, had remained little more than a trip-wire for the American nuclear forces. Britain very quickly responded to this situation, and in February 1969 announced its agreement to contribute to the establishment of a new on-call Allied Naval Force in the Mediterranean and to make other improvements in its conventional commitment.[20]

The overwhelming feeling among NATO members was that the invasion of Czechoslovakia would highlight the military role of the alliance to the exclusion of its *détente* policy, which stemmed from the Harmel Report of December 1967.[21] But it remained their conviction that NATO should continue to seek and to become concerned with political movements that might affect the conditions of European security. It therefore remained the political goal of the allies to seek 'secure, peaceful, and mutually beneficial relations between East and West',[22] and work was to continue on formulating policies for *détente* that could be put into effect when the political climate between East and West was more favourable. What was not foreseen was the speed with which a climate conducive to the resumption of *détente* policies was to re-emerge.

The first indication that Czechoslovakia was not to hinder significantly a development of East–West political accommodation, or at least an accommodation between United States and Russia, was seen in statements concerning the proposed openings of talks on the control of the strategic arms race. In October 1968 William Foster, the Director-General of the US Arms Control and Disarmament Agency, stated that the occupation of Czechoslovakia should not be used as a reason for delaying the start of talks so vital to the security of America.[23] In November the Soviet Union announced that it too was ready to start serious talks with the United States on nuclear weapons. The Strategic Arms Limitation Talks (SALT) opened on 17 November 1969 at Helsinki as an exclusively bilateral affair, but with obvious implications for the security of Europe, and NATO very quickly became the mechanism of consultation and information between America and her European allies.

For the West European States, one of the implications of the Czechoslovakian crisis and the opening of the SALT talks was that the Soviet Union and the United States placed the certainty and lack of mutual risk associated with the *status quo* above the probable benefits of unchecked political development and change in Europe. It also fostered the thought in many European minds that America was willing to settle issues vital to Europe's security over the heads of her allies, if this meant a reduction of the burden and the risks of her military involvement in Europe. The West European governments have used NATO as a lobby through which they can exert concerted pressure on the United States to recognize and respect their special defence interests, and at the same time as an organization for the co-ordination of their defence efforts aimed at assuming a greater burden of the defence of the alliance to reduce the probability of United States' troop withdrawals in the future. It is significant that Britain who, as a nuclear power had a very deep interest in the progress of the SALT talks, clearly felt that her relations with Washington were not sufficiently deep to ensure that all her interests would be considered, and became the leading advocate of the creation of a 'European defence identity' within NATO to ensure that the European members could maximize their influence on these negotiations by consulting together and speaking with a common voice.

Equally as important for the European members of NATO was the beginning of a series of negotiations that became known as the 'Bonn bilaterals', negotiations that have led to the signing of treaties aimed at the normalization of West Germany's relations with its East European neighbours and, more important, with the resolution of some of the outstanding European frontier disputes that have been the crux and the symbol of Europe's political problems since 1945. The first bilateral connection that Bonn re-established after the invasion of Czechoslovakia was that with Moscow, and this occurred as early as January 1969, but it was not until Herr Willy Brandt took office as Federal Chancellor on 21 October that real progress was made in the *rapprochement* between West Germany and its East European neighbours.

Within a month of taking office, Brandt declared his willingness to sign the Nuclear Non-Proliferation Treaty, if this would help in the opening of talks with the Soviet Union. He also developed his thesis of 'two German States in one nation', which has marked a dramatic step forward in terms of West Germany's willingness to recognize the *de facto* political realities of post-war Europe and the necessity of tackling the central problem of West German and East German relations as a lasting foundation for political harmony between the two halves of Europe. In November 1969 he proposed the opening of talks with Warsaw to discuss frontier issues and the prospect of economic and political co-operation between their two governments.

The speed with which Brandt's *Ostpolitik* has deeply affected political relations in Europe has been truly remarkable. On 28 November 1969 West Germany signed the Non-Proliferation Treaty, preparing the ground for the formal opening on 8 December of the Bonn–Moscow talks on the renunciation of force. This series of talks reached fruition on 12 August 1970, when Brandt signed a Treaty in Moscow. Although his government depends upon a very small majority which itself turns upon a coalition with the Free Democratic Party (FDP), Brandt has pressed on with his *Ostpolitik*; and on 7 December 1970 he concluded and signed a treaty in Warsaw which confirmed the Oder–Neisse line as Poland's western boundary and looked forward to the growing economic co-operation between the two countries.

The *rapprochement* between West Germany and both the Soviet Union and Poland and the prospect of some agreement between Bonn and the governments in Pankow and Prague are of enormous political importance to the rest of Europe, and carry with them the seeds of real political agreement between East and West, including the proposal to convene a European security conference. Such a conference could lay the foundation, if not of a new political order, then of new political arrangements in Europe to improve and make more certain the condition of East–West military security. Again Britain and her European allies have come to regard membership of NATO as an invaluable channel of communication and influence with respect to these negotiations, and regard it as a particularly useful forum in which they can exchange and also harmonize their views and interests.

The Brandt government has been the pacemaker of *détente* in Europe, but realizes that it cannot be the arbiter of so important a process. Ratification of the Bonn–Moscow and the Bonn–Warsaw treaties has been made dependent upon satisfactory progress being made in the Four Power Talks on the future status of Berlin that were begun on 30 September 1970. This has brought the United States and Russia, and to a lesser degree France and Britain, into the centre of the movement towards *détente*. It is upon their negotiations that the consolidation of the political accord already achieved in Europe depends. Berlin has become the crucial test of the Soviet Union's sincerity in seeking political accommodation with the West, and agreement over Berlin is not regarded by NATO's members as an extension of the *Ostpolitik* that Brandt has carried so far, but the threshold through which the Soviet Union must pass if *Ostpolitik* is to be confirmed and allowed to bear fruit.

Britain's interest in *Ostpolitik* stems not only from the effect it is having on the prospects of *détente*, but from its obvious effects on Britain's bilateral relations in Europe. The Bonn–Moscow Treaty has virtually confirmed the *status quo* in Europe and has reduced the priority that Russia attaches to her relations with Britain, and also France, who in the past were regarded as the two European allies most able to contain expansionist West German policies within the framework of alliance policy. Britain will value her involvement in NATO as a way to contain West Germany's influence upon the military and political developments in Europe; and Britain and France, aware of West Germany's growing influence, have gone a long way to reconcile their differences in foreign policy, and regard their participation in the Four Power Talks on Berlin as vital for the protection of their interests and influence.

Against the background of these developments, Britain's interest in the military security of Europe remains vital, but Britain's political stake in NATO has increased beyond all measure. If the atmosphere of *détente* that certainly exists is ever to be translated into political reality, it must inevitably involve the North Atlantic Alliance. For the West European States, including Britain, the best way to influence the shape of that political reality is to work within NATO rather than outside it. Any British government will be concerned to retain a position of influence in an organization deeply involved in an ongoing political process from which new security arrangements for Europe could emerge. The price of retaining that influence is to assist in the making of and to implement the Alliance policies that have emerged in response, first to the Czechoslovakian crisis and later to *détente*.

The political and military implications for the alliance of seeking to maintain its capability for defence whilst pursuing *détente* was exhaustively examined by the NATO ministerial meeting at Brussels in December 1970. Emphasis was laid upon the fact that 'there is a close inter-relationship between the maintenance of adequate defensive strength and the negotiation of settlements affecting the security of member states'.[24] In terms of defence, it was stressed that conventional capabilities must remain adequate to render viable the alliance strategy of flexible response but, because of the continuing increase in the military capability of the Soviet Union and the Warsaw Pact, attention was drawn to the necessity for improving and increasing existing levels of conventional forces. In addition to defensive requirements, the maintenance and improvement of force levels are viewed as the indispensable foundation for the success of negotiations between East and West; unilateral force reductions by the West would weaken the alliance, and remove the incentive for the Soviet Union to pursue *détente* seriously. In particular, the important allied goal of achieving balanced and mutual force reductions in Europe as part of an East–West agreement would be jeopardized if any NATO member were to withdraw its forces.

The evident need for a sound defensive deterrent posture for NATO has made the European members particularly aware of the special military and political roles played by the United States' forces in Europe. They are the essential political foundation of the Allied nuclear deterrent, and as yet they are irreplaceable. This role requires a substantial commitment of American troops to Europe, but a reduction of present levels would not necessarily undermine their deterrent effect. However, US force reductions could substantially and seriously deplete the conventional capability of the Alliance and thereby affect prospects of *détente*. President Nixon gave an assurance to NATO ministers that 'the United States will maintain and improve its own forces in Europe, and will not reduce them unless there is a reciprocal action from our adversaries', but demanded 'a similar approach from our Allies'.[25] The *quid pro quo* for this American undertaking has been set out in the European Defence Improvement Programme which Defence ministers of several European member countries[26] have agreed to implement at a cost of approximately 1,000 million dollars over the next five years, all of which is to be spent on improving

79

NATO's infrastructure and national forces committed to the Alliance.

British defence policy has for some time reflected the attempts to improve NATO's conventional capabilities. Between mid-1969 and mid-1970, the Labour government increased the strength of BAOR from 48,500 to 53,500, although over the same period the total strength of the army fell by 8,000.[27] The Conservative government has also declared the first priority of its defence policy to be 'the maintenance and improvement of our military contribution to NATO',[28] and has already made some additions to the forces committed to the alliance.[29] But the Defence Improvement Programme has called for further additions and improvements to national forces, including those of Britain. The terms of the programme are specific, and Britain's share, taken alone, would not greatly increase the cost of her military contribution to the alliance; but the spirit of the arrangement is clearly that America can be expected to maintain its NATO contribution only if the European allies refrain from unilateral withdrawals. For Britain this constitutes a strong political disincentive, over at least the next five years, to the revival of attitudes prevalent during the Cyprus and Malaysian emergencies that saw BAOR as a pool of manpower that could be drawn upon to meet the demands of commitments elsewhere. This might prove to be a serious handicap to the role that the government can expect of its forces in South-East Asia, and would render difficult the containment of more serious problems in Northern Ireland.

The decision to assume a greater share of the alliance defence burden has stimulated further the interest of the European allies in defence co-operation. This interest stems in part from the need to maximize the military efficiency and integration of national forces committed to NATO, and also from a strong desire, particularly in Britain, to contain increases in their individual defence budgets. A 'Euro-group' has been meeting regularly to explore the methods and grounds of defence co-operation within the alliance, and a range of issues have been discussed, including greater collaboration between European military staffs to correlate their tactical doctrines and ways of achieving logistic economies, but their discussions have centred on co-operative procurement of advanced weapons systems.

Britain has a strong interest in such co-operation, for she has faced for some years sharply rising research and development costs that have not been justified by the nation's limited requirement for high-cost equipment. Defence co-operation not only offers the prospect of economies of scale associated with longer production runs, but is essential if Britain's and Europe's technology-based industries are to withstand the competition from their giant American counterparts. For the Europeans joint production of high-cost military equipment is the only real alternative to a complete dependence upon the United States. Britain's commitment to such projects is well established: of the six major aircraft programmes listed in the Statement on the Defence Estimates for 1970, only three were for the production of entirely new aircraft, and all of them were joint European operations.[30] Britain is also a member of all seven aero-engine projects that are being undertaken by NATO members.[31]

It appears that Britain has accepted the economic and defence advantages of co-operation despite disadvantages that may become apparent only in the long term. One clearly is that Britain, with a wider range of interests and commitments than her Continental NATO partners, would like to procure equipment that is flexible and provides the possibility of deployment outside Europe. However, co-operative programmes have committed Britain to agreement on operational requirements and, for highly specialized weapons, to some agreement on the theatre in which they are to be used. The pressure from Britain's European Allies is almost invariably for equipment tailored for a European role; an example is the MRCA aircraft,[32] whose operational performance is likely to be little more than that of a close support tactical aircraft most suitable for forward deployment in Europe. It will not have the flexibility to fill the growing gap in Britain's long range strike/reconnaissance capability, threatened by the obsolescence of the Buccaneer and Phantom aircraft and by the cancellation of the TSR 2 and F III. This could mean that the reinforcement and air support of Britain's extra-European commitment in times of crisis may become an increasingly difficult affair.

However, Britain's involvement in such projects has brought some political advantages in Europe. As yet, defence co-operation has been based upon *ad hoc* arrangements, and has not involved the setting up of new political machinery, but it cannot be continued without significant political involvement and continuous political consultation. The promotion of the joint procurement of weapon systems has done much to establish Britain's *bona fides* for full participation in all the process of integration in Europe. It has been said many times that, if Britain is to become a member of the EEC, she must play her full part in the defence arrangements of Europe. However, there is now a reverse relationship, for any difficulties over the terms and conditions of Britain's entry into the Common Market could well jeopardize the political accord and co-operation that is so necessary in a period during which Europe hopes to shoulder a larger part of the burden of her own defence. The United States has an interest in the success of these small beginnings of European defence co-operation, and Britain might well find that she can best defend her close ties with America by fostering

F

closer links with Europe. The government might find that now Britain's 'Anglo-Saxoness' is pulling in the same direction as her 'Europeanness'.

Britain's defence policy closely reflects this developing economic and political relationship with Western Europe, particularly with the Six, and will also be influenced by the changing relationship between Europe and the United States; but the Conservative government has yet to declare what effect these relationships will have upon the role it expects of Britain's strategic nuclear forces. So far the commitment of Britain's Polaris fleet to the Western strategic deterrent has been maintained, and the arrangement under which her missiles are targeted collectively by the US Nuclear Targeting Committee, working with NATO's Nuclear Planning Group, continues. When in opposition Mr Heath questioned the government closely about the nation's ability to target her missiles independently,[33] but as Prime Minister he has yet to revive the concept of an independent nuclear deterrent. Alone Britain could hardly hope to make any threat credible against such sophisticated opposition as the USSR, particularly in the near future, when Polaris submarines *Repulse* and *Resolution* are due for major refits,[34] and there may be short periods during which no Polaris submarine is on operational patrol. In any event, in a crisis where Britain faced Russia alone she could not take for granted the survival of her small nuclear fleet, nor can Britain assume that her Polaris missiles will always be able to pierce the fast-improving Soviet missile defences. Britain's capability is unlikely to improve, since the government almost certainly will not purchase a fifth Polaris submarine or the improved Poseidon missile. It is doubtful whether Britain's nuclear weapons can provide even a semblance of independence associated with an ability to 'trigger' the United States deterrent; certainly her exclusion from the SALT negotiations suggests that her ability to act as a nuclear catalyst in a crisis is not greatly feared by the super-powers.

Mr Heath has spoken, however, of the possible creation of an Anglo-French deterrent held 'in trust' for Europe, but has offered few solutions to the problems involved in what is a complex situation. Anglo-French nuclear co-operation, without American assistance, could at best provide an industrial and technical base for the independent development of a mobile medium-range missile, but their joint efforts could not match the rate of innovation for offensive and defensive nuclear systems attained by the United States and Russia. There would be no certainty that an Anglo-French deterrent force would not be rendered obsolete and lacking in credibility by the time it was deployed, and it would inspire little confidence in Europe as a substitute for America's nuclear guarantee to NATO. For this reason alone, nuclear co-operation in Europe would require the full approval of the United States. This is a condition which France is reluctant to meet, for she would be required to rejoin at least NATO's Nuclear Planning Group and to renounce any pretence to an independent nuclear role.

The prospects for the creation of a viable European nuclear deterrent are distant, and without prohibitive expense Britain will not be able to render fully credible an independent nuclear strategy. The government may simply attempt to hold open Britain's nuclear options by supporting a national nuclear programme that will prevent her becoming too dependent upon the United States or totally enmeshed in European arrangements, whilst enjoying the present benefits of nuclear co-operation within the context of NATO. Britain's nuclear contribution, unique among the European allies, has enabled her to play a leading role in the dialogue between the United States and Europe within the Nuclear Planning Group, and has given her special access to and influence upon alliance nuclear planning. These remain important considerations, even though a serious European crisis would be rapidly dominated by the United States and Russia, making the exact implementation of agreed NATO plans and strategies uncertain. Nevertheless, continued nuclear co-operation within NATO provides the British government with a measure of influence upon European military and political events far greater than the influence she could hope to achieve by adopting an independent strategy with present capabilities: within NATO, Britain can hope to be consulted or at least informed; outside NATO, she would run the serious risk of being ignored.

Strategic and diplomatic developments in the last few years have combined to make NATO not only Britain's most important defence commitment, but the most demanding one as well. Britain plainly has a vital interest in the military security of Europe, which is still threatened by the considerable forces of the Soviet Union and the Warsaw Pact, and her contribution to NATO already accounts for the lion's share of her military capability deployed outside the British Isles. The only reasonable prospect of Britain reducing her contribution to the Alliance in order to revive an extra-European military role of substance would be if negotiations between East and West produce agreement to reduce forces in Europe in a mutual and balanced way. However, it is precisely this prospect of *détente* in Europe that makes Britain's present contribution to the military strength and political unity of NATO so important. If Britain is to retain a full measure of influence upon *détente* negotiations she and her European allies can expect only to increase and improve their military contribution to the Alliance. NATO will therefore continue to make heavy demands upon Britain's limited military capability and lack of manpower, for the armed forces and lack of money for defence budgets are likely to remain substantial barriers to a dramatic increase or improvement in Britain's military strength, and will inhibit the range of military commitments that can be safely accepted outside Europe. This, together with Britain's interest in becoming a member of the Six and also her involvement in joint military procurement projects with her European allies, will make it difficult for any British government to overlook the commitment to NATO in an attempt to achieve a greater military independence in the world.

Mr Heath nevertheless looks forward to a more vigorous international role for Britain, but is constrained to see it as a corollary of her becoming part of a more powerful Europe. It is perhaps significant that he gave as an example of Britain's new era of independent diplomacy the handling of the hostages affair in the Jordan War.[35] It was an act of great diplomatic skill, but an act that relied in no way upon Britain having military capabilities there. Whilst it is probable that the Conservative government may reverse the trend of diplomatic introversion implicit in the Duncan Report,[36] it seems less likely that the 'Europeanization' of Britain's defence policy can be greatly affected in the foreseeable future.

NOTES

[1] L. W. Martin, *British Defence Policy: The Long Recessional* (Adelphi Paper no. 61), p. 8.

[2] See Christopher Mayhew, *Britain's Role Tomorrow* (London, 1967), p. 131.

[3] Cmnd 3357, para. 3, July 1967.

[4] Cmnd 3515, para. 5, January 1968.

[5] Denis Healey, 'Britain's Defence Policy', *RUSI Journal* (December 1969), pp. 15–16.

[6] For suggestions that defence cuts were an economic necessity, see Cmnd 3515, para. 25, January 1968; and Denis Healey, ibid. For counter arguments, see David Greenwood, 'Economic Restraints and the Defence Effort', *RUSI Journal* (November 1968), pp. 328–30.

[7] Cmnd 4521, para. 2, October 1970.

[8] *The Times*, 10 October 1970.

[9] *The Times*, 29 December 1970.

[10] See *New Policies for Public Spending* (Cmnd 4515, October 1970).

[11] Cmnd 4521, para. 33, October 1970.

[12] For example, Edward Heath, *The Financial Times*, 28 May 1970.

[13] See *The Times*, 20 January 1970.

[14] *The Sunday Times*, 11 October 1970, and *The Times*, 12 October 1970.

[15] Cmnd 4521, para. 2, October 1970.

[16] *The Times*, 18 November 1970.

[17] Cmnd 4521, para 17, October 1970.

[18] For effects of 'overstretch', see Lt.-Col. J. H. B. Ackland's letter to *The Times* 15 August 1970.

[19] NATO ministerial meeting, final communiqué, Brussels, November 1968. See *NATO Letter* (December 1968), pp. 18–19.
[20] Cmnd 3927, para. 4, February 1969.
[21] See *NATO Handbook* (May 1970), pp. 42–5.
[22] NATO ministerial meeting, final communiqué, op. cit.
[23] Quoted in Robert Ranger, 'NATO's reaction to Czechoslovakia', *World Today* (January 1969), p. 25.
[24] NATO ministerial meeting, annex to the final communiqué (December 1970), para. 3.
[25] *NATO LATEST*, No. 18, 4 December 1970, p. 3.
[26] Belgium, Denmark, Germany, Greece, Italy, Netherlands, Norway, Portugal, Turkey and the United Kingdom.
[27] *The Military Balance, 1970–1971* (London, 1970).
[28] Cmnd 4521, para. 4, October 1970.
[29] Ibid., paras 25 and 32.
[30] The British–German–Italian MRCA aircraft, the Anglo-French Jaguar, and the Anglo-French WG 13 and Gazelle helicopters.
[31] See *The Military Balance, 1970–1971* (London, 1970), p. 114.
[32] See *The Daily Telegraph*, 21 February 1970; and *The Financial Times*, 10 March 1970.
[33] *The Times*, 27 February 1970.
[34] *The Daily Telegraph*, 12 February 1970.
[35] *The Sunday Times*, 11 October 1970.
[36] *Report of the Review Committee on Overseas Representation, 1968–1969* (Cmnd 4107).

V Retreat and Reappraisal in South-East Asia

MICHAEL LEIFER

The approach to foreign policy of the Conservative administration which assumed office in June 1970 has been distinguished by a pronounced concern with Britain's international standing. This has been expressed in a determination to retain a permanent military presence in South-East Asia, thus reversing the policy of the previous administration. This essay, which reviews the course of British military policy in its residual *imperium* in South-East Asia, sets out in particular to identify the sources and nature of constraints which may affect the latest phase of such policy. Because of earlier reversals justified on economic grounds, there has been a tendency to assume that such constraints stem only from British economic circumstances. Without denying the relevance of economic limitations, this essay points to other factors – especially the circumstances of involvement – which may well be equally constricting.

The establishment of a British military presence at the eastern exit of the Indian Ocean was a consequence of imperial design in the sub-continent. In 1786 Sir Francis Light acquired rights to the island of Penang in order to provide shelter from the north-easterly monsoon for the naval squadron allocated to the defence of the east coast of India. In 1819 the island of Singapore was secured with a view to trade following the flag. But in time its strategic position and naval facilities were geared also to the forward defence of India, and in the 1920s Singapore became the object of a debatable military investment. At the outset of the Pacific war, this ill-fated fortress fell with startling speed to the sound of Japanese cannon and a Churchillian lament.

After the Japanese capitulation in August 1945, the British returned in some force to refurbish their military complex in Singapore, indicating an intention to retain these facilities for some time by excluding the island from proposals for constitutional change for the Malayan mainland to which it was linked by a causeway. The function of the British presence changed somewhat, however, with the acquisition of political independence by India, Pakistan, Ceylon and Burma. The Indian Ocean was bounded in Asia by non-British territories and,

86

although 'Commonwealth' served initially to substitute for 'Empire', Commonwealth defence in Asia had a restricted application.

The British military presence in Singapore and on the Malayan mainland was related, in the main, to the protection of trading routes to the antipodean dominions and the internal security of a residual *imperium*; fulfilment of the latter function during the emergency in Malaya proclaimed in June 1948 involved heavy demands on local manpower and a substantial reinforcement from Britain. The previous month Britain had entered into informal arrangements for associated defence of her holdings in South-East Asia with Australia and New Zealand, made more concrete in 1955 with the establishment in Malaya of the Commonwealth Strategic Reserve. In September 1954 Britain enlarged the scope of its military commitments to become a member of the South-East Asia Treaty Organization (SEATO). In October 1957, following the political independence of Malaya, a specific military undertaking was provided in the Anglo-Malayan Defence Agreement with which both Australia and New Zealand became associated.

The accelerated movement from Empire had transformed the British role to the east of the Indian Ocean. Although there was a general commitment to a regional defence organization there was limited enthusiasm for its containment function as perceived by the United States. In effect, SEATO was not much more than a planning staff, and in time proved itself a feeble alliance deficient in cohesive qualities. Military presence was more directly related to a residual *imperium*; a specific commitment existed to a former colonial possession, plus responsibility for the island of Singapore and the territories of North Borneo including the Protectorate of Brunei, and on the periphery were obligations in Hong Kong and Fiji. In addition, there was an involvement in the forward defence of Australia and New Zealand. These responsibilities and attendant roles were assumed without serious question despite reservations held about the utility of SEATO.

When the Malaysia scheme for the political unification of Malaya and residual British possessions in South-East Asia was proposed publicly by Prime Minister Tunku Abdul Rahman in May 1961, the British government responded with enthusiasm. Here was an opportunity for painless decolonization which would provide a framework of political stability for vestigial colonies in North Borneo as well as encapsulate a potentially turbulent Singapore. The scheme offered also the prospect of trimming a military presence, though not a military role. With the agreement on Malaysia in London in July 1963, the application of the Anglo-Malayan Defence Agreement was extended to incorporate all the territories of the new federation. Britain retained the right to bases and facilities in Singapore as it considered necessary, not only for the defence of Malaysia, but also 'for Commonwealth defence and for the preservation of peace in South-East Asia'.

If the onset of Malaysia offered a prospect of political retrenchment and a reduction in the scale of military establishment, the implementation of the scheme ran into difficulties because of the militant opposition of Indonesia abetted in less vociferous manner by the Philippines, which contested sovereignty in North Borneo. The British military presence, concentrated mainly in Singapore but augmented across the South China Sea, did not serve to prevent Indonesian insurgency in Northern Borneo or feckless military penetrations of the Malayan mainland; but substantial reinforcement of all arms of the services led to the effective containment of confrontation to no more than nuisance level until in August 1966, following internal political change in Indonesia, it was brought formally to a close. The experience of such military containment was mixed for the British governments which honoured their responsibilities for the defence of Malaysia. It demonstrated that Britain was capable, in the special circumstances of confrontation, of dealing with insurgency with skill and measured response. It demonstrated also the heavy demands in men and resources, including an annual foreign exchange cost of about £100 million at the peak of the operation, which could follow from maintaining and honouring the type of open-ended commitment contained in the Anglo-Malaysian Defence Agreement. At the time, however, this burden was sustained without question. The nature of the military action was such that casualty rates were exceedingly low, and there was no domestic reaction against the involvement. When the role of defender of Malaysia was assumed by the Labour administration of Harold Wilson, it served as a valuable symbol for a political party which felt a need to demonstrate its national credentials. What could be better than to stand by a justifiably aggrieved Commonwealth country which, at the time, could be represented as a model in race relations and parliamentary democratic practice?

During the early years of the Wilson administration the commitment to an east of Suez policy soared to new heights, at least in rhetoric, exemplified in the claim in January 1965 that Britain's frontiers were on the Himalayas. But, from the time of the Defence Review in 1966, a strong sense of economic weakness induced a climate of opinion whereby party political considerations dictated an attenuation of role. This brought about in January 1968 – in the wake of the devaluation of sterling – an abrupt reversal of a policy formerly represented as an act of faith. The consequence was a scar on the face of British credibility.

At the beginning of 1966 government emphasis on the management of public spending had produced a ceiling for defence expenditure, but without any corresponding reappraisal of commitments. The separation of Singapore from Malaysia the previous August in a context of intercommunal acrimony had already increased the difficulty of defence planning. None the less, in the months before the formal termination of confrontation, a military role was reaffirmed for Britain in South-East Asia, on the condition that military facilities would be utilized only with the willing agreement of the local governments concerned.

Increasing economic difficulty reflected by the crisis of July 1966, a need to conciliate those in the Labour party attached to social priorities, together with a conviction that Britain was not prepared virtually unassisted to assume again the burden of containing the equivalent of Indonesian confrontation, produced a reappraisal of policy within a year. In July 1967 the Wilson administration announced a decision to withdraw all military forces and facilities from Singapore/Malaysia by the mid-1970s. The question of cost bulked large in the public explanation of the decision, without acknowledgement of the argument that 'unless the total strength of Britain's armed forces is reduced, very little economy can be achieved simply by cutting commitments'.[1]

The decision to withdraw the military presence was greeted with genuine concern by the local governments, but in the main there was a willingness to accept it with good grace, because the period of rundown before final evacuation was considered sufficiently extensive to permit provision for alternative arrangements. Also, the terms of economic compensation most necessary in the case of Singapore, which had depended on the British base complex for employment, were felt to be generous in the circumstances. The July 1967 decision, however, was not to be the final word from the Labour government, which found itself obliged to devalue sterling in the following November in spite of a fervent commitment to maintain its world price. Within two months, the 'east of Suez' policy was modified further in terms of rundown of military presence; without consultation or warning, the decision was announced to expedite the process of withdrawal by advancing the date of its completion to March 1971. An additional nine months' grace was secured, however, through the intercession of Lee Kuan-yew, the Prime Minister of Singapore, which introduced the possibility of a further reappraisal of policy following the next British General Election.

The decisions taken, especially that of January 1968, suggested a piecemeal and hasty process, and not the product of cool minds. They produced some debate, and a minor revolt within the Admiralty.[2] The reasoning of a cabinet involved with pressing domestic matters appeared to owe little to any serious consideration of the function of the

British military presence. Painful recognition of economic limitations encouraged by the social priorities of a vocal wing of the Labour party, combined with a perception of the European Community as a viable going concern set aside earlier aspirations that one author has ascribed to Harold Wilson's streak of romantic conservatism.[3]

With the decision to withdraw militarily from east of Suez (including the Persian Gulf), the two major British political parties were not to be distinguished by radically differing attitudes to defence policy. Both government and opposition were committed to entry into the European Economic Community, and there was a common recognition of the absence of the resources to sustain a general capability which could permit substantial military investment in both European and Asian theatres. The Defence White Paper of 1970 made this explicit for the government in stating: 'The broad direction of our defence policy for the new decade is set. It will be a European policy firmly based on NATO.'[4] A tangible indication of the change in emphasis was the additional information that the government had ceased to declare ground forces to the contingency plans of SEATO from 31 March 1969. If in presentation January 1968 had signalled the end of a British presence in South-East Asia, the 1970 Defence Estimates indicated a vestigial if ambiguous role. Denis Healey, the British Defence Minister, announced in March that the government would seek release from the commitment contained in the Anglo-Malaysian Defence Agreement, described as 'a blank cheque'. At the same time, the government would retain a capacity to operate outside the NATO area. To demonstrate its ability to reinforce rapidly by air from the general capability, a large-scale combined exercise at brigade level involving this facility was held in May/June 1970 in North-Eastern Malaya, in association with units from Malaysia, Singapore, Australia and New Zealand.[5]

On a more permanent basis, the Labour government promised to retain a continuous training presence with a rotation of three infantry battalions annually in passage through the jungle warfare school in Johore. An air force maintenance unit would be kept in Singapore to service stop-over facilities at one military airfield for planes using the Masirah–Gan route to Hong Kong, where the garrison was to be raised to a level of 10,000 men. A small naval liaison team would also be in Singapore to supervise any necessary repairs on ships expected to call regularly. The difference between this package and what the Conservative opposition were prepared to offer involved a difference of form rather than one of major substance. Edward Heath, as leader of the opposition, had denounced the decision of January 1968 as a breach of undertakings to friends and allies and a dereliction of duty towards British interests. In August, while on a visit to the Australian capital, he made it clear that a Conservative government would provide a small but permanent military force within the context of a five-power military arrangement between Britain, Malaysia, Singapore, Australia and New Zealand. The rationale then for this alternative programme was that a tangible presence 'on the spot will be needed, if threats to stability are to be contained before they become serious, and if the general capability to reinforce is to be credible to those who are most concerned in this area'. Sir Alec Douglas-Home, then principal opposition spokesman on Foreign Affairs, saw the projected presence as a modest one whose function would be to provide confidence and to enable Britain's four Commonwealth partners to develop their full defence potential.

In the event, the muted debate about the merits and demerits of alternative policies became of academic interest. The Conservative party won the General Election of June 1970 to assume office, having declared in its manifesto: 'We have proposed a five-power defence force to help maintain peace and stability to South-East Asia. We will discuss this with our allies and Commonwealth friends – Australia, New Zealand, Malaysia and Singapore.' Prior to the election, for obvious reasons, no commitment was made to any precise scale of military presence. In Canberra in August 1968, Mr Heath had indicated that the implementation of policy would be bound by certain constraints. He remarked: 'It will depend on the equipment and manpower available to our armed forces. It will have to take into account the state of the economy of our country.' The precise nature of the British contribution was to be dependent also on consultations with those countries which had expressed a willingness to welcome what was described in Conservative publications as 'a continuing British military contribution to the security of the area'.

The bare bones of Conservative policy began to be fleshed out during July 1970, when the new Minister of Defence, Lord Carrington, visited Singapore, Malaysia, Australia and New Zealand to explain his government's proposal for a five-power force centred on Singapore/Malaysia. The underlying premise of this proposal, reaffirmed constantly during the course of his tour, was that Britain would be 'an equal partner with the other countries who are concerned in the defence of the area'. In terms of military substance, the British government's proposals were of a modest order. The package made public in October[6] included a 'detachment' of four Nimrod jet anti-submarine and long-range reconnaissance aircraft drawn from North Atlantic service – a complement to the two squadrons of Mirage strike aircraft which the Australian government had already committed in 1969. The function of the Nimrod needs no explanation, and has special relevance to the surveillance of the Straits of Malacca and the eastern extremities of the Indian Ocean. In addition to this aerial capacity, there was included a flight of Whirlwind helicopters for air-sea rescue. There was also to be a small naval presence of frigates and a submarine (in addition to two ships from Australia and New Zealand) on station between the Indian Ocean, Singapore and Hong Kong. On the ground, one battalion group of infantry plus an artillery battery with support facilities were to be stationed in Singapore in a combined force with two battalions from Australia and New Zealand, while it was hoped that a rotating number of approximately 3,000 troops would be able to pass annually through the jungle warfare school in Johore, which subsequently became a Malaysian military establishment.

Lord Carrington made the offer in the context of the termination of the Anglo-Malaysian Defence Agreement, with its open-ended commitment, and its replacement by a much looser consultative arrangement. The Conservative Defence Minister, like his Labour predecessor, recognized that the size of the general capability could only permit limited demands on military manpower, especially in view of the persistent internal security problem in Northern Ireland, which had strained the contribution to NATO in Europe.

Among the other four members of the projected five-power force, there had been general and undisguised pleasure at the success of the Conservative party in winning the British General Election. Such pleasure was to be diluted to some extent, however, when the precise terms of Lord Carrington's proposals were made known to two of the governments concerned.

Lord Carrington went first to Singapore. It had been clear on the island, since the time of separation, that lip service only was being paid to the dictum that for defence purposes Singapore and Malaysia were indivisible. Under the impelling force of the *rapprochement* between Malaysia and Indonesia and subsequently of Britain's decision to withdraw her military presence, Singapore had sought an independent defence capacity with great vigour and limited tact. The prime concern of its government was with island defence and, in particular, with creating a credible deterrent geared, above all, to the prospect of a revival of Indonesian militarism. In the wake of the initial and subsequent British decisions to withdraw, there had been a successful adjustment to the new situation and an advance in military preparedness. Prior to the electoral success of the Conservative party, there was little, if any, sense of reliance on Britain's ability to intervene from afar in the absence of a permanent military presence. Following the Carrington visit, the Singapore government, in pragmatic fashion with its own plans for defence policy well in hand, did not appear at all disturbed at the prospect of the termination of the Anglo-Malaysian Defence

Agreement. With its own conception of threat, it saw the practical value of a permanent – albeit modest – presence as worth more than a formal treaty commitment, although disappointment was expressed that the contribution was not to include Lightning strike aircraft, especially as the bulk of the Australian Mirage squadrons were to be stationed at Butterworth in Malaysia.

If the government of Singapore appeared reconciled to the proposed form of the intended British military presence, the government of Malaysia received Lord Carrington with mixed feelings. Despite the changing orientation of Malaysian foreign policy expressed in a venture into the world of non-alignment, the Anglo-Malaysian Defence Agreement, with its automatic commitment, had been regarded as a tangible asset. The British proposals, involving an alternative system of consultation, were regarded as disappointing and as only of token value not differing greatly from the intermittent presence promised by the Labour administration. The modest substance of revealed Conservative policy contributed to a growing conviction that Malaysia was not only on its own, but ought to demonstrate a greater ability to fend for itself.

Following the termination of confrontation, Malaysia's conception of her security problems changed, encouraged by the pace of *rapprochement* with Indonesia. Commonwealth defence had been regarded with increasing scepticism since 1968 when, during one of the periods of quasi-crisis arising out of the Philippine claim to Sabah, Malaysian appeals did not meet with the desired response. In May 1969 Malaysia had experienced a violent inter-communal clash, and had been obliged to suspend its normal governmental processes; from that juncture, the energies of its Malay ruling élite had been directed towards internal priorities, including combating the revival of Communist insurgent activity along a common border with Thailand. Security was conceived predominantly as an internal problem unrelated to the role of a Commonwealth force of limited substance. If at one level satisfaction was expressed at Lord Carrington's visit, together with a willingness to participate in subsequent discussions on five-power defence, there was only limited enthusiasm for the undertaking. Indeed, when Tun Razak succeeded Tunku Abdul Rahman as Prime Minister of Malaysia in September 1970, he laid emphasis on the independent course of his country's foreign policy and its developing relationship with countries in Eastern Europe, but made no mention whatsoever of Malaysia's Commonwealth links or the five-power force.[7] Subsequently a proposal for the neutralization of South-East Asia was publicized; and in private the view was expressed that, if neutralization was accepted, then a five-power agreement would not be necessary.

By contrast, the governments of Australia and New Zealand were more genuinely pleased at the decision to retain a modest British military presence. It made their own limited involvement[8] appear less isolated, but more importantly they were most agreeably disposed to the underlying premise of the British proposals, which involved the substitution of a consultative arrangement for the Anglo-Malaysian Defence Agreement.[9] Both Australia and New Zealand had second thoughts about military involvement without Britain, in the wake of racial upheaval in Malaysia in May 1969. Indeed, only the following month, the Australian Prime Minister, John Gorton, went out of his way to draw a distinction between his country's commitment to the defence of mainland Malaya and the Borneo territories, in part a subject of dispute with the Philippines, an ally of Australia within SEATO and in South Vietnam.

Interestingly enough, Indonesia, which had once led a rhetorical onslaught on the British military presence in South-East Asia on the grounds of imperialist encirclement, did not raise objections to the policy of the British Conservative government. Lord Carrington's tour followed soon after Indonesia had, with no real success, taken a diplomatic initiative to contain the extension of military conflict to Cambodia. Indonesia's growing concern with regional security encompassed also an apprehension over the prospect of a recurrence of racial violence in Malaysia. In the event, the reaction of the Indonesian Foreign Ministry to British policy was to let it be known, in Anglo-Saxon understatement, that it was not displeased.

Lord Carrington's visit within South-East Asia and to Australasia initiated serious discussions on the five-power force proposal. It was followed in January 1971 by a meeting of officials in Singapore and in April by a conference at ministerial level in London. The April meeting formalized arrangements for command structures for joint land, sea and air forces and, besides establishing an Air Defence Council, set up also a Joint Consultative Council to provide a forum for regular consultation at the senior official level on matters relating to the defence arrangement. At the same time an obligation only to consult was substituted for the automatic commitment of the Anglo-Malaysian Defence Agreement.[10] The whole arrangement was to come into force on 1 November 1971.

Up to now we have considered the course of the reappraisal and revision of British policy in South-East Asia and the nature of the military contribution to the five-power force. It is time to discuss the rationale and utility of such policy and contribution in the light of the possible problems which might be encountered.

It was stated above that Conservative policy makers did not differ greatly from their Labour counterparts in an assessment of the availability of military resources. Few took seriously the earlier pretension of the Wilson administration that the general capability was of sufficient substance to permit a major reinvestment east of Suez.[11] Lord Carrington's proposals were for a very modest presence by previous standards, and for a minuscule one compared to the investment of forces at the peak of confrontation. Given the limited scale of intended British military involvement, albeit in association with a modest contribution from Australia and New Zealand, together with a progressively enhanced defence capacity by both Malaysia and Singapore, one is faced with the germane question of the intended and likely function of such a presence.

The major purpose of the British military presence has been represented as a contribution to stability. It has been acknowledged that 'the forces involved are not expected directly to defend British interests in the sense that they will protect the oil installations or rubber plantations by physically defending them. How could they?'[12] The assumption was that stability would follow from a presence 'on the spot'. It was argued further that 'it is the Conservative contention that a general capability based on the UK, distant in time, lacking in local experience, unacclimatized, and bereft of equipment in the area, will contribute little to stability'. Although such argument (directed against the policy of the Wilson administration) would appear to have lost some force in the light of the modest size of the additional presence offered, its underlying essence has remained. 'The nub of the Conservative argument, therefore, is that British interests in these areas can only flourish in conditions of stability, and that a British military presence will make a significant contribution to this.'[13]

Stability, which is the key consideration upon which Conservative policy purports to turn, is not a very precise expression. It tends to be identified by its absence rather than by its presence; in general terms, it infers the preservation of a tolerable political order in the face of serious challenge, either from internal or external sources. British success in resisting such challenge is attested by reference to the periods of emergency and confrontation. As the Conservative party has argued, 'it must be accepted that, without British intervention, it is highly likely that both Communist insurrection and later Indonesian confrontation would have succeeded in South-East Asia'. Such contentions are beyond dispute. None the less, it should be stressed that both operations involved a large-scale investment of men and resources in circumstances where success was in part a product of the overall direction of military planning residing in British hands. During the major part of the emergency, Britain was the sovereign power in Malaya,

95

while at the outbreak of confrontation Britain was the sovereign power in the North Borneo territories. But, as the memory of confrontation begins to recede and Malaysia, in particular, seeks to demonstrate greater self-reliance, the prospect of equivalent British control in military operations, whether in the unlikely case of aid to the civil power or in the unexpected situation of acting against an identifiable external aggressor, becomes increasingly remote. Indeed, the British government has made it abundantly clear that it does not intend that its forces should play a predominant role, and that a major investment of the order necessitated by the onset of confrontation is not contemplated.

Defence *per se* was not represented as the prime function of the British contribution; rather it was argued that 'a military presence can often prevent a situation developing in which disruptive elements can thrive. In short, a military presence on the spot can avert trouble.' Stability was to emerge from the aspect of deterrence provided by a combined presence incorporating the contributions of Australia, New Zealand and local forces. It was explained: 'Conservative policy is therefore to make an existing deterrent more viable, not to provide that deterrent alone.' The deterrent argument, however, would seem to be lacking plausibility, especially in relation to the examples cited above. British military strength prior to the advent of the emergency and confrontation was clearly in excess of the level of contribution envisaged in Conservative policy. And in both cases the military presence had to be substantially reinforced to contain the situation.

Deterrence in relation to external aggression is a fanciful prospect; and provision for effective defence is an uncertain activity, especially in South-East Asia, where scenarios are easily provided requiring substantial resources. But the framework for British policy is one which does not envisage a tangible threat to either Malaysia or Singapore from a third power within the next ten years. Balanced assessments of Chinese capacity and intent do not contemplate the prospect of the People's Liberation Army moving *en masse* in a southerly direction, while any analogy with past Japanese practice is misleading. Similarly the present modest and unadventurist orientation of the current government in Indonesia and its co-operative association with Malaysia does not foreshadow any early return to a mode of confrontation, even if its revival cannot be ruled out entirely.

The logic of all this is that the modest British military presence as a contribution to a five-power force can not be considered adequate to help deter or to meet a substantial threat. Also, if such a threat materialized there would be no guarantee that reinforcement would follow automatically, given the condition of the general capability and the

96

government's decision to economize on air support facilities. Given, however, that such a threat is not contemplated, except possibly by Singapore with its anxious view of Indonesia, then the British military presence would seem irrelevant in terms of the key objective of Conservative policy, namely to make an existing deterrent more viable. The local governments, for their part, give the impression of believing that a combined presence will have some deterrent effect but, except in the case of Singapore's obsession with Indonesia, deterrence is perceived in terms of a measure of psychological comfort rather than a substantive commitment based on a serious and uniform conception of threat.

The argument for deterrence has limited relevance also in relation to an internal threat. Communist insurgents will decide when and where to take up armed struggle on the basis of their own capacity, but importantly also with reference to what they would see as a revolutionary situation. A British military presence quartered on a permanent basis in Singapore, no more than American presence in Vietnam, is not likely to bulk large as a constraint on such action if the internal political condition is ripe for exploitation. More important perhaps than the question of deterrence is the fact that it is extremely difficult to contemplate a counter-insurgency function for the British presence which could be differentiated from an internal security role. And intervention to deal with the latter situation has been ruled out by the Malaysian government.[14]

Because of the nature of racial arithmetic and communal antagonism in Malaysia – particularly in the light of the experience of the emergency and in the aftermath of May 1969 – it would be exceedingly difficult to draw a line between counter-insurgency and assistance to the civil power inevitably against local Chinese. The political condition of Malaysia makes for clear disadvantage for any outside power seen to be acting to reinforce a political *status quo* perceived to be in the primary interests of only one community. In terms of fact this may not be so, but an external military presence in South-East Asia, however modest, is vulnerable to the force of polemic playing on prejudice. Of course, involvement in counter-insurgency operations cannot be ruled out altogether. However, such involvement would be most likely in circumstances where the scale of insurgency had passed beyond the capacity of the Malaysian government to contain it with its own resources. In such circumstances the demands of the situation would require an order of involvement not contemplated in Conservative policy.[15]

Up to now, we have considered only negative aspects of the British policy for a military presence in South-East Asia. There are, however, certain positive features which, in justice, ought to be assessed before

G

passing judgement. For example, while it is not anticipated that the presence will serve as a direct physical protection to British economic interests in Malaysia and Singapore, there is some expectation that the fact of the five-power force including a British contribution could be an inducement to investment. Such investment, of course, would come not only from Britain and its Commonwealth partners but also from other countries who have not required the presence of their own flag to assist in the safeguard of economic interests. The primary benefit of such investment would accrue, of course, to Malaysia and Singapore, and would be of only limited value for Britain.

In promoting the five-power force, the British government will be relieved of the automatic obligation of the Anglo-Malaysian Defence Agreement. The British presence will also ensure the involvement of Australia and New Zealand in regional security, as well as assist the overall relationship between London and Washington, which has relevance to undertakings in Europe.

But perhaps the most cogent argument in favour of the retention of a British military presence within a five-power force – and one related to that elusive notion of stability – is that it will contribute to the co-ordination of local military planning, especially in the deployment and use of sophisticated weapons systems. It is suggested that this aspect of the five-power force will induce a process of political reconciliation and co-operative association between Singapore and Malaysia whose relationship has been very strained, and yet who both pay public respect to the indivisible character of their defence problems. The cogency of this compelling argument is undermined somewhat, however, by the fact that the prospect of reconciliation and co-operation would seem to hold equally under the arrangement envisaged by the Labour party for the withdrawal of a permanent military presence by the end of 1971.

Following the decision of January 1968 to accelerate the process of British military withdrawal, a five-power conference was held in June in Kuala Lumpur, at which the British government's representative promised to make available a ground-to-air defence system for Malaysia and Singapore, together with the necessary expertise for instruction in its operation. The effective functioning of such complex electronic equipment would require co-operative association between Malaysia and Singapore in the absence, as well as in the presence, of a permanent British military contribution. While keen to encourage the placement of British striking power in Singapore, the government of the island has been especially aware of the need for co-operation between itself and Malaysia in technical provision for ground-to-air defence systems where geography dominates politics. Indeed, recognition of this aspect of indivisibility has been responsible for the element of dualism in the defence policy of Singapore. The government of Singapore, stimulated by the sound advice of its High Commission in Kuala Lumpur, is aware also that it cannot isolate itself from the racial problems that could beset Malaysia in the future. An increase in private conversations between senior ministers of both countries has indicated a growing awareness of common problems, although not an easier relationship. For example, in September 1970, a prearranged visit to Kuala Lumpur by Lee Kuan-yew had to be cancelled at the last moment, as a consequence of over-zealous conduct by members of the Singapore police force in detaining three Malaysian youths and then cutting their somewhat lengthy locks.

It has been suggested that a British presence within a five-power force could prove to be a factor for restraint, and thus contribute to that elusive stability so desired by Conservative spokesmen. Such a role, however, is fraught with danger. For example, Britain could find itself caught up in any embroilment which might ensue between two countries with different political cultures and interests; such was certainly its misfortune at one juncture during the Wilson adminis-tration.[16] Entanglement in any such reoccurrence would offer little profit and much risk. One doubts also whether racial passions if aroused would be calmed by the presence of an additional battalion of British troops stationed in Singapore. If the visit by the Prime Minister of Singapore to Malaysia could be cancelled on the strength and repercussions of the hair-cutting incident mentioned above, then the prospect for Britain as moderator of conflict would appear to be both near impossible and unenviable.

In the wider context of any grand strategy, the British military contribution does not represent much by way of purpose or substance. Views have been expressed to the effect that it might serve to prevent the emergence of a vacuum in the Indian Ocean which the Soviet navy would be eager to fill. There is no doubt that the few Nimrod anti-submarine and reconnaissance aircraft, together with the small naval presence, have a surveillance function in the Straits of Malacca and the eastern extremities of the Indian Ocean. However, such a modest force has no real relevance to matching an increasing use of the Indian Ocean by the Soviet navy. Such use will be determined by factors like the possible reopening of the Suez Canal and the availability of base facilities in prospective sites such as India and Mauritius. Much of the talk about a Soviet naval threat has been in the form of polemic to sustain a case for selling arms to South Africa, and such polemic has been adequately refuted elsewhere.[17] Meanwhile, even the Conservative government has not shown itself completely of one mind on this

99

question: in October 1970, following his return from a tour of the Far East, the Minister for the Navy, Peter Kirk, expressed the view that exaggerated attention had been given to the Soviet naval build-up; the report of his comments made it clear also that his view reflected that of the Chiefs of Staff.[18] It is interesting to note, however, that American naval opinion has welcomed the British decision to retain a military presence in South-East Asia, and that President Nixon has expressed a willingness to finance a naval communications facility on the island of Diego Garcia within the British Indian Ocean territories, which were constituted by the Wilson administration with such a purpose in mind. None the less, what Britain has offered to contribute to a five-power force is not going to affect significantly the balance of naval power in the Indian Ocean area.

All in all, the British military presence will be little in substance, and will add materially only to a limited extent to what the Malaysians and the Singaporeans are developing by way of separate defence infrastructures. The scale of the presence offered, costed at approximately an additional £6–7 million annually, has been determined by economic stringency expressed in terms of what can be spared from a depleted general capability strained in particular by the demands of internal security in Northern Ireland. Constraints on British action and initiative, however, do not derive only from limitations of resources or even of political will. It would be ridiculous to criticize in the manner of a Dean Acheson in terms of losing an empire and not yet finding a role when the constraints on roles are determined, not only by economic weakness, but also and importantly by the circumstances of involvement. The British military role in South-East Asia, although not faced by the order of problems experienced by the United States in Vietnam, is not free of such dangers where involvement might be contemplated. Indeed, it is almost certainly true to say that involvement is the last thing expected of a military presence whose stay in South-East Asia could be a limited one.[19]

The most that can be said for the proposed British presence is that it is acceptable with reservations to local governments in countries which Britain purports to know well. It is claimed that it will provide a measure of psychological assurance which cannot be expressed in precise or tangible terms. Its failings as they appear to this writer derive from the fact that the character of the contribution and the context of operation do not lend themselves to practical function. Indeed, the intended presence does not appear likely to be able to provide either for deterrence or for defence.

In effect, the British military presence is envisaged in symbolic terms. If the role remains one of symbol, then modest window dressing will suffice splendidly to underpin a policy which serves to demonstrate continued interest in South-East Asia and international standing. But if the demands of the situation of involvement take on a different cast, then the alternatives could involve either an entangling commitment from thinly stretched capability, or yet another scar on the face of British credibility.

NOTES

1 Hugh Hanning, 'Britain East of Suez: Facts and Figures', in *International Affairs* (*Britain East of Suez*, special issue, April 1966), p. 253.
2 See Christopher Mayhew, *Britain's Role Tomorrow* (London, 1967).
3 Neville Brown, *Arms Without Empire* (London, 1967), p. 28.
4 *Statement on the Defence Estimates 1970* (Cmnd 4290, 1970), p. 14.
5 The preparations for this exercise were begun fifteen months in advance. The results indicated that, if there was to be any rapid reinforcement from the general capability, it would be possible only if a Brigade headquarters were established in advance of deployment.
6 *Supplementary Statement on Defence Policy 1970* (Cmnd 4591, 1970). See also *Statement on the Defence Estimates 1971* (Cmnd 4592, 1971), which provides additional detail.
7 See Ian Ward in *The Daily Telegraph*, 23 September 1970.
8 Prime Minister John Gorton, speaking in the Australian House of Representatives on 25 February 1969, pointed out that 'it is no longer a contribution to the efforts of a major power which we will be called upon to make. It is a substitute for the efforts of a major power. And such a substitute must fall far short of what previously existed and be of a different character.'
9 Gorton also pointed out, in connection with the Anglo-Malaysian Defence Agreement: 'Should that Agreement in the future cease to be operative, we would wish general understandings rather than specific treaty obligations to be worked out with the countries concerned and ourselves'.
10 The Communiqué stated *inter alia*: 'The ministers also declared in relation to the external defence of Malaysia and Singapore, that in the event of any form of armed attack externally organized or supported or the threat of such attack against Malaysia or Singapore their governments would immediately consult together for the purpose of deciding what measures should be taken jointly or separately in relation to such attack or threat.'
11 For a criticism of the strength of the general capability by a serving officer, see a letter from Lt.-Col. Ackland to *The Times*, 15 August 1970.
12 Miles Hudson, *East of Suez* (Old Queen Street Paper no. 9, April 1969), p. 9 and passim. (Mr Hudson is in charge of external affairs in the Conservative Party Research Department.)
13 A corresponding view can be found in Phillip Darby, 'Beyond East of Suez', *International Affairs* (October 1970), p. 658.
14 See the letter from the Information Division of the Malaysian Ministry of Foreign Affairs, in the *Far Eastern Economic Review* (12 September 1970).
15 A more general consideration of this point has been well made in L. W. Martin, *British Defence Policy: the Long Recessional* (Adelphi Papers no. 61, London, 1969).

[16] See Michael Leifer, 'Astride the Straits of Johore', *Modern Asian Studies* (July 1967).
[17] Laurence Martin, 'The Cape Route', *The Listener*, 23 July 1970. See also J. E. Spence, 'South Africa and the Defence of the West', *The Round Table* (January 1971).
[18] Colin Legum and Andrew Wilson in *The Observer*, 11 October 1970.
[19] Henry Stanhope, Defence Correspondent of *The Times*, has commented: 'British forces will probably have been withdrawn from the area by the mid-1970s, and there are those who will heave a little sigh of relief when they have succeeded in getting away without being involved in something that is too hot to handle.' (*The Times*, 13 April 1971.)

VI The 'Special Relationship'

CORAL BELL

Since the beginning of this century, the dominant factor in the relationship between Britain and America has been a steely British determination to assume that there is between the two powers an underlying common interest, more important than the often sharp clashes of particular interests, or sharp differences of interpretation of particular situations. This is in itself so unusual an assumption between sovereign States as to warrant the phrase 'special relationship', though the particular concrete meanings attached to that term will be looked at in due course. The point to note for the moment is that the vital question initially is the assumptions behind policy. Whether any reality has matched these assumptions is another question, which will be taken up presently. The other immediate point is that it has been the *British* choice of assumptions that was, or is, decisive. In any alliance, one may argue, whether tacit or formalized, it is the weaker partner which makes the crucial choice. The dominant power in an extensive alliance system, like the United States, is somewhat in the position of a skipper in a sailing boat. His interest lies unambiguously in having the members of his crew put their respective weights behind the courses he has decided upon; but the crew members, for their part, have to make the decision between staying with the boat or constructing their own canoes to paddle – or, at any rate, rocking the boat. It is a continuous act of choice. In the British case the choice, I shall argue, was until 1971 favourable to the American connection *above any other.*

Before setting out to adduce evidence on this point, I should perhaps indicate the argument for regarding this as a true constraint on British foreign policy. It has operated, to my mind, to rule out a number of theoretical options which might have been considered in the absence of this assumption of parallel strategic interests with the United States. No doubt most of the possible alternative courses of policy were based on alternative assumptions about the nature of the world which would not be particularly acceptable to British decision-makers, or to the British electorate. But the fact is that these alternative assumptions have been, not so much considered and rejected by British policy-makers, as dismissed out of hand, or deemed unworthy of consideration, because they would have required the discarding of a framework of assumptions which has been familiar now for seventy years, and has only very occasionally shown signs of weakness. If it were not for this framework, there might have been more recruits, even in official circles, to a right-wing or Gaullist nationalism which would hold that Britain might pursue its own national interest more effectively by balancing between the dominant powers than by accepting the status of lieutenant to the United States. On the other hand, there might have been more recruits also to the view maintained by many left-wing groups, even in America, that to contribute to the strength of the United States in the management of the world is to contribute to the upholding of a structure of international injustice; and that the moral duty as well as to the true national interest of Britain is to assist the forces of revolutionary change in the society of States, from which alone can come justice for the world's peoples. These two extreme viewpoints, which one might describe as 'right-wing Machiavellian nationalist' and 'left-wing idealist-Maoist', have had only faint approximations among political groups of any importance in Britain, and would hardly appear in the schedule of possibilities of, say, a member of the policy-planning staff of the Foreign and Commonwealth Office. (Oddly enough, the actual impact of either of these possible attitudes on the society of States would be much the same: destabilizing in a greater or lesser degree. The right-wing nationalist line might well be more so than the left-wing line. It is not coincidence that China's most valued European friend has been France.)

It is easier to understand the later influence of the basic assumption of an overriding common interest between the United States and Britain than to give adequate reasons for its initial historical emergence. The period is clear enough (about 1895–1900), and perhaps the psychological mechanism, in that both powers then found themselves to some extent 'in the dock' to the rest of the effective world opinion of the time, the Americans over the Spanish–American war and the British over the Boer War. But what can only be described as the steady course of appeasement pursued by Britain, then the dominant power of the society of States, towards its up-and-coming and eventually successful competitor for that role remains historically surprising. One might instance the difference in attitudes towards Germany as a potential naval rival, and the United States as the power which did finally take the naval crown, almost without resistance, from Britain's grasp. Indeed, this naval example might be pursued historically up to the present as a microcosm of the general direction of British diplomatic attitudes: there was some anguish at the loss of Atlantic supremacy in 1919, more resignation over the Pacific in 1922, positive enthusiasm about the Mediterranean growth of US strength in recent years, and for the Indian Ocean qualms of anxiety in case the United States should remain reserved in its attitude to the area, and that it might by default become a Russian lake.

Within this overall context of, as I said, a progressively hardening British determination *not* to identify the United States as a potential military adversary, there have of course been periods of sharp friction, sharp enough to seem at the time likely to erode it away. Some post-war episodes of this sort will be discussed in more detail later, but it should be noted that no crisis since 1945 has been attended by such real mutual ill-feeling as those earlier in the relationship we are considering. If one contrasts Anglo-American relations in the period before US entry into the First World War, with that before US entry into the Second World War, or the friction over war-debts after the First World War, with the friction over the American loan after the Second World War the comparison is enormously in favour of the later period in every respect. The sense of common interest is not only firmer and less darkened by doubts on the British side; it has spread to the American side. President Wilson in the early stages of the First World War did not believe that any American interest would be served by participation, and he almost came to a rupture with Britain over the blockade. President Roosevelt in the Second World War obviously took a diametrically opposed view, and there was no crisis of feeling equivalent to that of 1916.

If one were drawing a graph of the role of the 'special relationship' as an influence on British choices in foreign policy, one might show it as establishing a fairly gentle rise, with some declivities, from 1895 or so to 1917; then a short high plateau to the end of the peacemaking, followed by some decline in the 1920s and 1930s, followed by a new and much higher plateau from 1941 to 1956. It is possible to argue that, even from 1956 to 1970, the decline was so slight as to be unimportant, and certainly the evidence appears to show that this relationship remained a more vital influence on British policy choices than any other – more important, for instance, than the relationship with the Commonwealth, or France, or the EEC, or European Free Trade Association (EFTA), or the UN. As for the relationship with the North Atlantic Treaty Organization (NATO), that to my mind is primarily the present form taken by the strategic part of the relationship with the US.

The sense of parallel strategic interests has been always the most visibly effective element in the general mesh of assumed common interests. It is true that the economic relationship between the two has been enormously important, especially to Britain, and that in both world wars and the aftermaths of reconstruction, the British economy has been heavily dependent on the American. But this economic dependence has generated much more resentment than the strategic one:[1] it has been seen by influential British policy-makers more as a dangerous weakness than as an advantage, whether the question has been post-war loans, or the connection between the dollar and sterling as reserve currencies, or the vulnerability of the City to movements on Wall Street. There has not been nearly so much ambivalence about the strategic connection, except among a small group on the Left and an even smaller one on the far Right. Yet this basic consensus – the assumption that US military power is a shield, not a threat – depends in turn on the more indefinite substance of a sense of common values. If one asks *why* British decision-makers and the British electorate were prepared to fight to the death against a world dominated by German military power, and at least moved determinedly to build a coalition against the prospect of a world dominated by Russian military power, yet accept placidly (with qualms only among relatively impotent minorities) a world basically dependent on American military power, the answer can only be because German or Russian military power served, or serve, political values felt to be alien and/or repugnant; American military power serves political values felt to be familiar and acceptable.

This submerged premise probably has depended, in turn, on what Bismarck assumed would be the most important political fact of the twentieth century: that America and Britain both speak English. The arguments of the minorities who have dissented from this premise, and held, in particular episodes or in general, that American power was serving policies that were morally unacceptable, or incompatible with British interests, will be considered presently. We have first to define more clearly what the common interest has been seen to be, in the view of the effective British decision-makers.

Taking the post-war period as a whole, I think one can hardly define this assumed common interest more specifically than as the rational management of world politics, with a view to avoiding both war and defeat without war. In the early part of the post-war period, roughly 1946–55, this general objective was expressed principally by a drive to build a balance-of-power coalition, to set inhibitions on the further growth of the Soviet power-base in Europe. That phase was more or less completed with the accession of Federal Germany to NATO in 1955. In the fifteen years since, lacking any dramatic new threat, the coalition has certainly suffered some internal decay, but not so much as to render it ineffective. By the historical standards of military alliances in peacetime, it has shown remarkable longevity. And certainly British policy has hardly wavered, through the twenty-five years since the idea first began to be turned into policy, from the notion that a military alliance, tying American power unambiguously to the defence of Western Europe, must be the sheet-anchor of British security.

It is interesting to speculate what the choice of British policy-makers would have been if the two halves of this convenient arrangement (on the one hand the unambiguous American commitment, and on the other the Continental forward-defence line) had seriously pulled apart; if NATO, for instance, had been captured by some radical nationalist European grouping, determined to exclude American influence and power from the affairs of Western Europe. Would Britain – given that either option, but not both, was available – have chosen its American connection or its European alliance? In the period to 1971, one may say, the answer was always in favour of America. A pale symbolic shadow of this question came up in 1962, when the decision to depend strategically on an American weapons-system, Polaris, for the future of British nuclear strike-power, rather than to build a European delivery-system in conjunction with France, was seen by President de Gaulle as a reason for excluding Britain from the EEC. To judge by his memoirs, de Gaulle believed till the end that this was then, and essentially remained, the British choice when the crunch came in that form: he wrote in 1970 that the 1962 decision 'justified his circumspection' about British membership of Europe.

One may contrast this, as an appreciation of British priorities in the post-war period: for instance, the clear preference for the cultivation of hopes *vis-à-vis* Europe over those *vis-à-vis* the United States which was indicated by the snub to Roosevelt's initiative of January 1938.[2] This contrast is not surprising, since it was the Second rather than the First World War which 'imprinted' in British decision-makers the judgement that the American connection was Britain's most vital last-ditch strategic asset. After all, if there was any single strategic meaning to the war-time experience, it was that Britain had survived unbeaten the loss of all her traditional allies on the Continent and the trauma of seeing her adversary control the Channel ports for most of the war, and had yet, with American help, kept her place as one of the architects of victory and of the post-war balance. Thus in the aftermath of the war, as the European movement began to get under way, it would have been a direct contradiction of their personal histories for the British decision-makers of the time to rate the prospective European grouping as more vital to Britain than the American connection. Certainly neither Attlee nor Churchill was ever tempted into ambivalence on this point: with Macmillan, Wilson and Heath new elements arose to complicate the question.

Remaining for the moment with the early post-war years, one

might argue in criticism that British decision-makers of the time were so impressed with the strategic moral of the Second World War that they failed to appreciate the importance of its political or psychological result: that the nation States of Western Europe had been brought to a condition in which they were prepared to contain or forget their ancient tribal feuds in a new economic and diplomatic framework, and that this mood represented a change in the British environment which warranted questioning the priorities which the war had established in their minds.

At any rate, the British reluctance to become wholehearted Europeans had from the earliest days of 1946, whether mistakenly or not, a strong element of determination not to strengthen the European tie in any way that might weaken the Atlantic one. The major tactical point with British policy-makers was to maintain that no tension existed between the two, and thus to avoid being forced into a choice.

Looking back over these twenty-five years as a whole, one might claim as a substantial success for the people concerned that, in fact, no such choice has even been imposed beyond evasion: the Atlantic connection is still there, and so, more or less, is the forward defence-line in Europe, despite the little local difficulties with France. But Britain has, of course, suffered an economic penalty for this strategic success; perhaps the policy-makers concerned were less than realistic about the country's ability to sustain the double role economically. Mr Macmillan used to propound a view of Britain's position as being at the point of contact between three circles – Europe, the Atlantic, the Commonwealth. Such a situation may indeed have had a number of advantages, but they have proved expensive.

It would be misleading to imply that the 'special relationship' with America has been a constraint on British policy in Europe in any sense that might seem to hint at American reluctance to see Britain join the Six. Quite the contrary has been the case: the State Department has on the whole been far more firmly convinced than the Foreign Office that the road into the EEC was the right road for Britain. The same has been true of many of the top-most American decision-makers such as President Kennedy. With the advantage of being more remote than, for instance, British prime ministers from the actual problems of British readjustment to life within the Market, they have been a good deal more convinced of its essential advantages to the West as a whole. Dean Acheson's remark, painful though it was to British sensibilities, that Britain had 'lost an empire without finding a role', was only an unusually blunt reiteration of a view that had been conveyed for years from American to British participants in the policy-making machine.

A more accurate way of putting the situation between the two powers would be to say that the dominant British estimate of Britain's national interest (as formulated by the actual decision-makers of the time) assumed that the tie with the United States was more vital than the tie with the Continental powers (though both were very important): the dominant American estimate of the American national interest was that the strengthening of the European end of NATO and the preservation of its Atlantic orientation would be best served by British membership of the EEC. Most of the American policy-makers concerned also quite honestly believed that the British national interest, as well as Western political strength, would be advanced by this event; but, of course, it was not their national foot that had to be fitted into the European shoe.

During the 1960s, as the non-European world began to seem to American policy-makers more likely to provide the crises of the future than Europe itself, there was some change in the judgements of the most strategically sophisticated Americans as to where the British presence, militarily speaking, was most useful to Western purposes. Mr McNamara said that the British troops east of Suez were more valuable, man for man, than those on the Rhine: President Johnson and his Secretary of State were grievously disappointed that not even the smallest of token British forces could be obtained for Vietnam.

One may, in fact, make a general historic contrast between Europe (where Britain and the United States in two World Wars and the Cold War have shown consciousness of a parallel interest in combating powers which had some apparent potential for sweeping out of Central or Eastern Europe to the conquest of Western Europe) and the non-European world (which has characteristically been a sphere of economic and diplomatic rivalry, and quite often differences of political judgement. This is true even of the post-war period). The crises of the Anglo-American relationship have almost all been extra-European in origin: Palestine, Suez, the Congo, the Yemen, Vietnam, the Bay of Pigs, the Dominican Republic. The two powers had reason to understand that they needed each other in Europe, since the potential adverse powers there looked so formidable. This is still not true of non-Europe: even China does not yet in reality look formidable if your base point of reference is Britain.

For the post-war period the Middle East and, to a lesser extent Africa, have been the only genuine areas of contest, since Britain no longer has the economic or political strength to be a major factor in Latin American or Far Eastern affairs, as it was in the nineteenth and early twentieth centuries. Thus British public attitude on Vietnam or Laos or Cambodia, or on the Bay of Pigs and the Dominican Republic, though it certainly stung American policy-makers, especially President

Johnson, to some rage, did so rather because it was painful to their sensibilities or politically damaging than because it represented any real obstacle to their purposes. As Mr Healey once tough-mindedly observed, a nation's power in any particular sphere is dependent on its ability to help a friend or harm an enemy. By the 1960s, this power for Britain had vanished in the Latin American sphere, and was undergoing its presumed last exercise in Asia.

The process of Britain's withdrawal back to its European base did, however, show its effects more slowly in the Middle East, and one might class the Suez adventure of 1956 as the one episode in all this historical disinvolvement during which the British government yielded temporarily to the illusion that it could re-enter the non-European world by force of arms. (There have been other episodes in which Britain has successfully used armed force to delay withdrawal of influence over the post-colonial outcome, but that is a different question.) The fascination of Suez as a case-study in Anglo-American relations is, not only the clarity with which it shows British policy as subject to American veto (since it was certainly, despite some policy-makers' denials, the American attitude which induced the British government to abandon the project at a point at which temporary military success was almost within its grasp) but also the questions it raises about why the veto was so slow in making itself effective. The ambiguities of diplomatic finesse even between close allies – in fact, especially between close allies – have never been better illustrated. Failure of understanding is usually taken to arise from lack of communication, but in this case one might be tempted to put it down to a surplus of communication: the decision-makers concerned could not see the wood because various ingenious people were working so hard at pointing out the trees. Mr Harold Macmillan's memoirs make this clear almost comically. He writes for instance of the vital first American reconnaissance, by Robert Murphy: 'We certainly did our best to frighten him or, at least, to leave him in no doubt of our determination. . . . He must have reported in the sense which we wanted.' On the American side, Dulles certainly imparted some ambiguity to his own signals, seeming at one point deliberately to convey the impression that the US might acquiesce in the use of force ('a way must be found to make Nasser disgorge'), and at another point sending the reverse signal (the statement that he had never intended that there should be any teeth in the Canal Users' Association). I would be inclined to class this as an example of his use of ambiguity as a technique of crisis management, intended in this particular case to delay any action at least until after the American presidential election. On this point it was a failure. The reason for the precise timing of the Anglo-French–

Israeli action is still somewhat obscure: why so disastrously *that* week rather than a fortnight later? It must have been the Israeli decision to mobilize on 27 October which determined the military time-table of the other two, but one would assume that any adequate set of consultations on collusion ought to have taken note of the one certain political fact: the date of American elections. Mr Macmillan seems to have recognized later that he had missed the vital signal in his September talks in Washington: 'Except for the plea that we should try to avoid pressing the issue until the election was over, there was no hint in this talk that Dulles did not recognize our right, and indeed our need, to resort to force if necessary. Perhaps I should have attached greater weight to the date of the Presidential election . . . I felt that the American government, while publicly deploring our action, would be privately sympathetic, and thus content themselves with formal protests'.[3]

Beneath the failure of understanding, however, this crisis[4] in Anglo-American relations turned around a genuine asymmetry of national interests or assumed national interests. The British decision-makers of the time assumed that the British national interest required that the Canal be kept in the control of Western governments or a Western-oriented Egyptian government. The American decision-makers assumed that the American national interest could not be served by so traditional a piece of European plundering in the non-European world. Fifteen years after, with the Canal again just a fortified ditch, and with no prospect of its being reopened save under a joint Soviet–American guarantee, one can make a case for the original Eden assumption that its operation could not be assured by the local powers alone. But there is now no special British interest in seeing it open, and a possible American interest in doing so is just emerging. The original asymmetry of interests as between Britain and the USA has vanished.

One could call this symptomatic of the general process by which the occasions of conflict between British and American interests in the non-European world have been reduced. As Britain 'draws in her horns', there remain fewer and fewer areas in which a serious clash of interests is possible. Bearing in mind Palestine and the Yemen as well as the undercover competition in the oil States (oilmen cut each other's throats in gentlemanly quiet), it seems perhaps surprising that the endemic Middle Eastern frictions of the period 1945–60 did not produce rather more irreparable holes in the general fabric of Anglo-American relations. In the case of Suez, this must be put down to a piece of rapid and skilful invisible mending on the part of Mr Macmillan. (One might argue that the survival of the 'special relationship' owed even more to him than to Churchill.)

In fact, to change the metaphor, he may well be regarded as the most skilful practitioner on this particular fiddle, reaching an even finer hour in his art over Skybolt than after Suez. Along with the Multi-Lateral Force (MLF) and the 'centralized command and control' problem, both of which also belong to the Macmillan era, Skybolt illustrates the strength of Whitehall's determination to keep British and American strategic interests parallel. I use the term 'Whitehall' deliberately, because I think this is one of those spheres of policy in which the arguments of, say, a tough-minded senior civil servant in the Ministry of Defence or the Foreign Office may have had more influence on the way things finally went than the Cabinet or the parliamentary party, or opinion generally.

The issues on which this can happen are usually so specialized that they require intensive study, and sometimes 'restricted' information. But though they are 'technical' in this sense, they may also in the nuclear age involve the largest issues of possible life or death for whole populations. It is in this field, to my mind, that one can see most clearly one of the facets of the 'special relationship'; it has been, among other things, a relationship between the 'intelligence communities' of the two countries. No doubt the Central Intelligence Agency (CIA) and the Special Intelligence Service (SIS) compete in many areas, like other branches of American and British endeavour, but it is clear from such scraps of knowledge as the outsider can gather that there is also a considerable 'pooling' of information in Washington and London. The system seems to have been established during the Second World War, and not to have been much dismantled since. One would estimate it to be closer than that between Britain and any other power – even, for instance, Australia or Canada. It is a sort of official and 'undercover' counterpart of a general intellectual relationship, which the shared language makes more readily available between these two powers than any two others of comparable importance. Even for those with no access to 'restricted' information, its influence can be felt in the small international strategic community, whose largest elements are American and British. This might not seem important, but in fact it is vitally so, because the process of debate within this group has been a major formative factor in the way in which the decisions of, say, Mr Denis Healey or the policy advice of Professor Henry Kissinger may be formulated.

It was this factor, to my mind, which prevented any real friction over the 'central control' doctrine of Mr McNamara's time. (The doctrine enunciated in his Ann Arbor speech of June 1962 laid down the principle that 'our best hope lies in conducting a centrally controlled campaign against all of the enemy's vital nuclear capabilities, while retaining reserve forces, all centrally controlled'.) Theoretically, since the British nuclear strike-force was actually in being, while the French force was just a determined gleam in the eye of President de Gaulle, this evolution in American policy offered an opportunity for a much sharper and more immediate conflict of interests with Britain than with France. In fact the opposite proved to be the case: the Anglo-American 'joint targeting' system, which presupposes close co-operation between the military intelligence establishments concerned, seems to have continued unimpaired, whereas France set out on the road of doctrinal nuclear independence.

It was again this issue which underlay the Skybolt/Polaris debate, and the difference between British and French attitudes towards the American offer. When British decision-makers first began to understand that Mr McNamara might mean what he was saying about cancelling Skybolt, on which they had relied to prolong the life of the V-bombers into the early 1970s, the situation appeared a textbook illustration of the French thesis that reliance on American technology might mean a disastrous collapse for the nuclear force concerned. No doubt Mr Macmillan's attitude of wounded astonishment, and fear for his own political survival, represented the most appropriate diplomacy for Nassau; it was eventually successful in extracting the offer of Polaris as a substitute, and though Polaris was initially more expensive, it had a far longer term of viability as a weapons system. (In fact, if Skybolt had been delivered on time, the Labour government of 1964–70 would certainly not have moved towards an alternative system, so that Britain's nuclear strike force would have been phasing out by the early 1970s, leaving France as the sole European nuclear power, and in a situation to remake European strategy to her own prescription.) If the United States government had refused Polaris to Britain (it was also offered to France) as some State Department men wanted the President to do, it might of course have forced the Prime Minister into the choice of France, instead of the United States, as Britain's primary strategic partner, and so reversed in 1960 the whole trend of British policy since 1945. But Kennedy rejected this advice, under the influence of Macmillan's persuasive diplomacy, and so the British reliance on the American strategic weapons systems was enhanced rather than diminished during the 1960s. It may be prolonged as Poseidon succeeds Polaris, unless a bargain is struck over British entry to Europe, on the basis of a French style of nuclear force. Since land-based systems now look much more vulnerable than they did in 1962, such a system might well be submarine-based, not greatly different from Polaris, though certainly less advanced than Poseidon.

Some well-informed Europeans have argued that the Nassau agreement was the rationalization rather than the reason for de Gaulle's veto in 1962; that if Macmillan had been refused Polaris he would not have got entry to the EEC either. De Gaulle would simply have found some other reason for the rejection.[5] This may be so, but British nuclear co-operation would have been so valuable to France at this point that it is difficult to believe that even de Gaulle would have opted for total independence.

In any case, Mr Macmillan did not regard it as a reasonable bargain for Britain. On a technological and economic basis it could not be, since Britain has been undoubtedly a net beneficiary from the enormous American research effort in weapons development. An independent project, even sharing costs with France, would have been a far more expensive way of keeping up any kind of strike system.

But, though the objective basis for Mr Macmillan's decision may be clear enough, there is exemplified in this crisis and others of his time a factor which must be mentioned: personal relationships between President and Prime Minister, Foreign Secretary and Secretary of State. The bad personal relations between Eden and Dulles played some part in the Suez catastrophe; the good personal relations between Macmillan and Eisenhower, and Macmillan and Kennedy, played some part in the repair of Suez, in the Polaris offer, and in the Cuba crisis of 1962. Probably the personal factor is more often overrated than under-rated, but it ought never to be disregarded. Mr Harold Wilson's abortive attempt to act as a mediator in the 1967 crisis of the Vietnam war probably never had much chance of success, since neither party at that time had much intention of moving the conflict from the military to the political plane. But the President's personal suspicions of the British participants in these efforts ('working on getting their Nobel Peace Prizes') probably vitiated what slim chances there were, and ensured that the effort ended with maximum confusion and resentment all round.[6]

Mr Nixon as President and Mr Heath as Prime Minister seem to have enough in common to prove compatible: both moderate, un-charismatic conservatives, grappling with essentially similar problems of inflation, communal friction and over-commitment abroad. The first visit of Mr Heath to Washington in December 1970 illustrated neatly how the balance of political and diplomatic usefulness of President and Prime Minister to each other shifts from time to time, and affects the way in which they speak of the connection between their two countries. On this occasion it was Mr Nixon who spoke warmly of the 'special relationship', and Mr Heath who retreated modestly to the phrase 'natural relationship'. Mr Heath's choice of vocabulary may have been influenced by a consciousness that many of the pro-European segment of his own party have come to regard the British assumption that the connection with Washington is the most important of the country's diplomatic and strategic connections, as the principal obstacle to Britain's taking up what they see as its only satisfactory future role, in Europe. Given their premise that a strong, united 'third force' Europe will prove an unmixed diplomatic blessing, they are probably right in believing that undue British stress on the relation between London and Washington has been counter-productive to their hopes. Whether they can convert the stalwarts of the party, or still more the strategic back-room boys permanently to their assumptions is another question. For the benefits of the European connection are still somewhat a matter of faith to be proved after joining, whereas the advantages of the American connection, at least in the strategic field, can already be demonstrated over the whole post-war period.

The usual counter to this observation, in London or in Washington – though not in Paris – is that there is no incompatibility between the two. The fairly near future may put that claim to an inevitable test. One of the implications of the Strategic Arms Limitation Talks (SALT), the American–Soviet *détente*, and the possibility of some American withdrawal of forces from Europe, is a rise in the potential importance of European nuclear power. As the American strategic guarantee to Europe, which has been the whole basis of its defence since 1947, begins to look less absolute, the case for its being reinforced by some degree of European independent nuclear strike-forces looks more plausible, in several respects, than it has done since 1947. The credibility of the existing European strike-forces is also much affected by some of the possible SALT decisions, especially the decision on anti-ballistic missiles (ABMS). Assuming that any American–Soviet agreement is for a light symmetrical deployment of ABMS around their principal cities *only*, as appears probable, a European nuclear strike capacity retains some credibility. But what should be its nature? It could remain as at present, in two nationally controlled independent forces, British and French (the British is at the moment much the stronger). But there may appear a case for a single jointly-targeted force. The difficulty is that the British force is still based on American technology, whose secrets are forbidden by the American legislation concerned to be shared with any other power, including France. Thus while for France an *entente nucléaire* with Britain could have great technological advantages, for Britain it might have a very high technological cost: the loss of access to American advanced weaponry. In the circumstances, the bargain will be hard to sell to British decision-makers. The American government could force the choice, if it so wished, by modifying its own legislation and policy, either to include France in the magic circle of technological secrets,[7] or to exclude

Britain. If there really is to be a European deterrent strong enough to enable some degree of American withdrawal from European affairs, then the American interest would seem to require that it be strong enough to offset any Russian advantage in Europe, without being strong enough to encourage any kind of European adventurism. It will be a difficult balance to strike, and even after the Americans have made their decision, the essential problem for Britain may still be the same. Considering how often the French concept of the European interest has been at odds with the British concept of it over the past twenty years, why should British decision-makers assume that they will see eye-to-eye with their French counterparts on the very difficult and dangerous problems of the strategic field for the foreseeable future? And if they do not believe this, what reason could there be (other than a forced choice) for making the disadvantageous bargain of France instead of the United States as Britain's closest strategic partner? Some of the decision-makers concerned will remember that the last time that partnership operated, it produced Dunkirk.

The United States could, as I said, force the choice by its own administrative or legislative action, and if enthusiasm for 'United Europe' remained as high in Washington in the 1970s as it was about 1960, it might logically do so. But experience, first with France and more recently with West Germany, has cast some shadow over the original US assumption that the strengthening of the European movement is always unalloyedly in the American national interest. Both President de Gaulle and Chancellor Brandt have shown, in their separate ways, that strong European personalities, playing in their respective fashions for their own concepts of the national or the European interest, can devise policies disconcerting to American decision-makers, and damaging, as Washington sees it, to American management of the situation *vis-à-vis* the Soviet Union. There is an American phrase which indicates the likely choice among rival Presidential candidates: 'the most available man'; the phrase implies a more complex and subtle balancing-out of future possibilities as between the contenders than the words themselves may seem to convey. In rather the same way, though it is at times overshadowed by France or West Germany, Britain has in fact persisted in emerging, on balance and over the long term, as 'the most available ally'. This is not only continuously true in the non-European world; there are possibilities in the present European reshuffle which might make it as vital a consideration there at some future date as it was in 1947, when Britain was the only firm American bridgehead to a Europe whose political shape was still indeterminate.

Let us now look at the degree to which it is likely that the 'special relationship' will continue to influence British foreign policy choices. Despite all that has been written to prove that it can no longer exist, if it ever did, my own view is that its influence may persist for the foreseeable future almost undiminished, even assuming British membership of the EEC. If we drop the phrase 'special relationship' and talk merely about 'the American connection' as an influence on British policy, it is rather difficult to see exactly why it should be expected to decline. The United States is still the dominant power in the alliance system which Britain sees as vital to its own security, and the security of all the powers in which it has a special interest (such as Australia, New Zealand, Canada, Western Europe, and the powers which lie around the Indian Ocean). Therefore the sustaining of American strength, and access to the policy-making machine in Washington must continue to be objects of British policy. (I am, of course, assuming that there is unlikely to be a revolutionary change in the British decision-making élite; if there were such a change, as in Cuba with Castro's victory, the objects of policy would no doubt change also. But the level of probability of this development seems so low as to justify disregarding it.) Even after British entry into the EEC, it is difficult to see that the familiar objectives will change in the short run. The British are not likely to believe that the American commitment to Europe has ceased to be necessary to the stability of the world balance of power; President de Gaulle himself did not believe that. Nor is it likely that Western Europe will come to find the political values of Moscow more congenial than those of Washington, unless there is a sensational mellowing of the one or a sensational deterioration of the other.

It is theoretically possible, of course, that over the long term the European grouping including Britain might undergo such a phenomenal growth in political cohesion and will, economic strength and military power that it would look like an equal or more than equal to the Soviet Union, and could afford to be genuinely indifferent to any American strategic help or guarantee. As far as Western Europe's resources and its people's skills go, such an outcome is quite on the cards; but whether the general peace would be better assured by the resulting situation is another question, and the British attitude to it might therefore remain ambivalent, as it always has been to 'European third force' notions.

One might reasonably maintain that generation change will affect these calculations. The line of argument would be that the belief that American strength in the world was a British interest became 'imprinted' in the Second World War generation of policy-makers (who now have almost passed from the scene) and 'reimprinted' in the Cold War generation of policy-makers (who are now edging towards retirement) during unambiguous struggles against political systems (Hitler's Germany and Stalin's Russia) which the decision-makers concerned, and the electorate in their time, saw unambiguously as dangerous to the survival of Britain and to all reasonable political values. These generations, whether of decision-makers or electorate, are not likely to change their minds; the imprinting has gone too deep. But the generations which arrived at political consciousness only in the 1960s and 1970s (for example those born after 1945) have had no such personal imprinting with this experience; the Second World War – and even the Cold War – are just old men's tales to them. Their 'crystallizing' experience of American purposes in the world, indeed their whole image of America, has been created by the moral and political disasters of the Vietnam war and the racial strife of the late 1960s in the United States. So they have no such reasons to identify with America, as had earlier British generations in this century. If they identify the British national interest with any outside power, it will be with Western Europe.

All this seems quite possible, and might be accounted the main question-mark from the British side over the future of the 'special relationship'. There are likewise some question-marks from the American side, mostly having to do with the decline of Britain as a power in the world. In the immediate aftermath of the Second World War, American policy-makers to some extent still felt themselves newcomers to the corridors of power politics, and in need of some guidance through them. So there was scope for considerable British initiative, and if one looks at Ernest Bevin's role in the Marshall Plan, or Churchill's, or Macmillan's role in the processes that created the *détente*, it is apparent how important these were. But what is the role of the marriage-broker once the engagement has been announced? Since 1962 the US–Soviet relationship has found its own logic, and no intermediary has been required.

The two great functions of British policy-makers with respect to American policy in Europe – first moving it towards the balance-of-power coalition, and then moving America and the coalition towards *détente* with the Soviet Union – are both completed, for the time being. The system may break down, and then a new function for Britain might emerge, but nothing of the sort seems likely at present. In the world outside Europe, American attitudes to British policy have passed through two main phases: first, suspicion at their presence (up to the early 1960s) and, later, alarm at their withdrawal. With the return of the Conservative government in 1970 the situation has become fluid again; it seems probable that Britain will play at least a minor role in affairs 'east of Suez'. The Indian Ocean could become an area of considerable general interdependence, and one which might prove of some importance to the general balance of power in the world. American development of a communications facility on the British island of Diego Garcia may prove an appropriate symbol for the future in that area.

There are many uncertainties here. Either country could develop its own brand of neo-isolationism. In Britain's case, it would probably be of a European sort, refusing to notice any security problem more distant than the Mediterranean; in America's, it might be imposed by domestic difficulties, rising even towards the level of civil war. If both developments occurred, the Third World would be left to whatever political winds blow through it. One cannot say for certain that this would be inimical to peace – only that its results would be unpredictable. The strength of the 'special relationship' is that it is not a construction, but a capacity – a capacity to see the elements of common interest in whatever international storms the time may bring.

NOTES

[1] The case of the RB 211 contract and its disastrous effect on Rolls–Royce and Lockheed offers a classic illustration of the way in which an effort to cultivate the American market may produce a crop of dismay and resentment on both sides.

[2] See Sumner Welles, *The Time for Decision* (New York, 1944), pp. 64–8.

[3] *The Wind of Change*, vol. 4; *Riding the Storm 1956–1959* (London, 1970), pp. 136, 149.

[4] See Richard E. Neustadt, *Alliance Politics* (New York, 1970), for a full account of this crisis.

[5] Pietro Quaroni in *The World Today* (October 1970).

[6] An account of this episode has been published by the former CIA man involved, Mr Chester Cooper, in *The Lost Crusade: American Policy in Vietnam* (New York, 1970). See also Mr Wilson's account of the events of Kosygin's visit in his political memoir, 'Our Days in Power', *The Sunday Times*, 16 May 1971.

[7] In this case some difficulty might arise over the Non-Proliferation Treaty and the SALT negotiations.

VII Britain and the Commonwealth

PETER LYON

We all have different problems, not excluding Britain. But we live in one small world. If we can give the Commonwealth a new relevance, a fresh validity, it will be a more agreeable place for all of us.

From Lee Kuan Yew's address of welcome at the opening of the Commonwealth heads of government meeting in Singapore, 14 January 1971.

The Commonwealth is a mystery. It is mysterious because it is so complex and ever-changing; it defies simple explanations. This is why so many statements about it are simple – indeed, oversimple. The contribution of British ideas and practices to the Commonwealth of the recent past and the present has been, and is, profound; British public interest and understanding of the Commonwealth has mostly been perfunctory. The purpose of this chapter is to try to explain this paradox, and to assess the nature and importance of Commonwealth links for Britain in the present and in the immediate future.

Despite the title of the chapter, it should be said at the outset that it is this writer's view that very often use of the phrase 'the Commonwealth' can be an impediment to realistic understanding and to intelligent policy, unless the context makes the connotation entirely clear. Used as anything more than as a convenient shorthand label for purposes of general identification, 'the Commonwealth' needs to be supplemented, even if not replaced, by careful consideration of British interests in relation to particular Commonwealth connections.

Britain and thirty other countries[1] were represented at the Commonwealth Prime Ministers' Conference in Singapore in January 1971. All thirty had been governed before their independence by Britain; but their assembling together in Singapore cannot be explained adequately in terms of their once having the same colonial ruler in common. Each freely chose to become a member of the Commonwealth at the time of gaining their independence (as Burma and Sudan did not), and each has freely chosen to stay in this Commonwealth company (as Ireland and, perhaps, South Africa did not). There was, and is, thus some presumptive interest in the continuance of the Commonwealth for each of its members, though undoubtedly for different reasons and with different degrees of enthusiasm.

Britain's present interests and involvements in the Commonwealth cannot be adequately understood without some considerable knowledge of history; but that discipline is a very ambiguous and equivocal guide to present policies, and even more so for those of the immediate future. The Commonwealth is no mere vestigial reversionary of Empire,[2] though quite often nowadays it is wrongly regarded as this only – not least because some of its most persistent residues are those of Empire. To understand British policy in regard to the Commonwealth requires some general appreciation of the numerous factors, including ideas, by which it is conditioned, and the main methods and instruments which are employed in seeking to safeguard and promote the national interest. It would be foolish to embark on any analysis of Britain and the contemporary Commonwealth without first emphasizing the very close and many-sided interdependence of Commonwealth and world affairs.

A complete study would need to assess the quality and significance of Britain's relations with each of the thirty-one erstwhile colonies that are now members of the Commonwealth, to compare and contrast these bilateral relationships with the many Commonwealth and other multilateral links in which they are enmeshed, then to try to aggregate these adequately and finally to view Britain's Commonwealth interests and involvements comprehensively in the general context of her domestic and international relations and resources. All this obviously cannot be achieved in one short chapter.

The preference of this writer is for piecemeal analysis preceding any general judgements. But a case for impressionism as sufficient in itself has been strongly made, surprisingly enough, by one of Britain's leading international lawyers and theoreticians of power politics, in the following terms:

'Little would be gained by attempting to define the Commonwealth by any piecemeal analysis. It is more promising to try to grasp the specific character of this elusive and dynamic phenomenon in a more impressionist manner. In this perspective, the most striking features of the Commonwealth are its apparent illogicality, informality and spontaneity. It appears illogical because it is so thoroughly empirical and pragmatic. It is informal to the point of appearing shapeless. Relying as it does on complete spontaneity, it gives, at times, the impression of being dormant, fading away, or having ceased to exist.

'The Commonwealth is ever-changing. Thus, to observers with

static minds, it is elusive, if not incomprehensible. They tend to concentrate in their analysis on its past.'[3]

Even so, it remains the present writer's contention that the Commonwealth will not adequately yield her full character in sketches and etchings, for these can too easily become either caricatures or else mere eulogies. For the Commonwealth has been much exposed to writers, and to very little sustained analysis in depth. Thus it ill behoves the present writer to complain of the inevitable inadequacies of short treatments and then to perpetrate another, but this is at least the main reason why I have felt it necessary to festoon this chapter with so many notes and references.

Britain is the founder member of the Commonwealth, and in 1971 had the largest Gross National Product (GNP) of the thirty-two members, although this will probably be surpassed by Canada during the 1970s. Territorially she ranks about seventy-fifth in size among the countries of the world, occupying only about 0.18 per cent of the world's land area, and more than half a dozen fellow members of the Commonwealth have national territories of their own larger than Britain's. In population size she ranks tenth in the world, with about 2 per cent of the world's inhabitants; and in density of national population she is fourth, behind Japan, Belgium and the Netherlands. In the relative volume of her world trade, Britain ranks third in the world, accounting for nearly one-tenth of the total, taking about one-fifth of the world's exports of primary products, and providing about 8 per cent of the worlds' exports of manufactured goods.[4] The United Kingdom is also the central banker of the sterling area, and the City of London is one of the world's greatest centres for international investment, insurance, and financial expertise. These facts at once indicate why, for most of its members, the Commonwealth is still, in economic terms, if less and less in political terms, Anglocentric. But in general the notion that there is a single major centre is becoming less and less important.

In terms of national income per head, the United Kingdom ranked in 1971 appreciably below the United States; some way below Canada, Australia, New Zealand, Sweden and Switzerland; and slightly below France and the Federal Republic of Germany. It is thus no longer the case that Britain is the greatest economic power in the Commonwealth in every sense. Demotion from her former and short-lived position as richest country in the world, whether in terms of GNP or *per capita* income, occurred in the nineteenth century. Not that these particular – and crude – measures of international status were fashionable in the nineteenth century;[5] but they are today, in an age when well nigh universal deference is paid, at least verbally, to the value of universal adult suffrage and to improving material welfare in measurable ways.

It is wrong, however, to regard Britain's present role and relations with all other Commonwealth countries, and in the world at large, as solely, or perhaps even substantially, attributable to her own actions, initiatives or inadequacies. The transformation of what was only thirty years ago still the largest Empire in the world into the present Commonwealth, with some small remaining dependencies, is the result of changes (particularly in military power, in patterns of trade and investment, and in dedominionization[6] and decolonization) which have been at work for more than a century.

The essence of the British Empire was its exclusiveness, the predominance of a single metropolitan centre and the compulsory membership of its subordinate parts; the essence of the contemporary Commonwealth of Nations is that it is a voluntary association of formally equal members acknowledging no common superior or single centre – despite the continuance of some considerable London centricity. It is curious that this unique and voluntary and versatile Commonwealth of nation States should have emerged out of the dissolution of such a ramshackle Empire, providing it thereby with a protracted and diverse series of obituaries and a degree of posthumous vindication.

Ideas

'The British Commonwealth sometimes professes to be an empire of ideas; but the ideas, when one examines them, seem to be subtle, if not elusive – they are ideas about the forms and spirit of procedure, about methods of legal redress and political behaviour, about toleration, moderation and persuasiveness. They may be ideas which sensitive and intelligent people value highly, but are they ideas which will awaken the fervour of the masses ?'
W. K. Hancock (1937)

For the British people the Commonwealth today, like the British Empire before it, is usually regarded and understood, if at all, unselfconsciously and most times with quiet geocentricity. Insular idiom can be, and is, veneered with myths that are in part self-indulgent and in part self-demeaning. The two qualities are not necessarily far apart. Self-deprecation can be a form of self-flattery; it can be a thinly disguised way of quietly advertising how much can be shed without real loss. Such thoughts may provide balm and solace in days of imperial decline and decolonization, of national uncertainty and of recurrent national economic difficulties, especially when the considerable differences between Empire and Commonwealth are not widely appreciated. The British Empire is now entirely dead; the Commonwealth is now a post-imperial and evolving association after Empire, and Britain still has a few remaining colonies.

The British are poor ideologues: there are many British political ideas, but no one dominant British idea. That is why ideologues are distrusted in Britain, and are distrustful of Britain. Ideas of Empire and of Commonwealth, however, have played a part in British life – sometimes harmoniously, sometimes in conflict – for centuries.

Imperial idiom once was Britain's most self-conscious and assertive ideology. But imperial ideology enjoyed a popularly ascendant vogue in Britain for only about fifty years, from the 1880s onwards; the Empire, for better or worse, indubitably was British. The Commonwealth (which by custom and usuage fairly swiftly ceased generally to be known as the 'British' Commonwealth in the late 1940s) has become less and less a British preoccupation.

The idea of Empire[7] was not unknown even to Anglo-Saxon England. It was party based on and fortified by myth. One belief was that King Arthur had made himself Emperor by asserting his independence of the Caesars; and the Statute for the Restraint of Appeals in 1532 began by declaring that 'by divers sundry old authentick histories, it is manifestly declared and expressed, that this realm of England is an Empire, and so has been accepted in the world'. Thus in Henry VIII's reign 'Empire' at least signified a single sovereignty. When, a century later, Milton wrote of 'this Britannick Empire with all her daughter-islands about her', he was thinking only of Britain and her offshore islands – Ireland, the Isle of Man, the Channel Islands, and even the Hebrides, the Orkneys and the Shetlands – which were her satellites. But he saw further and deeper; for he also envisaged an Empire and Commonwealth rather like that actually brought into being later by the British, or at least as seen by them in their most self-congratulatory moments: 'Surrounded by congregated multitudes, I now imagine that I behold the nations of the earth recovering that liberty which they so long had lost: and that the people of this island are disseminating the blessings of civilization and freedom among cities, kingdoms and nations.' In this view and its later equivalents, has not the Empire-become-Commonwealth truly served as a nursery of nations?

Milton's most famous exhortation, calling upon England to teach other peoples how to live,[8] and to spread the blessings of freedom, was very English, very arrogant – even very European – in character; for Europeans have since ancient times believed in their civilizing mission as a duty to the world. The British governing classes have been deeply imbued with such a belief, in this rivalled only by their French counterparts; but in both countries the desire to rule realms overseas seems swiftly to have evaporated in the late 1950s and early 1960s.

For prevailing fashions in ideas can change very markedly and swiftly. In early to mid-Victorian times a Gladstonian–Athenian conception of an Empire and Commonwealth, of a loose confederacy of free or would-be free peoples, held sway in Britain. This then soon gave way after 1870 to a swelling apolaustic imperialist-nationalism: popular imperialism first reared its head. At the start, the word 'Imperialism'[9] was used to castigate neo-Bonapartism and French imperial ambitions; soon afterwards it became a self-congratulatory label, a movement – a faith – for those, such as Dilke and Disraeli, who hymned of a Greater Britain that would emulate Greater Rome. The Empire that the English had so empirically, so haphazardly, put together, and had hitherto described so often in sonorous but pragmatic terms, now became lacquered, eulogized and stereotyped by convention and ceremony. In 1876 Queen Victoria was named 'Empress of India' by Act of Parliament – a title which British monarchy kept until 1947. Thus there was in mid to late Victorian Britain a kind of Roman interlude, particularly when transported and transmuted to India,[10] with men such as Macaulay, Sir Henry Maine, James Fitzjames Stephens and George Nathaniel Curzon playing prominent roles as participants – and sometimes as beneficiaries – in chief.

But the high noon of Empire also was the early morning of the modern Commonwealth. In its contemporary sense, the word 'Commonwealth' was first used, or at least anticipated, by Lord Rosebery in a speech in Adelaide in 1884 when he was on a private visit to Australia. He said to his audience:

'Does this fact of your being a nation – and I think you feel yourselves to be a nation – imply separation from the Empire? God forbid! There is no need for any nation, however great, leaving the Empire, because the Empire is a Commonwealth of nations.'[11]

Thus a British liberal-imperialist almost accidentally became the putative godfather of the modern Commonwealth. There have been many varied, and sometimes ingenious, subsequent attempts to invest the contemporary Commonwealth with an intellectual pedigree: John of Salisbury,[12] Halifax the Trimmer,[13] and Edmund Burke[14] are among the British philosopher-publicists who have been enlisted in this cause; Aristotle and Augustine can be conscripted if there is a desire to stress the more generally European origins of venerable ideas relevant to the Commonwealth today.

Undoubtedly, however, the idea of this Commonwealth of nations was taking shape as a fact long before it was coined as a phrase, even though the phrase achieved general currency only after 1949. 'Commonwealth is a distinctive English word current from the fifteenth century onwards',[15] wrote Sir Keith Hancock, the most penetrating and original of all the historians of the British Empire and Commonwealth between the two World Wars.[16] And he sought to show how the word became the vehicle for ideas and aspirations whose history stretched far back into classical antiquity, an 'irrepressible word' that 'persisted in breaking bounds', the watchword of England's 'greatest creative age', the seventeenth century, 'a standard and a manifesto' in the sixteenth and the twentieth centuries. When writing his magisterial survey of the Commonwealth in the middle 1930s, Hancock insisted that there was no necessary incompatibility between Empire and Commonwealth, that recent experience had helped to 'cut the claws of sovereignty' and, indeed, had reduced the pretensions of the doctrine of sovereignty to 'its own proper dimensions as a juristic hypothesis'. Refreshed and fortified by copious draughts of English Common Law, the jurisprudence and political practice of the Commonwealth on this view owed as much, and perhaps more, to the notions of Camden, Coke and Burke, as to those of Hobbes, Austin and Dicey; since 1949 the reverse has been true, but this may now change again in view of Britain's prospective entry into the European communities.

Hancock's persuasive writing was suffused with the conviction that the true purpose and end of the Empire/Commonwealth was the 'government of men by themselves' (a phrase, incidentally, which he seems to have got from Lionel Curtis, but then fitted it into a rather different philosophy of Empire and Commonwealth), that most colonies were embryonically independent States possessed of inchoate Commonwealth status. Implicit in this interpretation also was the notion, though not the phrase, of 'dedominionization' which in later years came to be described as 'autochthony'[17] – that is, 'springing from native soil'.

Decolonization[18] and assisting in the development of her former colonies might be said to have been twin and principal challenges and opportunities for British statecraft within the Commonwealth ever since 1945. There is little doubt that much more time and energy has been devoted to the first than to the second task by British leaders.[19]

No one who has even a superficial awareness of the speed and extent of decolonization since 1960 in the once very extensive British and French Empires can doubt that empires, as well as kingdoms, in the words of a familiar hymn, can swiftly 'wax and wane'. Lord Rosebery used some prophetic and presently relevant words in that self-same speech at Adelaide in 1884 in which he said:

'I confess I think that each day we live we shall be more and more unwilling to see this ancient Empire of ours – raised with so much toil, colonized with so much energy, cemented with the blood and sweat of so many generations – pass away like a camp struck noiselessly in the night, or split into isolated and sterile communities, jealous among themselves, disturbed by suburban disputes and parochial rivalries, dwindling possibly, like the Italian States of the Middle Ages, into political insignificance, or degenerating into idle and polite nonentity. And let me remind this assemblage of the fact that empires, and especially great empires, when they crumble at all, are apt to crumble exceedingly small.'[20]

Such sentiments should not be entirely dismissed as an isolated example of Rosebery's own encroaching misanthropy. Even among the enthusiasts for the British Empire and for the Commonwealth a sense of morbidity, of the imminence and likelihood of death has been recurrent. Kipling, the poet laureate of British imperialism, also wrote 'Recessional'. It is almost as if repeated public disavowals of one's own disillusion are necessary in order to forestall or reverse any trend towards dissolution,[21] or so as not to seem to be taken by surprise.

Even at moments of apparent triumph and self-confidence a sense of pessimism and uncertainty is often not far below the surface. Mr Harold Macmillan on his return home from a uniquely triumphal tour of the Commonwealth in early 1958, the first British Prime Minister to engage in such extensive Commonwealth travels whilst in office, none the less confided in what was then his private diary:

'There is no doubt that the tour has been a great success – far greater than I or any of my advisers thought possible – so far as the various Commonwealth countries are concerned. What is unknown to me is whether it has any impact at home. People at home seem to be in a very cynical and defeatist mood about everything.'[22]

This was yet another sombre reminder of the politician's pervasive awareness that foreign (and we may add Commonwealth) policy, begins, and ends, at home.

Whether or not Sir John Seeley was right when he said that Britain acquired in the eighteenth century an Empire almost 'in a fit of absence of mind',[23] it is certainly true that in the second half of the twentieth century it has only been found possible to divest Britain of overseas Empire decently by trying to display and practise much presence of mind. Even today there is still no smooth and swift way of completing British decolonization entirely. Tethered by the most Lilliputian of her colonies, Britain is still constrained to remain a colonial power for some considerable time to come, the least of her colonies remaining to the last.

Granted that Britain still has a few continuing colonial responsibilities,[24] some problems persist. In virtually all of the territories retaining any close association and constitutional subordination to Britain, the need of economic aid will be permanent; indeed, with growing population and with an undoubtedly rising level of expectations and demands, the bill must be expected to increase.

It would be quite possible to assemble a large anthology of intemperate and abusive criticisms volleyed at British governments or at aspects of British policy by fellow members of the Commonwealth in recent years. But to believe that these were without precedent before 1939 is to be remarkably ignorant of the history of the Empire/Commonwealth, even between the two World Wars. The Irish alone provided many spicy examples of uninhibited criticism, but they were not the sole skilled practitioners of this ancient art. What is different today is that there are many more voices raised, and more easily and loudly amplified, in criticism. The views of such critics are more swiftly and easily transmitted, and perhaps more people hear than ever before in Britain and elsewhere in the world.

Imperial thinking, Winston Churchill told Walter Lippmann in August 1939, 'means to think always of something higher and more vast than one's national interests'. British imperialists were, in fact, the custodians and champions of a comprehensive concept of 'British interests' they had themselves invented or zealously adopted. Empire inevitably produces imperialists. In Britain since 1945, and especially since the Suez war of 1956, the Commonwealth has seemed less and less capable of producing many ardent British 'Cth-men' – merely a few among the skittish at Christmas-time in the editorial offices of *The Economist* (as, for example, on 20 December 1958 and 21 December 1968).

Today, in Whitehall and Westminster the Commonwealth at large probably is seen principally as a kind of awkward octopus. Undoubtedly it is a beast with some occasionally friendly propensities, but nevertheless is hard to handle, and capable of delivering blows from almost any direction. Such a view does not preclude particular attempts at co-operation and joint ventures, but tends to assume that these will necessarily diminish as the beast gets older, larger and more ungainly.

Instruments

'We cannot work out a coherent foreign policy unless we are able to take fully into account the non-Commonwealth interests of

Commonwealth countries and to deal with them in their regional or world context. . . .

'The political and economic considerations dominant in determining British interests overseas increasingly cut across the divisions between Commonwealth and foreign countries. . . .'

Plowden Report (1964) paras 42 and 45 (6)

'The Commonwealth has no legal definition, and until recently has had no formal institutional expression. Inter-governmental consultation is its principal mode of operation, and this is carried on both by direct inter-governmental correspondence and by the periodic Commonwealth Prime Ministers' meetings.'

A Year Book of the Commonwealth 1971

These are two familiar and authoritative statements of prevailing Whitehall orthodoxy. The first line of thinking helped to hasten the death of the Commonwealth Relations Office (CRO), the second passage is to be found enshrined in various editions of the CRO (then the CO) yearbooks, and now appears in the *Yearbook of the Commonwealth*, thus carrying the *imprimatur* of the Foreign and Commonwealth Office, and having survived the demise of the Commonwealth Relations Office.

On 6 July 1960 Lord Home (as Sir Alec Douglas-Home then was called) had made his final Parliamentary speech in the House of Lords as principal spokesman for the Commonwealth Relations Office. On that day he told the House of Lords that a Secretary of State for Commonwealth Affairs 'must secure that the Commonwealth aspect is appreciated by every other department in Whitehall, both when they are taking their day-to-day decisions and in the framing of UK legislation; and he must be certain that the interests and views of Commonwealth governments are kept at all times before his colleagues in the Cabinet when they are framing United Kingdom policy'.[25]

This was a straightforward statement of the standard pro-Commonwealth view of those British politicians and public servants who wish to see the Commonwealth accorded prominence in British official thinking and decision taking; this company has become much smaller in numbers and influence during the past ten years. To promote such views effectively did and does not necessarily require that there be a separate Department of State specifically devoted to Commonwealth relations, but undoubtedly the existence of such a Department is an indication of the prominence and distinctiveness successive British governments had attributed to Commonwealth affairs since 1947. Thus the official demise of the Commonwealth Office as a separate Department of State in October 1968 was a great and significant change in Britain's governmental and bureaucratic treatment of Commonwealth affairs.

I

It was the culmination of several years of quasi-official, quasi-public debate[26] about how best to administer and deal bureaucratically with Britain's external relations. It was also a decisive moment in a series of rather similar administrative rearrangements.[27] The Commonwealth at large now counts for much less in Whitehall and Westminister than it did ten years ago.

Even so, it is still official orthodoxy, apparently, to insist that there are some persisting and significant differences between a British Embassy and a High Commission overseas – that is, between a diplomatic post in a foreign and one in a Commonwealth country. This difference was explained more than ten years ago, and similar versions have been authoritatively repeated on many subsequent occasions in the following terms:

> 'The principal difference between a High Commissioner and a foreign Ambassador in a Commonwealth capital is that, whereas the Ambassador must do all his business through the Department of External Affairs, the High Commissioner is entitled to deal direct with other departments of government. The result is that the High Commissioner and his staff at appropriate levels have contacts of an informal sort throughout the machinery of government.'[28]

And in a memorandum to the Estimates Committee of the House of Commons in 1959, the Commonwealth Relations Office claimed that 'the UK High Commissioner has closer and more frequent contact with the Prime Minister of the Commonwealth country in which he is serving than is the case with foreign heads of mission' – though it was admitted that practice, even in this regard, varied considerably.[29]

No doubt the intensities and relative importance of these special Commonwealth intimacies and mutual ease of access do vary considerably in various parts of the Commonwealth. For Britain today they are in general much more extensive and intimate with Canada, Australia and New Zealand than with other members; but even these are now declining as particularly intimate special relationships with Britain. For example, Canada's then newly installed Defence Minister, Donald Macdonald, said during a newspaper interview in February 1971: 'a lot of Canadians have a mistaken estimate of the regard in which we are held by Britain. I think we will have to expect a new relationship with Britain – they want it that way.'[30] Macdonald argued that this affected military relationships. He noted that the Canadian armoured force in Germany no longer served with the British Army on the Rhine; that it had moved south, and was now under an overall American command. He also commented that old Centurion tanks were the only major piece of British equipment the Canadians were still using. 'If the British come up with a good piece of equipment, we will buy it – but not just because it is British', he said. Similar instances could be given of declining intimacy in Britain's relations with each of the 'old Dominions'.

Britain's links with the rest of the Commonwealth and the world at large are much more extensive than those of any other member; but there is little doubt that the present British government, like its immediate predecessor, regards Britain's role in the Commonwealth as constituting obligations and constraints much more than opportunities and advantages. This point of view was put implicitly but very forcibly by the Secretary of State for Foreign and Commonwealth Affairs, Sir Alec Douglas-Home, in an address to the Commonwealth Press Union at their quinquennial conference in Scotland on 7 October 1970, when he stressed with pride Britain's aid to other Commonwealth countries, even in times of domestic financial stringency. 'Some day', he predicted, 'there will be a cross fertilization – a flow of capital and expertise between the various partners. But till then it is Britain and a few others in the Commonwealth who must carry the cost.'[31]

If the British government had been governed by a narrow conception of British interests, Sir Alec declared, it would not be making such efforts to seek protection for certain essential Commonwealth interests in its negotiations for entry into the Common Market, nor would it have taken so 'positive a lead' in the second United Nations' Conference on Trade and Development (UNCTAD) scheme for generalized preferences for the Commonwealth; nor would Britain be devoting 'so much of its resources to all forms of development assistance, and concentrating this on the Commonwealth in preference to other countries of the world'. Britain trades more, for its size, with the developing world than does any other industrial country; most of this trade was 'deliberately cultivated' with the Commonwealth countries of Asia and Africa. For seventeen of these Commonwealth countries, Britain was still the principal supplier, and the principal market for fifteen. This gave these countries, Sir Alec claimed, something which no aid could supply, and of which they stood most in need – a trade surplus. In 1969 Britain bought £130 million sterling more than it sold in Commonwealth Africa. And the flow of British aid was not restricted to capital and trade, but included people. There were over 14,000 British teachers or technical advisers working in the Commonwealth under government schemes, and in 1969 there were over 40,000 Commonwealth students at institutions in Britain.

Without the Commonwealth, Sir Alec concluded, it would be harder for a British government to receive the backing of public opinion for aid on the present scale, especially in time of financial stringency at home. 'The Commonwealth idea carries with it in the public mind a sense of historic obligation which makes sacrifice justified, and we can do, under the Commonwealth umbrella what we could never do for commonwealth countries if that umbrella was taken down....' All these comments were addressed to the underlying theme of how much Britain actually does to help fellow members of the Commonwealth. Nothing was said to suggest that Britain extracted anything of value for herself from the Commonwealth. Selflessness, indeed self-sacrifice, is now the prevailing tone of most British official statements about the Commonwealth. This may partly account for the apparent decline of the Commonwealth at large in the popular appeal of the British public during the past ten years.

Since October 1968, then, Britain's governmental-bureaucratic relations with specific Commonwealth countries have been dispersed in the different regional departments of the Foreign and Commonwealth Office. The only office in Whitehall now specifically charged with taking a pan-Commonwealth view is the – rather small – Commonwealth Co-ordination Department, which has the following responsibilities and interests:

> 'Constitutional questions, and policy, procedures and practices, affecting the Commonwealth as a whole. The Monarchy in relation to the Commonwealth. The position of the associated States and dependent territories within the Commonwealth, including their representation at Commonwealth meetings. Co-ordination of constitutional development in the dependent territories and of any dependent territories' questions falling outside the scope of other departments. Commonwealth Prime Ministers' meetings. The Commonwealth secretariat and other intra-Commonwealth organizations not separately allocated, the Commonwealth Parliamentary Association, the Commonwealth Foundation, and the Commonwealth Institute. Liaison with Commonwealth Societies. Commonwealth Gifts Scheme.'[32]

What then is left, if anything, of the old claim that Britain grants to members of the Commonwealth a range and ease of access to its government and administration not comparably available to other, non-Commonwealth, countries? It is difficult to test the truth and relevance of this doctrine today; but there can be little doubt that the sheer increase in membership of the Commonwealth since 1960 and the transfer of pan-Commonwealth 'management' functions from Whitehall to the Commonwealth secretariat since 1965 have greatly accelerated the general assimilation of Britain's Commonwealth and international relations, and has reduced any peculiarly pan-Commonwealth content. In the last resort, special privileges and access Britain grants to and receives from each fellow Commonwealth country now and in the future mostly depend on the prevailing degree of mutual trust, respect and reciprocity in their respective bilateral relations.

Trade

For well over a century, international trade has been of vital importance to Britain's economy[33] and it continues, of course, to be so today. The Empire and Commonwealth have loomed large in Britain's international trade position, and still do – Canada, Australia, South Africa and the Republic of Ireland are still among Britain's most important trading partners, though since 1957 the United States has been Britain's largest single market and source of supply. Britain relies upon imports for about half its total consumption of foodstuffs and nearly all the raw materials needed for industries. Exports of goods and services together represent about one-fifth of the gross national product (GNP). Britain is the world's largest market for foodstuffs (mostly bought from Commonwealth countries), and among the largest for metals and ores, textile raw materials, petroleum, and many other products. In recent years the expansion of domestic agricultural production has reduced Britain's dependence on imported food supplies, and the proportion of imported foodstuffs to total imports has fallen from 39 per cent in 1954 to 23 per cent in 1969, when imports of foodstuffs (including beverages and tobacco) were £1,934 million. There has been a similar downward trend in the proportion of basic materials imported – from 30 per cent in 1954 to 15.1 per cent in 1969; a major reason for this is the growing use of synthetic materials to replace such imported natural materials as rubber, wool and cotton. Thus, the structure of British import demand has changed quite considerably over the past decade; put crudely, but in a way which conveys a sense of this important change of emphasis, we can say that since 1945 the British economy has changed basically from one founded on coal and cotton to one reliant on chemicals and synthetics.

Britain's position in Commonwealth and world trade is affected by a multiplicity of factors, of which her aid and investment patterns are part; but broader historical and political connections between the UK and its former dependencies, and the legacies of British predominance in world trade and manufacturing during the eighteenth and nineteenth centuries, are also of continuing consequence. The development of the great London commodity markets and networks of British services over the Commonwealth – in banking, insurance, merchanting and shipping – are at once illustrations and reminders of this.

In general, however, the informal and historical, peculiarly intimate links between Britain and members of the Commonwealth are weakening, as are the formal connections provided by Commonwealth Preference and other special imperial arrangements. In the past twenty years there has been a noticeable tendency for British exports to do best in the less commercially developed, less competitive markets of the Commonwealth (Ceylon, for example, rather than Australia). The more rapidly the character of a market is changing, the less well the UK has tended to do. British business undoubtedly has failed, in many ways, to adapt itself to changing conditions in the Commonwealth – though, as with all generalizations, there are some notable exceptions. In general, it does seem true that Britain's post-war generally sluggish performance as a manufacturing and trading nation has tended to weaken its economic position in the Commonwealth very considerably. These recent trends are not inevitable or irreversible, but there are no significant signs at present that they are changing. Even if there were continued reductions in the relative magnitude of trade between Britain and members of the Commonwealth, this trade could still be substantial and important for the British economy.

Aid

Aid is employed as an instrument of foreign policy, but whether and how it actually advances or retards the interests of donors and recipients is usually very difficult to determine; inevitably it is a controversial subject.

The aid relationship is the most difficult form of diplomatic relationship to operate satisfactorily, whether one considers this from a donor or a recipient viewpoint. It is certainly not self-evidently true that disbursing aid directly increases diplomatic friendships and influence. Aid flows usually are symptoms, rather than causes, of good or bad inter-governmental relations. It was the considered view of a senior British official, expressed to the present writer, that the role that British aid had and could play in cementing Commonwealth ties is a neutral one, in itself containing neither marked diplomatic advantages nor disadvantages.

Britain's aid programme to poorer countries overseas consists of loans and grants for economic and social development, technical assistance, budget support, and contributions to multilateral agencies providing financial aid and technical assistance. Historically, Britain's aid programme began as part of its policies towards her colonies and dependencies, and even today most of British aid is distributed within the Commonwealth and to the remaining dependencies. In 1969 £157 million (88 per cent) of Britain's official bilateral aid was disbursed to Commonwealth countries and to dependencies.[34]

Investment and banking

Private British investment in the Commonwealth was more than £3,000 million in 1970, which is more than 40 per cent of Britain's total overseas assets. At the Singapore Conference in January 1971, Mr Heath claimed that private investment could be important in assisting the economic development of the poorer Commonwealth countries. But a number of other Prime Ministers expressed strong doubts about the usefulness of private investment as a substitute for official government aid. A Pakistani minister said that, quite apart from the value of private investment in assisting economic development, he doubted whether Britain would have much available for the developing world if she joined the EEC.[35] The essence of the disagreement between Mr Heath and his critics on this particular issue is that he appears to regard private investment as a solution to many development problems, while many other Commonwealth leaders are acutely aware of its shortcomings. A case against private investment was strongly expressed by Mr Forbes Burnham, the Prime Minister of Guyana, at Singapore, when he said that too few investors were willing to 'share the cake' fairly with their hosts, while too many were apt to claim extra-territorial rights or call in their own governments to protect their interests.

Many further doubts about the efficacy of foreign investment were expressed during the brief plenary discussion of economic problems in Singapore. There were many references to the targets proposed by the UN for the 1970s as a 'second development decade'. These require, *inter alia*, that developed countries should not only transfer 1 per cent of their GNP to the developing world by 1975 (which Britain has promised to do), but should also ensure that no less than 0.7 per cent of the GNP should be devoted to official government aid. At Singapore none of the speakers demanded, or probably expected, that Mr Heath should accept the 0.7 per cent target which had been rejected by the British delegation to the UN the previous autumn. There was no doubt, however, that general dissatisfaction was expressed, and lingers, about Britain's policies on aid and investment. This was not dispelled by Mr Heath's contention that British aid terms are generous, and that British investors are conscientious about ploughing back their profits.

From the late nineteenth century until the First World War British overseas banks provided international banking services from the main trading centres then within the British Empire, and also from those areas where Britain had large interests, such as Latin America. Later they expanded to provide branch banking networks in some countries. Since 1947 several British colonies, just before or just after their independence, have received advice and other forms of assistance from the Bank of England to help them set up their own national central bank; now many overseas branches of British banks are reverting to something rather like their earlier role. There is still, however, a considerable difference between overseas banks, mainly in the old Commonwealth (especially in Australasia), and those (such as National and Grandlays and the Bank of London and South America) mostly concentrated in the developing countries of the Commonwealth and the Third World generally. Indeed, a number of interested bankers have insisted that the main threat that their banks face is not only, or even mainly, nationalization, but economic sluggishness or stagnation. Lord Aldington, the chairman of National and Grindlays, said in his 1970 annual report that he welcomed the spread of nationalism into banking and that overseas banks should not attempt to run national branch banking networks in overseas countries, but concentrate on providing new international investment finance for their host countries and other customers.

These 'vulnerable' banks have the greater incentive to change, develop and specialize – particularly by attempting to provide international finance for these countries. Thus some of Britain's overseas banks and branches have become principally vehicles within the international money market for financing trade and investment throughout the world, instead of only in old imperial and other traditional territories. Both BOLSA and National and Grindlays now make more than half their total profits from their London head offices rather than from their branches abroad; this is of some significance when we recall that world international investment in the late 1960s was increasing at twice the rate of world trade.[36] In the future, British overseas banks and investors in the Commonwealth and elsewhere will need, more than ever before, to be sensitive to the requirements and susceptibilities of their host countries. While the hosts may need the co-operation of international banks and investors for many years to come, these international banks need not necessarily be British; they could be Japanese, German, American, or of some other nationality. Thus common membership in the Commonwealth now confers no particular or exclusive advantages in banking and investment matters, for markets and customers are sought on a world-wide or regional basis; the Commonwealth is of declining importance as a significant crucible.

Migration
Migration was an issue of major importance in imperial relations.[37] It is of increasing sensitivity and importance in present British[38] and Commonwealth politics[39] and, in part, though only in part, has been heightened by Britain's attempts to secure entry to the EEC.

British governments in the main have experienced, and expect, both immigration and emigration as processes involving settlement, usually at least until retirement age, and thus as trends to be assessed in terms of decades and years, not in months or weeks. Within the Commonwealth this situation was closely related to the always somewhat qualified, and now defunct, idea of universal British citizenship for all members of the Commonwealth.

The operative principle of the EEC's Labour legislation is to treat foreign workers as transient 'guests'. This rule is now incorporated in the regulations for alien workers in Britain, and is extended to all 'non-patrial' Commonwealth citizens under a new Immigration Bill in 1971. The Bill's slow and complicated progress in the House of Commons* in the second quarter of 1971 has impeded any clear negotiations and agreed definition between Britain and the member governments of the EEC on the movement of labour, but the British government has accepted the Community policy in principle. It seems probable, at the time of writing (July 1971) that there will be a legislative distinction between 'patrials' and 'non-patrials', by whatever definition Parliament finally adopts. Any such definition would exclude all those non-patrial Commonwealth citizens living in Britain who do not want to, or are unable to, acquire UK citizenship, for which a five-year residence qualification is required.

It has been authoritatively estimated[40] that in 1969, excluding movements between the United Kingdom and the Irish Republic, some 293,000 people emigrated from the United Kingdom compared with 206,000 arrivals, resulting in a net outflow of 87,000. This compares with the net outflow figure of 56,000 people in 1968; the increase resulted from a larger gross outflow and a smaller gross inflow. The fall in the gross inflow mainly reflected a drop in the number of Commonwealth immigrants, particularly from India, Pakistan and Ceylon, while the rise in the gross outflow was largely a result of an increase in the number of UK citizens emigrating to Australia.

The rights and privileges which the 'decision on the freedom of movement of employees within the Community' at present gives to the citizens of member countries of the EEC are considerable and go beyond what was foreseen in the Rome Treaty. Unless a member invokes an escape clause, it has to give any citizen of an EEC country the same competitive access to any job as its own nationals (given the assumption of equal qualifications). People are thus free to move from one member-country to another in search of work. If dismissed, they are allowed to stay in the host country for twelve months without a job.

* The government's definition of 'patrials' as people with at least one grand-parent born in the UK was thrown out at the Committee stage, and a less generous definition allowing a connection through the parents only was substituted.

Two diametrically contrasting viewpoints have been expressed by British opponents of their country's entry into the EEC, in respect of labour regulations.[41] These may be termed the 'invasion' fear and the 'exodus' fear: the first conjures up the image of vast hordes of foreigners from Europe swamping the British labour market; the second postulates a mass exodus of British workers into Europe in search of the greater riches available in more dynamic economies. Both views rest, of course, on the dubious assumption that mobility of labour is always principally motivated by economic factors; if recent trends persist, both fears seem exaggerated. If, as at present, prevailing levels and trends in wages and living standards are generally considered better in Western Europe than in Britain, then it is unlikely that cohorts of 'blackleg' labour will come flooding into Britain.

Many labour economists and other experts have their doubts about the validity of the opposite theory: that thousands of both British and Commonwealth workers will pack their bags and emigrate to Germany as a direct consequence of British entry into the EEC. While the 'pull' factor of demand does exist at present, the 'push' of unemployment is not considered big enough, and is unlikely to be allowed ever to grow to proportions that would thereby prompt mass migration from Britain into Western Europe. Some economists, however, do think that the lure of better wages alone may persuade perhaps as many as 200,000 skilled and semi-skilled British workers to go to Germany, whether Britain joins the EEC or not; early in 1971 there were some 15,000 British workers in Germany. But against these trends and possibilities is the fact that there are no traditional ties (particularly of kinship and language) to encourage and facilitate large-scale movement between Britain and the EEC without the spur – or sweetness, depending on one's viewpoint – of British membership of the EEC. French experience in labour mobility since 1957 has shown how tenacious traditional ties can be in determining migration. Thus those British workers who are emigration-minded most likely will continue to prefer the traditional countries for British emigration such as Australia and South Africa, for which more than 100,000 British people have departed annually during the past six years, apparently regardless of the fluctuations in the economic situation at home.

Interests and Involvements

'We have no eternal allies, and we have no perpetual enemies. Our interests are eternal and perpetual, and those interests it is our duty to follow. . . . With every British Minister the interests of England ought to be the shibboleth of his policy.

'I hold that the real policy of England is to be the champion of justice and right: pursuing that course with moderation and prudence, not becoming the Quixote of the world, but giving her moral sanction and support wherever she thinks justice is, and whenever she thinks that wrong has been done.'

These were the words of Palmerston in the House of Commons in 1848. They were resurrected and quoted with approval by Mr Edward Heath, in an article written for an American journal[42] about a year before he became Prime Minister of Britain. At the Singapore Prime Ministers' conference in January 1971 he voiced very similar sentiments, apparently with such fervour and sense of defiance that his nineteenth-century predecessor would have purred his approval.

But 'interest' is not made incorrigible or self-evident merely by calling it 'national', nor does such an invocation infallibly locate 'national interests' in some inviolate realm remote from competitive politics.[43] Every country – and government – has a multiplicity of interests, and if political activities and standards are to be resolved according to 'interests', then attendant problems have to be similarly assessed too, because each claim has a distinct particularity and priority in relation to any other. To be satisfactory and utilizable in a sophisticated way, the notion of 'national interest' needs to be comprehensive and evaluative as between different competing component interests. A real danger and depravity arises when politics are expressed as nothing but the pursuit of material interests, for this is a doctrine which is both shallow and immoral, denying as it does that there are any binding standards of obligation.

It has been, and is, a persistent British assumption that Commonwealth affairs should be quietly and intelligibly ordered, and that it is right and proper for Britain usually to play a prominent – if not always the foremost – role in this regard. The first opinion is nowadays more strongly held than the second; thus noisy, declamatory, openly disputatious diplomacy is regarded with distaste by most British officials and politicians as somehow alien to the proper conduct of Commonwealth affairs. Particularly since 1960, noisy public disagreements have been regarded by British governments as the unwelcome intrusion of bad 'UN' habits into an association which could do much better without such malpractices. Hence the predictably approving words about the quiet and mostly unpublicized special meetings of Commonwealth lawyers or Ministers of Education, or Finance, or some other commendably quiet example of inter-governmental or non-governmental co-operation within the Commonwealth. It is a view of politics consistent with the conclusion expressed by Balfour in his introduction to the Report of the Research Committee of the 1926 Imperial Conference (which emerged, so Leopold Amery tells us, as a result of judicious manoeuvring by Amery and his associates on the Empire Marketing Board) – 'Let us cultivate easy intercourse, and full co-operation will follow';[44] it is also the view of politics articulated in a dilute form by Mr Edward Heath at the Commonwealth heads of government conference in Singapore in January 1971.

In outlining his own conception of the Commonwealth's position and future to a plenary session of the Singapore conference on 15 January 1971 Mr Heath explained why he was in favour of what we may call a 'low-key' Commonwealth in the following terms:

'The future of the world is dominated by three problems – the challenge to international security by internal and external violence; the relation between the races of the world; and economic development. The Commonwealth can make a real contribution to the "successful management" of the two latter.

'It is the more important to strengthen Commonwealth links, because the world is now changing rapidly. Values for which the Commonwealth has stood are under challenge. The worth of the individual, the value of independence of judgement and decision, of mutual tolerance, respect and goodwill are coming under an increasing challenge. If we allowed our values to be eroded by neglect, or our basic principles to be distorted by passion, we would play into the hands of those who would like to see the Commonwealth destroyed and a very different international system take its place.

'The Commonwealth does not depend on contract or treaty, nor is it a deliberative assembly with rules of procedure required by a constitution to reach decisions on debated issues. Nor is it a market place for financial and commercial exchange, nor yet a joint enterprise in which the partners contribute prescribed stakes for a share of the profits. Nor is it even a court of appeal with a prescriptive right to sit in final judgement on the policies and actions of its members.

'To me it is a body of friends brought together by history, free to come and go as they wish, to contribute as much or as little as they can, but always concerned, as all friends are, with one another's welfare.

'We should think carefully before allowing this friendship to be fragmented by misunderstandings. If this is not to happen, we need to treat each other in the true manner of friends, as we have in the past. We must not seek to bind one another or deny others freedom of judgement and choice on matters each rightly reserves to himself.'

This speech was characterized in several newspapers as Britain's declaration of independence from the Commonwealth – a notion, of course, which is in itself an admission of British dissatisfaction with Commonwealth ties. But Britain's interests and involvements throughout the world are still considerable, and her continuing links with each and all of the countries and institutions of the Commonwealth provide at once contributory measures and searching tests of her international capabilities and standing.

In recent years official British conceptions of and policies towards the Commonwealth often have not been stated with sufficient precision, nor urged with sufficient conviction, nor pursued with the sufficient determination and realism to command the general support and respect from fellow members that might have been won. British policy has been too often merely reactive and insufficiently purposeful; it has been found too insular, wanting in imagination and foresight. In 1971, looking back at the previous decade, this seems particularly true of Britain's policies in regard to decolonization in southern Africa, but not perhaps in regard to the attempts to secure full membership in the European communities.

Regionally the great failures of British imperial and post-imperial endeavours have been in the Middle East.[45] Politically, perhaps the greatest series of failures have been the many abortive or shortlived experiments in establishing federations. When we recall that India 1935–47, Malaysia 1961–5, the West Indies, Nigeria, Central Africa, and the Persian Gulf sheikdoms have to be included in any comprehensive survey, and that this is far from a complete list, we can begin to gauge the scope of this theme. There is a certain historical irony in the efforts of successive British governments to create balanced, viable successor states out of the dissolution of an Empire which had to some extent depended on the principle of division. Certainly it was believed by many, perhaps most, responsible British officials and politicians throughout the 1940s and 1950s that there should be no decolonization, no full formal transfer of power, without a considerable chance of subsequent viability for the colony concerned; this was believed in as a prudential and a moral imperative. Federation often seemed to be the only constitutional device which promised unity in diversity, stability and viability. What viability actually meant in detail, and in political terms, often remained mysterious, and was never fully discussed in public. Since 1960, and in the face of a clamorous anti-colonial majority in the UN which insists on the irrelevance of all so-called requisites for independence, Britain has seemed to pay less heed than hitherto to the concept of due preparation;[46] from Aden to Anguilla,[47] tergiversation and improvisation have been triumphant in her latest acts of decolonization. Little real thought or hope seems to have been entertained that there are any real alternatives to continuing colonial status or to granting independence to even the most minuscule colony.

In the late 1960s British trade with and investment in black Africa had grown faster than with the Republic of South Africa; in 1969 Britain imported about £100 million more from Commonwealth countries in Africa than from South Africa. If recent trade trends persist then it may not be long before British exports to these Commonwealth countries also surpass in aggregate those going to the Republic.[48]

A major question is, of course, whether present trends will persist, or whether the present British government's determination to sell arms to South Africa, as part of their interpretation of obligations stemming from the Simonstown agreements, in consequence will have adverse repercussions on British interests in Africa. There is most unlikely to be some concerted breach in economic relations between all the African members of the Commonwealth and Britain; they have never been, and are unlikely to be, all in close agreement concerning their relations with Britain. What is more likely is the increased application of what are sometimes called 'salami tactics'; in this case, it would mean more countries taking control of British investments in their countries and the reduction of Britain's opportunities for future expansion. In East Africa, where feelings of opposition to South Africa run very strong, there are already examples of both: Lonrho, Barclays Bank DCO and Zambian Anglo-American have all experienced Africanization in varying degrees. Perhaps the clearest example hitherto of cutting back on opportunities for expansion came from President Kaunda, who in 1970 prohibited British Leyland from building a new plant in Zambia, to show his distaste for current British policies.

There is a case for and against Britain supplying South Africa with maritime arms.[49] Commercial profit and honouring the obligations explicit (and Mr Heath might add those 'inherent' too) in the Simonstown agreements seem to be the main arguments for supplying the arms, though the British government publicly urges the second, not the first, and adds that there is a serious need to patrol the main searoutes in the Indian Ocean and to keep a careful watch on growing Soviet naval activities. Nothing said at the Singapore conference seems to have converted anyone from previously held views. The British press seemed to believe almost unanimously (with, perhaps, only The Daily and The Sunday Telegraph constituting exceptions) that Mr Heath, for all his declared dislike of apartheid, had failed to demonstrate adequately to British and international opinion that the advantages of supplying arms would outweigh the disadvantages. Most British press comment said specifically that to persist in a policy of supplying arms to South Africa could not but invite the construction that support, if not approval, was being given by Britain to the government of South Africa. Seretse Khama of Botswana expressed a general Commonwealth misgiving when he said at Singapore that the South Africans wanted the supplies from Britain, not for the arms themselves, but for the advantages they hoped would thereby flow; 'these are principally a certificate of respectability, an enhanced role for South Africa in Western security arrangements, and an escalating Western commitment to the South African *status quo*'. To the extent that this view is widely shared, it is difficult to see how Britain's interests will best be served by a policy which can be so interpreted.

When Britain first tried formally to join the EEC in 1961–3, British negotiators felt impelled to take considerable account of a very comprehensive range of Commonwealth interests. Ten years later many interests and attitudes in Britain are less agitated about the probable impact of British entry upon Commonwealth connections; and anxieties in most Commonwealth countries are considerably less than they were in 1961.[50] The major growth in Britain's trade in the past ten years or so has been with Western Europe; in 1958 37 per cent of Britain's total exports were to the Commonwealth; in 1970 only about 20 per cent were. The relative decline of intra-Commonwealth trade perhaps has been considerably affected by the preoccupation since 1960 of successive British governments and business men with expanding trade and investment in Europe; but it has also been accentuated by the palpable failure of the Commonwealth tariff preferences to compete with changes in the global tariff structure – meaning particularly the General Agreement on Tariffs and Trade (GATT), the Kennedy Round cuts, and the proposals of the United Nations' Conference on Trade and Development (UNCTAD). If Britain joined the EEC, all the remaining Commonwealth tariff preferences would have to be phased away.

The Commonwealth exists at different levels in interaction for Britain much more than for its other members, and the specific importance of these levels has been, and is, subject to considerable and sometimes rapid change.

The champions of the British Empire in the early twentieth century boasted of an Imperial defence system – though it needed no latter-day Voltaire to point out that this was hardly Imperial, or even a system. The Commonwealth is not a military association at all, even though on rare occasions it has been found convenient to use a Commonwealth label, as with the Commonwealth Reserve in Malaya from 1955, or more ambiguously and recently with relevance to ANZUK. But in 1970 about half the net deficit in respect of governmental expenditure related to military outlays overseas. If we accept Mr Denis Healey's aphorism that the defence budget is the prime cost of foreign policy, then we should add that in the past twenty years Britain's military activities in the Commonwealth[51] (as in Malaya 1948–60 and Malaysia 1963–6, East Africa 1964, and in Aden, the Persian Gulf and Anguilla) have been a very sizeable proportion of these costs, and concern about this exercised considerable influence on British reappraisal of her commitments overseas in the late 1960s.

The British have not notably indulged in sophisticated public ruminations and analyses about the nature of the Commonwealth. Among academics, Professors Hancock, Miller and Mansergh – two Australians and an Irishman – have made the most substantial contributions, though all three know Britain well, and Mansergh (now Master of St John's College Cambridge) has spent most of his life in Britain. Among British politicians, Mr Patrick Gordon-Walker is in some ways a notable exception as a persistent analyst, as well as advocate, of the contemporary Commonwealth. Although based in London, the two most distinguished contemporary British newspaper correspondents on Commonwealth affairs, Patrick Keatley and Colin Legum, are by birth Canadian and South African respectively. And the late Leonard Beaton, that versatile and eloquent champion of the Commonwealth who died in 1971 while still a young man, was also a Canadian, albeit a very Anglophilic one. Many leading figures in British public life recently have admitted to the unfulfilled ambition of wanting to be Viceroy of India: Lord Butler, Enoch Powell, Lord Reith each vainly aspired to this now defunct office. How many Englishmen even aspire to be Secretary-General of the Commonwealth, or of any pan-Commonwealth association?

Perhaps the most neglected argument for Britain's continuous and active interest in Commonwealth affairs is a political/diplomatic one. It is that the Commonwealth is an admirable sounding board and testing ground for many, perhaps most, of her external policies; for to be able to command the support and respect of a large majority of one's fellow members of the Commonwealth in matters regarded as major by any incumbent British government, and by the British people, is important for Britain, and involves much more than mere vote-gathering or the politics of acclamation. It is the contemporary equivalent of Eyre Crowe's wise words, first written more than fifty years ago, that the jealousies which particularist policies can provoke are best averted or mitigated by being 'so directed as to harmonize with the general desires and ideals common to all mankind, and more particularly with the primary and vital interests of a majority, or as many as possible, of the other nations'.[52]

When any British government cannot command the respect of a majority in the Commonwealth on matters of prime importance, or when it ceases to regard Commonwealth approval and at least general tacit assent as important, then it will have failed to have placed itself, and perhaps the Commonwealth of Nations, in its proper place as part of the Commonwealth of mankind.

NOTES

1 The number becomes thirty-two if one includes Nauru, which became a member in 1970 but (because of its small size and population of only 6,000) was not represented at the heads of government meeting in Singapore in January 1971; [the member countries of the Commonwealth at that time were: Australia, Barbados, Botswana, Britain, Canada, Ceylon, Cyprus, Fiji, Republic of the Gambia, Ghana, Guyana, India, Jamaica, Kenya, Lesotho, Malawi, Malaysia, Malta, Mauritius, Nauru, New Zealand, Nigeria, Pakistan, Sierra Leone, Singapore, Swaziland, Tanzania, Tonga, Trinidad and Tobago, Uganda, Western Samoa, Zambia. (Pakistan left the Commonwealth in January 1972; Bangladesh joined in April 1972.)

2 This was Dean Acheson's main assumption in his much noticed speech at West Point on 5 December 1962:

'Great Britain has lost an empire, and has not yet found a role. The attempt to play a separate power role – that is, a role apart from Europe, a role based on a "special relationship" with the United States, a role based on being the head of a Commonwealth which has no political structure or unity or strength and enjoys a fragile and precarious economic relationship by means of the Sterling area and preference in the British market – this role is about played out.'

(Acheson, 'Our Atlantic Alliance: the Political and Economic Strands', *Vital Speeches*, vol. 29 (1963), pp. 163–4; also 'Losing an Empire, Finding a Role', *International Journal*, vol. 23, no. 4 (Autumn 1968), pp. 507–610.) In the course of the so-called 'great debate' on Britain and the EEC, Lord George Brown said: 'I have long smarted under Dean Acheson's remark.' See House of Lords Debates, vol. 323, no. 140, col. 59, 26 July 1971.

3 George Schwarzenberger, *Power Politics: a Study of World Society*, 3rd ed. (London, 1964), p. 76.

4 All the figures and comparisons given in this paragraph are taken from an official publication, *Britain 1971: an Official Handbook* (London, 1971).

5 For measures and assessments of Britain's international status in earlier periods, see A. J. P. Taylor, *The Struggle for Mastery in Europe, 1848–1918* (Oxford, 1954), pp. xix–xxxvi; H. C. Hillmann, 'Comparative Strength of the Great Powers', in A. Toynbee (ed.), *The World in March 1939: Survey of International Affairs, 1939–1946* (London, 1952), pp. 366–507; J. David Singer and Melvin Small, 'The Composition and Status Ordering of the International System, 1815–1940', *World Politics*, vol. 18 (January 1966), pp. 236–82. This last article includes the 'old' Dominions in its tables, and ranks them all very low in international status up to 1940. Britain is placed among the top three throughout.

6 This ugly but suggestive word was coined recently, as far as I know, by a

young Australian scholar, J. Davidson, who is already an authority on Trollope and the Colonies. In British imperial history 'dedominionization' refers to the old Dominions (Canada, Australia, New Zealand, South Africa) and their gradual constitutional evolution from dependency to full independence – from colonial to autochthonous countries. For some aspects of this still neglected theme, see J. D. B. Miller, *Britain and the Old Dominions* (London, 1966); Nicholas Mansergh, *The Commonwealth Experience* (London, 1969); Louis Hartz, *The Founding of New Societies* (New York, 1964); D. Harkness, *The Irish Free State and the British Commonwealth of Nations, 1921–1932* (London, 1968). For a crisp discussion of autochthony, see K. C. Wheare, *The Constitutional Structure of the Commonwealth* (Oxford, 1960), ch. 4.

7 See R. Koebner, *Empire* (London, 1961); Jack Simmons, *From Empire to Commonwealth: Principles of British Imperial Government* (London, 1949); A. P. Thornton, *The Imperial Idea and its Enemies* (London, 1959).

8 This rallying cry was quoted approvingly by Hugh Foot (Lord Caradon) in an article in *The Observer*, 3 February 1963, 'What's Left for Patriotism: Teaching the New Nations How to Live'. His views were considerably and eloquently elaborated in his memoirs, *A Start to Freedom* (London, 1964). Foot argues that too many people fail to see the potentialities of the Commonwealth because they are too busy regretting the loss of an Empire, and he dilates on the dangers that the affluent nations shall become soft, selfish, self-centred: 'We in Britain seem to be sinking into a new kind of surburban isolationism' (p. 231).

9 R. Koebner and H. D. Schmidt, *Imperialism: the Story and Significance of a Political Word* (London, 1964).

10 See Eric Stokes, *The English Utilitarians and India* (Oxford, 1959).

11 Crewe, *Lord Rosebery* (London, 1931), vol. I, p. 186. See also W. K. Hancock, *Survey of British Commonwealth Affairs*, vol. I: *Problems of Nationality, 1911–1936* (Oxford, 1937), p. 54.

12 One recently published massive history by a senior Australian-born historian and advocate of the Commonwealth is prefaced by this quotation from John of Salisbury:

'A commonwealth, according to Plutarch, is a certain body which is endowed with life by the benefit of divine favour, which acts at the prompting of the highest equity, and is ruled by what may be called the moderating power of reason . . . so that each and all are, as it were, members one of another by a sort of reciprocity, and each regards his own interest as best served by that which he knows to be most advantageous for the others.'

See H. Duncan Hall, *Commonwealth: a History of the British Commonwealth of Nations* (London, 1971).

13 See Hancock, op. cit., pp. 5, 6.

14 Ibid., especially pp. 18–19; see also pp. 8, 10 and 305.

15 Hancock, ibid., p. 56.

16 See Hancock [note 11 above].

17 See K. C. Wheare (note 6 above).

18 For a brief official outline, see *Britain and the Process of Decolonization* (Central Office of Information Reference Pamphlet 91), (London, 1970).

19 This lopsided emphasis extends also to scholarly writing. There are two valuable accounts and analyses of colonial issues in British politics since 1945, but not one with authority and detail concerning Britain and the Commonwealth. See J. M. Lee, *Colonial Development and Good Government: a Study*

of the Ideas Expressed by the British Official Classes in Planning Decolonization, 1939–1964 (Oxford, 1967); and David Goldsworthy, *Colonial Issues in British Politics 1945–61: from Colonial Development to Wind of Change* (Oxford, 1971). I would like to acknowledge a general intellectual debt to J. D. B. Miller for his writing and conversation concerning the Commonwealth. His works are one notable exception to the general poverty of writing specifically about Britain and the Commonwealth. From his assessments of British ideas and the Commonwealth I have derived advantage, particularly from his *The Commonwealth and the World* (London, 1958), ch. 7; 'Britain and the Commonwealth', in *South Atlantic Quarterly*, vol. 69, no. 2 (Spring 1970); and 'Politicians, Officials and Prophets', in *International Journal*, vol. 26, no. 2 (Spring, 1971).

20 Crewe, *Rosebery*, vol. 1, op. cit.

21 See Max Beloff, 'The Commonwealth: from Disillusion to Dissolution?', in *Commonwealth: The Journal of the Royal Commonwealth Society* (1971).

22 Harold Macmillan, *Riding the Storm* (London, 1971), p. 410.

23 J. R. Seeley, *The Expansion of England* (London, 1883), p. 10.

24 See note 19 above.

25 See Kenneth Young, *Sir Alec Douglas-Home* (London, 1970), p. 117.

26 See especially *Report of the Committee on Representational Services Overseas* (Cmnd 2276, February 1964), and *Report of the Review Committee on Overseas Representation* (Cmnd 4107, July 1969).

27 Her Majesty's Diplomatic Service, as presently constituted, was formed on 1 January 1965 by the merger of the hitherto separate Foreign, Commonwealth and Trade Commissioner Services, and this newly integrated service subsequently incorporated the staffs of the Colonial Office in London, which was absorbed within the Commonwealth Relations Office on 1 August 1966 to form the Commonwealth Office. The Foreign Office and the Commonwealth Office continued as separate Departments of State until 17 October 1968, when they combined to form the Foreign and Commonwealth Office (FCO), responsible to one principal Secretary of State, and in November 1970 overseas development also became the ultimate responsibility of the Secretary of State for Foreign and Commonwealth Affairs, still within the day-to-day charge of a Minister for Overseas Development, although without a separate ministry. The staff of the present Overseas Development Administration wing of the FCO are almost all members of the Home Civil Service, and not H.M. Diplomatic Service. Brief descriptions of the main departmental organization and formal responsibilities of the offices in London, brief outlines of the in-service careers of the members of H.M. Diplomatic Service, who in 1971 numbered about 6,000, may be found in *The Diplomatic Service List*, an official annual publication. See also J. A. Cross, 'Whitehall and the Commonwealth: British Departmental Organization', in *Commonwealth Relations, 1900–1966* (London, 1967).

28 See House of Commons, *Third Report from the Select Committee on Estimates* (session 1958–1959), p. 56, as cited by K. E. Robinson, 'The Governmental Machinery of Commonwealth Relations', in *A Decade of Commonwealth 1955–1964*, Hamilton, Robinson and Goodwin (eds), (North Carolina, 1966), pp. 89–123. Cf. *A Yearbook of the Commonwealth, 1971* (London, 1971), p. 5.

29 As cited by Robinson, op. cit.

30 *Ottawa Citizen*, 23 February 1971, p. 7 For the old Dominions in general, see J. D. B. Miller, *Britain and the Old Dominions* (London, 1966).

31 See *The Scotsman* and *The Times*, 8 October 1970; and cf. Sir Alec Douglas-Home's speech in *House of Commons Parliamentary Debates*, vol. 821, no. 185, cols 1705–15, esp. 1711–12, 22 July 1971.

32 *The Diplomatic Service List, 1971*, p. 5.

33 For general perspectives see H. S. Booker, *The Problem of Britain's Overseas Trade* (London, 1948); and Vivian Anthony, *Britain's Overseas Trade* (London, 1969). For Commonwealth patterns, see: Paul Streeten, 'A New Commonwealth', *New Society*, 3 July 1969; Michael Lipton and Clive Bell, 'The Fall in Commonwealth Trade', *Round Table* (January 1970); Commonwealth Secretariat, *Commonwealth Trade* (London, 1968), and *Commonwealth and Generalized Preferences* (London, 1970); John Pinder, *The Commonwealth in the Evolution of the World Economic System* (London, 1968); P. Streeten and Hugh Corbet (eds), *Commonwealth Policy in a Global Context* (London, 1971); Richard Bentley, *Promoting Commonwealth Development* (London, 1970).

34 See *Statistics of Economic Aid to Developing Countries, 1963–1967* (London, 1968), and *1964–1968* (London, 1969). See also *British Private Investment in Developing Countries* (Cmnd 4656, April 1971).

35 *The Financial Times*, 20 January 1971.

36 See John H. Dunning, *Studies in International Investment* (London 1970); and *Britain's International Investment Position* (COI Reference Pamphlet 98, London, 1971).

37 See, for example, W. K. Hancock, *Survey of British Commonwealth Affairs*, vol. 2. *Problems of Economic Policy, 1918–1939*, part 2 (London, 1942), pp. 149–76.

38 Robert R. Wilson and Robert E. Clute, 'Commonwealth Citizenship and Common Status' in *American Journal of International Law*, vol. 57, no. 3 (July 1963), pp. 566–87. E. J. B. Rose and Associates, *Colour and Citizenship: A Report on British Race Relations* (London, 1969).

39 See *Round Table*, no. 242 (April 1971), special issue on 'Commonwealth Migration'.

40 See the Registrar General's *Quarterly Return for England and Wales*, for March quarter 1970, no. 485 (London, 1970).

41 See *House of Commons Parliamentary Debates*, vol. 819, no. 159, esp. cols 387–97, 456–7, 449–50 and 573–80, 16 June 1971.

42 *Foreign Affairs*, October 1969.

43 Joseph Frankel, *National Interest* (London, 1970).

44 L. S. Amery, *My Political Life* (London, 1953), vol. 2, p. 351.

45 See Elizabeth Monroe, *Britain's Moment in the Middle East, 1914–1956* (London, 1963).

46 See B. Schaffer 'The Concept of Preparation', in *World Politics* (October 1965); and Thomas Balogh, *The Economics of Poverty* (London, 1968).

47 See Basil A. Ince 'The Diplomacy of New States: the Commonwealth Caribbean and the Case of Anguilla', in the *South Atlantic Quarterly*, vol. 69, no. 3 (Summer 1970).

48 For general treatments, see: Dennis Austin, *Britain and South Africa* (London, 1966); Roy Lewis, 'Britain, South Africa and the Commonwealth', in *Commonwealth* (December 1970); Michael Lee, 'La Politique Britannique à Liegard de l'Afrique Noire', in *Etudes Internationales* (1971), pp. 102–9; Barbara Rogers, *South Africa's Stake in Britain* (London, 1971); William E. Gutteridge, 'Can Africa's Armies Attack Southern Africa?', in *Commonwealth*, vol. 14, no. 5 (October 1970), pp. 179–84.

[49] Geoffrey Rippon, 'South Africa and Naval Strategy', *Round Table*, no. 239 (July 1970), and Julius Nyerere's eloquent pamphlet arguing against the British government's proposal to supply arms to South Africa, prepared for the Singapore Conference of January 1971 and reprinted in *The Far Eastern Economic Review* (30 January 1971). For dispassionate treatment, see Jack Spence, 'South Africa and the Defence of the West', *Round Table*, no. 241 (January 1971), and L. W. Martin, 'Britain and the Indian Ocean', in *Mimeo* (March 1971).

[50] Harold Husemann, *Britain's Political and Military Position in the Commonwealth and in the Western Alliance since 1945* (unpublished thesis, Kiel, 1970). Duncan Sandys, *The Modern Commonwealth* (London, 1962). Mr Sandys was then Secretary of State for Commonwealth Affairs and wrote *inter alia*: 'We have made it clear that if we were faced with the necessity of choosing between the Commonwealth and Europe, we should unquestionably choose the Commonwealth' (p. 20). Michael Stewart, 'Britain and Europe. Changes in Relationship with the Commonwealth', in *Commonwealth* (April 1970); Carol Ann Cosgrove, 'Britain, the Developing Commonwealth and the EEC', in *The World Today* (June 1970); *The Future of the Commonwealth: a British View* (London, 1963); *The United Kingdom and the European Communities* (Cmnd 4715, July 1971), especially paras 97–122.

[51] R. N. Rosecrance, *Defence of the Realm* (New York, 1968), and Neville Brown, *Arms without Empire* (Harmondsworth, 1969).

[52] Memorandum by Mr (later Sir) Eyre Crowe, 1 January 1907. See G. P. Gooch and H. Temperley (eds), *British Documents on the Origins of the War* (London, 1926), vol. 3, pp. 402–3. This famous memorandum provided the opening text for Sir Keith Hancock's magisterial *Survey of British Commonwealth Affairs*, vol. 1. *Problems of Nationality, 1918–1936* (London, 1937), pp. vii–ix.

VIII A Failure of Foreign Policy: the Case of Rhodesia

JOHN DAY

Rhodesia's successful defiance of Britain in seizing independence and determining its own constitution provides at least *prima facie* evidence of British weakness. After the British and Rhodesian governments had failed to agree on an independence constitution, Rhodesia declared herself independent on her own terms. The British government did not recognize the new régime, and tried hard, principally through economic pressure and by negotiation, to induce Rhodesia to return to legality and to accept a constitution which satisfied Britain. These strenuous efforts were without success, although Britain claimed sovereignty in Rhodesia and the difference in resources between the two countries is ludicrously large; Rhodesia's armed forces are modern and efficient, but minute compared with Britain's. Assessed on *per capita* income and exploited resources, Rhodesia is one of the richest African countries; but relative to Britain it is poor and underdeveloped. The total population of Rhodesia is about a tenth that of Britain, and the Rhodesian government directly represents only the Europeans, who form about one-twentieth of the people.

While investigating how far Britain's failure to achieve her ends in Rhodesia was the consequence of constraints on her policy, it is worth bearing in mind that constraints differ in the degree to which they are voluntarily accepted. Some constraints prevent statesmen from choosing to pursue certain policies: a State without a navy cannot fight a naval battle. Other constraints, however, do not destroy the power of choice: a small navy may act as a constraint on foreign policy by providing a strong motive to avoid naval war, but a State with a small navy may still choose to risk the danger of defeat in naval war if the prize to be won by victory is sufficiently large. The constraint in this case influences, but does not determine, the policy. Constraints on policy are of varying strengths whose effects on statesmen range from absolute direction through strong compulsion to weak persuasion. The strongest constraints allow no discretion to an actor in a particular field of action; other constraints provide motives for refraining from certain actions, but the final decision about policy remains with the actor who balances the cost or risk the constraint imposes against the probable benefits of the contemplated action.

A further distinction between kinds of constraint may usefully be borne in mind while discussing British policy in Rhodesia. To speak of a constraint upon an action usually implies the existence of a deterrent outside the actor. A foreign policy, for example, may be adopted after considering the diplomatic and military actions that a stronger power might employ against an alternative policy. Yet without violation to the language one can speak also of internal constraints by which the actor limits his own actions. Moral constraint, for example, may prevent a statesman using force. A policy he is considering is restrained by scruples within himself not by danger from outside.

To discuss merely the constraints on British policy in Rhodesia and ignore other motives of the British government would not show the relative importance of the constraints as determinants of British policy; for full understanding of the constraints one must see the interrelationship of all the motives of British conduct over Rhodesia. It is important, for example, to estimate how far Britain's decision not to use force was the result of constraints like fear of military setback, and how far it was the result of positive calculations of what Britain could achieve by means other than force. Similarly, one must ask to what extent Britain's failure on Rhodesia stemmed from constraints on her policy, and to what extent from misunderstanding or mismanagement of the situation. It can be argued, for example, that Britain relied on sanctions to bring down the Rhodesian régime, not because it was a second-class power, but because it depended on second-class advice. Assessing the operation of constraints on British policy in Rhodesia requires comprehensive explanation of that policy.

Rhodesian independence began to pose problems for the British government in March 1963 when the newly elected Rhodesian Front government made its first formal demand for independence. An *impasse* arose between the two governments because Rhodesia wanted independence under the existing 1961 constitution, while Britain demanded modifications to it; neither was prepared to make sufficient compromises to satisfy the other. Behind the disagreements and even the agreements on constitutional points lay deep differences about the role which Africans should play in Rhodesian government. The British government's wish to have the Rhodesian problem off its hands was perhaps the main force making for a settlement; the Rhodesian government's passionate desire for independence gave it some motive for negotiating a settlement, but at the same time made it less than determined to reach a settlement because it was prepared if necessary to seize independence without one.

The reasons why the Rhodesian Front attached such importance to independence are not immediately obvious, because it already enjoyed the substance of independence before it had the title. Under the 1961 constitution the Rhodesian government was in practice as unimpeded by the British government from outside as it was by the African people from within. The British government had given up the reserved powers that it had under the 1923 constitution by which it could veto potentially discriminatory legislation, and it had recognized explicitly the convention under which it did not legislate for Rhodesia without the consent of the Rhodesian government. Sir Edgar Whitehead, who negotiated the 1961 constitution with the British government, claimed that Rhodesia was virtually independent. Legal niceties apart, he was right: the only circumstances in which Britain might conceivably interfere in Rhodesian affairs was if the Rhodesian government blatantly infringed the constitution, for example, by a unilateral declaration of independence.

It might be argued that the Rhodesian Front sought formal independence in order to change those parts of the 1961 constitution which promised eventually to give Africans control of government. In return for removing its reserved powers, the British government in 1961 obtained the Rhodesian government's agreement to the introduction of fifteen African representatives into the legislature; the remaining fifty MPs were elected by those who had certain educational and income qualifications. In the early 1960s these voters were nearly all Europeans, and they ensured that the government remained in white hands for the present. However, when sufficient numbers of Africans acquired the income and education to qualify them to vote for the fifty seats, there would cease to be a European monopoly, and eventually Africans could expect to take over the government with a majority in Parliament. The Rhodesian Front did not believe that majority rule was valuable in itself, and was prepared to accept it only if it was 'responsible'.[1] This might seem to provide a motive for seeking independence: free from British sovereignty, the Rhodesian government could retard African majority government as long as it chose. It is doubtful, however, if this is a sufficient explanation of the strength of feeling with which the white Rhodesians insisted on independence. There was no immediate prospect of Africans taking over. Most Africans eligible for a vote did not use it, following the policy recommended by the African nationalist parties as a protest against the inadequate representation given to Africans by the 1961 constitution. Furthermore, Rhodesian governments between 1959 and 1964 banned five African nationalist parties and rendered African radical protest impotent, thus demonstrating their ability to curb 'irresponsible' African challenge to white dominance.

The white governments could also exercise some control over the pace of African economic and educational advance, upon which their political progress depended. Even without deliberate manipulation by governments and with full African use of the vote, it was doubtful whether the Africans could win a majority of seats in the near future. Estimates varied about how soon the Africans could reach majority rule under the 1961 constitution: some thought it might conceivably come within a few years, but the end of the century may be more realistic.[2] In addition, a strong government could, under the 1961 constitution, control African political advance by reducing the number of African seats to below fifteen. Such a constitutional change required a two-thirds majority in Parliament, which the Rhodesian Front had after the May 1965 election, when it won all fifty upper roll seats. The danger of African power was remote; the desire for independence was immediate. The Rhodesian Front did not need independence to hold back African rule. If the Africans had become a threat to the Rhodesian Front's control of the State, the government would have prevented the threat materializing, if necessary by violating the constitution. Fear of African takeover was not the motive which made independence a white hot issue for the Rhodesian Front.

The Rhodesian government did not demand independence because it felt vulnerable to British or African incursions under the aegis of the 1961 constitution. In 1961 the members of the Rhodesian Front had not supported the concessions to Africans made in that constitution, but by 1963 they were prepared to accept it as the basis for independence; soon after he became Prime Minister in 1964, Ian Smith defended the constitution because it ensured that government remained in 'responsible' hands.[3] The cause of Rhodesian passion over independence and of the Rhodesian government's readiness to risk the wrath of the world by declaring independence unilaterally was not calculation of political advantage but nationalist pride. Conscious of white Rhodesia as a nation, and having governed themselves since 1923, the white Rhodesians were no longer satisfied with the power of self-government, but craved also the title. They felt that the very possession of self-government entitled them to the dignity of independence. When Rhodesia determined to be independent, it was not seeking status or recognition from others; it certainly obtained neither by UDI. It was the Rhodesians' self-esteem which required the full panoply of independence; the hostility of most of the rest of the world to the white Rhodesians strengthened their determination and increased their self-consciousness.

The humiliation of being denied independence was deepened by the readiness of Britain to grant independence to countries having

African governments, with much shorter experience of ruling than Rhodesia; in 1964 the neighbouring territories of Zambia and Malawi celebrated their independence with African leaders who had had only a year or two in government. The Rhodesians bitterly resented being treated by Britain as less responsible than Africans, whom they regarded as unstable as well as inexperienced.

The nationalist pride which led the Rhodesians to insist on independence also made them reluctant to accept any liberal modifications to the 1961 constitution as conditions of independence. They felt that Rhodesia had made sufficient concessions to Britain in 1961, and that nothing more could reasonably be demanded.

Naturally, Britain was much less emotionally involved than Rhodesia in the issue of Rhodesian independence, but it was not prepared to yield everything the Rhodesian government demanded. The British government was morally committed to majority rule, as the Rhodesian government was to 'civilized' government. The principles of the British government led it to seek, as the cost to the Rhodesian government of independence, acceleration in African political progress and guarantees against later amendments which would retard it; the Rhodesian government made its stand from nationalist pride, and the British government out of self-respect and care for its prestige. Britain had not intervened in Rhodesian government, and did not intend to; but she felt obliged to make constitutional demands in conformity with its principles. Like Rhodesia, she was not trying to increase her power by an attempt to mould the independence constitution. The British government had no direct interest in the political fortunes of Rhodesian Africans, and it never tried to insist on majority rule as a condition of independence; its attempts to modify the Rhodesian political system were modest, and could bear fruit only in the distant future. In spite of the conflict of political ideologies, the British government did not aim at undermining the existing power of the Rhodesian government. Notwithstanding its later compromise of principle and loss of prestige, the British government's main motives in the Rhodesian affair were loyalty to principle and preservation of prestige.

When the Rhodesians raised the issue of independence in 1963, the British government's first impulse was to procrastinate; but after lengthy exchanges the Commonwealth Secretary, Duncan Sandys, stated frankly in a letter to Winston Field, the Rhodesian Prime Minister, that 'the present difficulty arises from your desire to secure independence on the basis of a franchise which is incomparably more restricted than that of any other British territory to which independence has hitherto been granted'.[4]

Little progress towards agreement was made in the drawn out

negotiations through 1964 and 1965. The Rhodesian government grew increasingly impatient with the delay in reaching agreement on independence; exchanges between the governments became increasingly acrimonious, especially when Smith had to deal with Harold Wilson after the Labour party's election victory in October 1964. As the British government saw the matter, 'the problems at issue are the pace of the transition to majority rule and the timing of independence in relation to it'.[5] For the Rhodesian government there was no problem: independence must come soon, and the pace of transition to majority rule must be dictated by the 1961 constitution.

During 1965 the British government clarified five principles on which it would need to be satisfied before it was able to contemplate the grant of independence:

i. The principle and intention of unimpeded progress to majority rule, already enshrined in the 1961 constitution, would have to be maintained and guaranteed.

ii. There would also have to be guarantees against retrogressive amendment of the constitution.

iii. There would have to be immediate improvement in the political status of the African population.

iv. There would have to be progress towards ending racial discrimination.

v. The British government would need to be satisfied that any basis proposed for independence was acceptable to the people of Rhodesia as a whole.[6]

In the September the two governments elucidated the Rhodesian government's position on each of these principles. The two sides were poles apart; for example, the Rhodesian government was prepared to work the 1961 constitution only 'provided that it is satisfied that the majority rule which may in time result from that constitution will be a reasonable and responsible one'. Furthermore, the Rhodesian government could not accept any form of constitutional safeguard which would prevent the Europeans in Rhodesia from altering the constitution if they deemed it necessary to prevent the premature emergence of an African government.[7] With this unpromising background Smith came to London in early October 1965 for talks with Wilson, at the end of which an agreed communiqué was issued admitting failure to agree.

This might have appeared to be the point beyond which talking was a waste of time, but the British government, led by Wilson, showed great energy and ingenuity in exploring every possible means of avoiding the unilateral declaration of independence which the Rhodesian government was considering if independence could not be negotiated. After the agreement to disagree, Wilson held a meeting with Smith 'to clear up any possible misunderstandings on either side' before Smith returned home. Wilson raised the possibility, not previously discussed, of a treaty as a guarantee against retrogressive amendment of the constitution. Smith, showing more realism and less hope than Wilson on this occasion as on subsequent ones in the month before UDI, pointed out that 'the treaty would represent a possible means of meeting the difficulties in relation to only one of the United Kingdom's five principles'.[8] Undeterred, Wilson rapidly flew another kite which Smith shot down.

The day after discussing a treaty, Wilson wrote to Smith proposing a Commonwealth mission to Rhodesia; but Smith, always resentful of Commonwealth interference, turned the suggestion down flat, replying spikily to Wilson's tone of statesmanlike politeness. Two more barbed letters were exchanged, and then, on 21 October, Wilson proposed that he should fly with the Commonwealth Secretary to Salisbury in the following day or two. This dramatic gesture underlined the importance that Wilson attached to preventing UDI.

Smith agreed to the visit, and during the discussions between the representatives of the two governments Wilson came up with another device which he hoped would help break the deadlock. He now suggested a royal commission with strong Rhodesian representation which would be asked to recommend an independence constitution which would be acceptable to the Rhodesian people as a whole. Smith, as realistic as ever, doubted if Europeans and African nationalists would agree, but Wilson's 'own feeling was that a solution would be found'.[9] Protracted discussions about the royal commission did nothing to bridge the gap between the two governments on an independence constitution. Towards the end of the talks Wilson said that he thought the discussions might have indicated a possible basis for further advance towards a settlement, but C. W. Dupont, a Rhodesian minister, correctly pointed out that there was still deadlock on the basic issue.[10] Wilson seemed anxious to keep open the possibility of agreement, no matter how remote it seemed. At times he seemed to forget or to ignore the ideological differences between the two governments, and the loss to pride or prestige which either might suffer if it agreed to a constitutional compromise which diverged too greatly from its principles. At one stage, Wilson said that 'it might be better that the two governments should try to abstract from their respective political philosophies, and to confine themselves to the more specifically constitutional problems which confronted them'. In the circumstances, this was a splendidly unpragmatic pragmatism, as Smith immediately recognized. 'What confronted them was precisely a question of political philosophy, not merely one of constitutional law.'[11]

Soon after he returned from Salisbury, Wilson wrote to Smith proposing that the royal commission should find out if the Rhodesian people wished to become independent under the very slightly amended 1961 constitution that the Rhodesian government proposed. If the commission was unanimous that the Rhodesian people did want this, it would become the independence constitution. Smith raised several objections to the details of the proposals. Behind his opposition must have been the knowledge that the commission would probably not unanimously find that the Rhodesian people as a whole wanted independence under the 1961 constitution, and the fear that the royal commission's inquiry would merely delay the independence the Rhodesian government was determined to have. Wilson continued to try to persuade Smith to accept a royal commission, although the Rhodesian government on 5 November declared a state of emergency, which was generally supposed to be preparatory to declaring independence. On 11 November Wilson took his last desperate measure to avert UDI when he telephoned Smith and tried to persuade him to accept the royal commission scheme. Smith was frank that the differences between them looked irreconcilable, which Wilson emphatically denied. He offered to send a senior minister to Salisbury to clarify any points. 'If anybody can now say that this position is irreconcilable or justifies illegal action, I think they want their heads examining, or they must have a death wish on them that is beyond what can be dealt with by ordinary rational argument.'[12] That morning the Rhodesian government declared itself independent.

In the month before UDI, Wilson showed great anxiety and went to great lengths to prevent it. He apparently felt an optimism about his chances of success that took account neither of the pessimism of the Rhodesian ministers nor of their impatience for a final decision on independence. He seemed to hope that by the device of the royal commission he could circumvent the repeated failures of the two governments to agree. He worked hard in pursuit of a shadow, trusting too much in the power of his own diplomacy. Smith, by contrast, appreciated the unreality and futility of protracted discussion of increasingly sophisticated devices to conceal fundamental differences of overall ideology and immediate policy.

When Rhodesia declared itself independent, the British government, as it had promised, refused to recognize the régime, and withdrew the economic privileges which Rhodesia had enjoyed as a member of the Commonwealth. Britain urged other States not to treat Rhodesia as a State, and to join with Britain in employing economic sanctions against

Rhodesia. The British government ruled out any possibility of using force against Rhodesia to obtain its return to constitutional government, and urged the rest of the world to employ economic sanctions against Rhodesia in an effort to make illegal independence untenable.

Initially the British policy seemed intransigent in contrast with its enthusiasm before UDI to negotiate. Yet early in 1966 it showed that it was prepared, while not abandoning the harsher method of sanctions, to seek a settlement by negotiation. The faith in talks which the British government had shown before UDI persisted after that dramatic event; the basic aim of negotiating an independence constitution remained, although now the British government also required a return to constitutional rule under a broadly based interim administration before an independence constitution was introduced. Although Rhodesia was diplomatically isolated and inconvenienced by sanctions, it showed less enthusiasm for reaching a settlement than Britain. The pattern of pre-UDI repeated itself, with the British government taking more initiatives than the Rhodesian government to find ways to agreement. Yet the prospects of success were worse unless, as seemed increasingly unlikely, sanctions made illegal independence intolerable for the Rhodesians. All the difficulties which prevented agreement before UDI were still present; in addition, the hatred and contempt each side felt for the other were intensified. Most important, the Rhodesians now had the independence they valued so highly, and would do nothing that might put this in the slightest jeopardy.

Soon after UDI, both sides made tentative advances about reopening talks, and subsequently each blamed the other for failure to find a satisfactory basis on which discussions could start. The British government's difficulty was how to talk effectively to a régime it did not recognize officially, but this did not prevent exploratory talks throughout 1966, first through civil servants, and in September by the Commonwealth Secretary. After long and complex discussions, in substance similar to those which preceded UDI, the British government arranged a meeting between the Prime Ministers, intended to be, in the words of the official British account, 'a final effort . . . to secure an honourable settlement'. It was not the first 'final' effort and it was not to be the last. Wilson arranged to meet Smith on the battleship *Tiger* off Gibraltar. Since the last meeting of the two men, the Rhodesian government had given up its insistence that an independence constitution should not take away its power under the 1961 constitution to reduce the fifteen African seats, and the British government in exchange had allowed the creation of a new category of seats reserved for Europeans. One effect of the proposed constitution was that more Africans would need to qualify for votes than under the 1961 Constitution or that proposed by the British government before UDI before Africans obtained a majority of seats, although a white Rhodesian government would now be unable, within the constitution, to reduce the number of seats reserved for Africans. The stumbling-block, however, was the British insistence that Rhodesia should return to legality under an interim government, while Rhodesian opinion was tested on the independence constitution. The *Tiger* talks formed a dramatic climax to the post-UDI year of negotiations; but predictably they failed because, as Smith had said earlier, 'Rhodesia was, and intended to remain, a sovereign nation'.[13] The Rhodesian government regarded the return to legality as 'unconditional surrender'.[14]

At the end of the talks on the *Tiger*, Wilson told Smith that, if there was a break then, there would be no more talks.[15] In fact, however, the failure on the *Tiger* did not dam the British government's enthusiasm for constitutional discussions, any more than did UDI. Each time the British government claimed that Rhodesia had slammed the door; but Rhodesia found the British government was prepared to push it open again. At first Wilson declared that his government was no longer prepared to compromise with the Rhodesian Front, and would insist that Rhodesia should not have legal independence before majority rule. However, an intermittent dialogue continued at various levels of unofficialness, including a visit by the Commonwealth Secretary to Salisbury in November 1967. By September 1968 the British government thought that the political climate in Rhodesia had changed sufficiently to justify renewed hope of a settlement. This supposed change – mainly based, it seems, on Smith's resistance to the most right-wing elements of his party[16] – was probably a less weighty cause of optimism about a settlement than the British government's willingness, shown in the next battleship summit conference on the *Fearless* in October 1968, to drop the requirement, which was largely responsible for the failure of the *Tiger* talks, that Rhodesia must return to legality before receiving independence under an agreed constitution. However, as Britain was prepared to concede more, Rhodesia seemed determined to demand more. The Rhodesian government rejected the *Fearless* proposals, principally on account of the provision for appeals to the Privy Council against infringements of the entrenched clauses of the constitution. This had been in the *Tiger* proposals, but Smith had not mentioned it when stating his government's grounds for rejecting the *Tiger* proposals.[17] It might appear that the Rhodesian government was seeking a pretext to reject the settlement, but it is not easy to see why it should. The Rhodesian government saw the proposals for appeals to the Privy Council as 'an unwarranted interference with the sovereignty of the Rhodesian parliament, and a negation of independence'.[18] This sounds authentic; national pride had been the main motive of the Rhodesian Front in all its behaviour over independence.

Even after the rebuff over the *Fearless* proposals, the British government did not entirely lose its appetite for discussing constitutional niceties. In November 1968 the Commonwealth Secretary went out to Salisbury for talks which proved unproductive. When the Rhodesian government decided to introduce a new constitution more illiberal than those of 1961 and 1965 (UDI), in that Africans could never obtain more than parity of seats with Europeans, the Labour government tired of ritualistic discussions. It could not accept such a constitution as a starting point of negotiation, and the Rhodesian government could no longer be expected to show interest in a modified 1961 constitution.

Before UDI the British government persisted with talks when they ceased to offer much prospect of a settlement; after UDI it continued negotiating with the Rhodesian government, in spite of still bleaker prospects. Accompanying the latter discussions was the more aggressive but equally ineffective policy of sanctions. In establishing itself as an independent State without Britain's consent, Rhodesia humiliated Britain; but the British government would not use force. Why was it content with talks and sanctions, when these served principally to emphasize Britain's impotence? Huffing and puffing on the *Tiger*, on the *Fearless*, and at the United Nations did not blow the Rhodesian house down.

Before UDI, one motive of Wilson in prolonging the negotiations and constantly engaging the Rhodesian government in the exploration of new routes to a settlement was probably the desire to postpone UDI indefinitely. Even if a royal commission would not lead to an agreed constitution acceptable to the Rhodesian people, the discussions about it, while still prolonged, prevented Rhodesia seizing independence. The British government had nothing to lose in the constant delay to Rhodesia's independence, and was probably not wholly confident of its ability to deal with UDI if it came. Wilson sounded indignant and incredulous when Smith refused to talk interminably and instead acted by declaring Rhodesia independent. Yet Wilson was wrong to expect that Smith would wait indefinitely or accept discussion as a substitute for independence.

It does seem as if the British government did not fully understand, or chose unwisely to underestimate, the strength of white Rhodesian nationalism, although this was the main force behind the Rhodesian Front's attitude to independence, both before and after UDI. Underestimating perhaps the emotion behind the demand for independence, the British government seemed constantly to overestimate its own chances of persuading Rhodesia to compromise. Immediately after UDI, Wilson confessed that he found the move incredible, and stated that his government had had many reasons to doubt whether Smith would declare independence illegally. Yet Smith had actually suggested, during his talks with Wilson less than two weeks before the event, that 'UDI, if carried out neatly, might still provide the best solution'.[19] Wilson incorrectly thought that the publication of the exchanges between the two governments would support his view that agreement was very close just before UDI. Wilson explained UDI as the irrational act of emotional racialists, but it is better understood as an act of rational calculation by nationalists determined to have national sovereignty. If Wilson had grasped this, he would not have hoped to reach agreement by constitutional logic-chopping, nor would he have been surprised by UDI; he would not have expected the Rhodesian government after UDI to surrender sovereignty, even temporarily.

One consequence of the British government's failure to realize the degree of nationalist determination in Rhodesia was the misplaced belief that the Rhodesian Front might be dissuaded from UDI, or persuaded back to legality by threats and warnings about what that action would entail. The British government hoped that the Rhodesians would be frightened by premonitions of post-UDI disaster, or by such a disaster itself. In fact, their reaction was more likely to be entrenchment than surrender, and increasing pressure would tend to toughen rather than weaken their resolve. Furthermore, the British estimates of how disastrously UDI would affect Rhodesia turned out to be less accurate than the more sanguine Rhodesian forecasts. Sandys in February 1964 and Wilson in October 1964 spelt out to the Rhodesian government the consequences of UDI in efforts to deter the Rhodesian government. In talks with Smith in London a year later, Wilson warned that UDI might 'set the whole of southern Africa, and even a wider area, ablaze'. Russia and China might intervene 'with incalculable consequences. Here lay a great danger – almost, perhaps, a probability. He feared a terrible conflict and bloodshed.'[20] Smith was confident that there would be no violence. In the Salisbury talks later the same month, Wilson described UDI as a drastic and dangerous step, and forecast that it would bring about majority rule quicker than any other course;[21] the Rhodesian government was unmoved by such arguments. After UDI the British government tried to make life uncomfortable for Rhodesia, chiefly through sanctions. In a speech in July 1966, Smith showed the futility of such relatively weak hostility: 'We have set our course and we have no intention whatsoever of deviating. We will never surrender to threats. We will never surrender to sanctions; in fact, we are not the sort of people who will surrender to anything.'[22] At the end

L

of 1966 the British government was still predicting terrible and incalculable consequences for Rhodesia if it did not return to constitutional rule;[23] on the *Tiger* Wilson tried to impress Smith with Britain's bulldog qualities: 'Britain had never been defeated yet on an issue to which she bent her strength, and their resolve would be inflexible to settle the Rhodesian problem in the way they thought right.' The British Prime Minister also warned that the régime should not assume that Britain would necessarily refrain from force in the future because it had in the past.[24] Smith was not impressed by veiled threats, any more than by protracted diplomacy.

Not only did Wilson underestimate Smith's coolness and resilience, but he also imagined that he might be able to isolate Smith from his party and do business with him. This image of Smith as a rational moderate in the temporary grip of wild extremists gave Wilson unreal hope of reaching agreement with Smith. Smith has said – and all the evidence supports his statement – 'As far as independence is concerned, I have led – and I have led the whole way; and I am a strong enough character not to *be* led. I won't be led.'[25] In his telephone conversation with Smith on the morning of UDI, Wilson tried to put the blame for the impending break, not on Smith, but on some of his Cabinet colleagues 'who have got the bit between their teeth'. Smith assured him that the majority of them were not determined on a break irrespective of what Britain offered, as Wilson suggested. Yet, reporting the conversation to the Commons, Wilson described Smith as 'a confused and unhappy man', who had 'been, in these past weeks, under intolerable pressures from some of his colleagues and from the unreasoning extremists'. Wilson maintained that Smith had admitted that the position was irreconcilable because of those in the Cabinet determined on a break at all costs; in fact, Smith merely admitted that a few might possibly fall into this category, but emphasized they were not in a majority.[26] Arthur Bottomley, the then Commonwealth Secretary, also believed that Smith was not wholly responsible for UDI; in his statement to the Commons afterwards, he related how Smith had confided to him that he had difficulties in his Cabinet. Bottomley advised him that, if he went to the electorate on his name alone, he could win without the support of his party.[27]

This journeying into dreamland continued after UDI. Smith has said that Wilson seemed obsessed with the idea that there were some members of the Rhodesian cabinet whom Smith would have liked to get rid of, and Smith could not persuade him otherwise.[28] On the *Tiger* Wilson indulged, apparently in all seriousness, in the ludicrous fantasy of the British government in alliance with Smith against the Rhodesian parliament. Wilson was prepared to see the parliament function in the interim period after Rhodesia had returned to legality, but before the independence constitution had been accepted by the people, 'provided Mr Smith could handle it and keep it under control. But if parliament became an embarrassment to Mr Smith, then he would have the course open to him of dissolving it and having a general election. If the worst came to the worst, the British could always help out with Special Orders in Council.'[29] Even after the *Tiger* meetings, Wilson speculated about the possibility of Smith making an agreement which his Cabinet disowned. This recurring dream that Smith might be won over could only have marred Wilson's judgement of what talks with Smith might achieve.

The British government not only seems to have overrated its chances of achieving a settlement by talks through misunderstanding its opponents, but also to have miscalculated the effects of sanctions. In April 1965, after discussing sanctions and other action that would be taken against Rhodesia in the event of a UDI Wilson announced: 'She cannot hope to defy Britain, the whole of the Commonwealth, nearly the whole of Africa, and the United Nations.'[30] Once Rhodesia declared independence, he was confident that sanctions would bring the rebellion to an end in weeks rather than months; of this he was quickly disabused, but, once it was seen that the Salisbury régime was surviving, the British government may have believed that sanctions and talks buttressing each other would bring the Rhodesian government to a reasonable compromise.

The initial mistake of believing that Rhodesia would easily fall to sanctions was the result of the government's following ill-informed advice from the Department of Economic Affairs in preference to the different opinions prevailing in the Ministry of Overseas Development.[31] The government's faith in sanctions was unduly sanguine, when so much scepticism about their efficacy was expressed within and outside government circles. The British government, because it did not fully grasp the fervour of nationalism throughout white Rhodesia, did perhaps not see that economic inconvenience and material discomfort would not end independence, but would strengthen the will to resist. Combating sanctions by developing the domestic economy had the effect, according to Smith, 'of strengthening the morale and determination of the people as a whole. It has brought us together as a nation in a way that I believe would not have happened had we not been faced with this exercise.'[32]

Although sanctions did not soften Rhodesia's will to resist, they may ironically have sharpened Britain's keenness to negotiate. On the *Tiger*, Wilson dismissed speculation about Britain's economic weakness. 'It is true that the loss of some £30 million of exports to Rhodesia in the last year was unfortunate', but total British exports had increased by nearly £300 million.[33] Yet it is arguable that Britain's willingness to treat and compromise with Rhodesia after independence stemmed partly from anxiety about the effects of sanctions on Britain's severe balance-of-payments problems. Such economic embarrassment may have been a constraint on Britain's policy, discouraging it from turning its back on Rhodesia if the faintest chance remained of a settlement, which would allow Britain to lift sanctions. In addition to the loss of export trade to Rhodesia, Britain lost invisible earnings because of Rhodesian retaliation against sanctions: the British Exchequer paid for the cost of airlifting oil to Zambia when the blockade on oil to Rhodesia cut off the normal supply route; the price of Zambian copper increased because the usual outlet through Rhodesia was closed. The direct cost to the Exchequer was £27 million from November 1965 to the end of November 1967, and the loss to the balance of payments in 1966 was about £40 million.[34] As sanctions were intended to coerce Rhodesia, Britain could not admit that they had a greater effect on British policy; but Wilson's conduct on the *Tiger* and the *Fearless* becomes more easily intelligble if it is assumed that he was anxious to remove the strain of continued sanctions on Britain's already precarious economy.

The explanations we have suggested for the British policy of continually prolonging negotiations may not altogether dissipate the feeling that the seemingly endless talks were not entered into by either side with the belief that a concrete agreement would emerge; there remains a feeling of unreality, of ritualistic movement rather than rational behaviour. To some degree Wilson's aim may have been to protect his reputation rather than to solve the problem; he had considerable success in presenting his recurrent attempts to negotiate a settlement as the serious efforts of a responsible government to obtain a moral and sensible settlement, which were thwarted by evil and senseless opponents, and, by presenting the confrontation in these terms, he obscured the fact that Smith took what he wanted and he could not stop him. The British government also successfully propagated the myth that agreement was better than disagreement, almost irrespective of its terms. Those who swallowed the belief that agreement was a good in itself admired the British government's persistence in seeking agreement, without worrying very much whether the content of such an agreement would compromise the principles from which Britain was allegedly acting or whether such an agreement was practical politics.

In addition, the constant activity of talks about talks and the high drama of battleship meetings concealed from some the essential weakness of the British government's position. This weakness lay in the inefficacy of talks and sanctions, and in the inability or unwillingness to coerce the Rhodesian government. Not only did the British government neither use force nor threaten to use force, but it categorically stated that in the event of a UDI it would not use force. It consequently removed any disincentive which uncertainty about the use of force might have provided. Britain made it clear that it would send troops into Rhodesia only if the Rhodesian government were unable to prevent widespread disorder: if an African uprising in response to UDI had dislocated the country, Britain would have moved in; also, if Rhodesia had cut off electricity to Zambia from the Kariba power station, Britain might have replied militarily.

Why did Britain deny herself the use of force in Rhodesia except in these special circumstances? One answer is that Britain hoped, if nothing more, that first talking and then talking with sanctions would bring Rhodesia into line. However, there were almost certainly other reasons before and at the time of UDI, and, once it was clear that Britain would win no easy victory by talks and sanctions, there must have been powerful motives why the government preferred defeat to an effort at victory by force of arms.

Britain was not constrained by fear of great power intervention against her: the super-power rivals were as united against UDI as they had been over the Suez invasion in 1956. Britain knew that world opinion would not condemn her for bullying a small country, for the former colonies demanded the use of force against Rhodesia. On the other hand, as Wilson feared that UDI might lead to a conflagration in southern Africa and provide a pretext for Russian military intervention, he may have calculated that, if Britain did use force against Rhodesia, this might precipitate the conditions of war which Britain's ideological enemies might exploit for their own purposes. It might encourage the United Nations to send its troops in support of Britain, and Wilson feared the presence in southern Africa of 'a Red Army in blue berets'. Of course, it could have been argued that Britain's decision not to use force might lead others to use soldiers against Rhodesia. However, Wilson may have calculated – and, if so, correctly – that others would not take the trouble, risks and expense of military action in Rhodesia unless Britain, who had the major responsibility, took the initiative and bore the main burden.

If Britain had fought in Rhodesia it would have been against the trend of imperial policy since the War of American Independence. Since that disastrous attempt to subdue rebellious colonists, Britain has not exerted herself to prevent colonists of British stock moving steadily towards independence. In the nineteenth century Britain was prepared to fight non-white 'natives' in order to hold colonies, and in the twentieth century to resist demands for self-government from coloured people rather more vigorously than those from whites; yet, even in these cases, Britain eventually transformed the expediency of retreat into the principle of self-determination.

Britain's imperial policy has been not to hold on to empire when it becomes too much trouble, and her attitude to Rhodesia from the earliest European settlement conforms to this general policy. At first Britain was reluctant to take on the responsibility for the handful of settlers in Rhodesia; but it did assert itself a little, principally in order to exclude Boer influence, to protect the settlers against the natives, and to protect the natives against the settlers. Even so, the British government ruled the country until 1923 through the agency of Rhodes's British South Africa Company, and then allowed the settlers to choose between joining the Union of South Africa and becoming an almost self-governing colony. They chose the latter, and under the 1923 constitution Britain held only a very loose rein over internal affairs; it merely scrutinized proposed legislation that might discriminate unfairly against the Africans, and the 1961 constitution removed even this power. With this history of Britain's minimal involvement in Rhodesia, the use of force even to counter the exceptional and unconstitutional UDI would have been a radical departure in British policy.

The purely moral objection to using force supported the policy indicated by Britain's traditional reticence in Rhodesia. As Britain had no police or soldiers in Rhodesia, UDI entailed no physical resistance to British authority; if Britain had attacked Rhodesia, it would have been meeting mere unconstitutionality with naked violence. To risk thousands of British and Rhodesian lives and the dislocation of Rhodesian society, the British government would have had to be very positive about the magnitude of what was at stake in UDI. A Labour government in particular would more likely eschew force in conformity with Labour's traditional ideological preference for rational means of settling international disputes.

A further constraint on military action was the knowledge that a vocal minority in Britain led by the Anglo-Rhodesian Society sympathized with the white Rhodesians, and would strongly deplore fighting them for asserting their independence. Many in Britain had friends and relations who had settled in Rhodesia; few members of the Labour government were likely to be influenced by feeling for their kith and kin in Rhodesia, but especially after the Suez crisis, would not wish to fight a war with a strong minority of the British people against it. Rumours that some British soldiers would not fight if ordered into battle against Rhodesians may have weighed in the government's calculations; the extent of this danger could not be known unless force was actually used against Rhodesia, but the government would not want to risk another Curragh Mutiny, which could seriously weaken any attack on Rhodesia and dangerously undermine the morale of the Army.

The Labour government may have been more worried about the effects of its Rhodesian policy on the electorate than on the Army. The election of October 1964 gave the Labour party a majority of only seven, and Wilson wished to have another election as soon as he felt confident of being returned with a safe majority; he may have feared that the use of force in Rhodesia might alienate too many voters and any military setback might further damage Labour's appeal. In Parliament the Conservative opposition might seriously embarrass the government if, with its precarious majority, it ventured on an unpopular military expedition. An apparently strong but flexible policy of talks and sanctions presented fewer risks to Labour's power.

After Wilson was returned in March 1966 with a greatly increased majority, he could afford to be less sensitive about the public reaction to his Rhodesia policy; yet, even then, he would have had to be convinced that the arguments in favour of force were very strong in order to overcome the objection that military setback or even military involvement in Rhodesia would create great administrative and political problems for the government. The Conservative opposition would have vigorously opposed the use of force, and Wilson avoided political difficulties by adopting policies which the Conservatives could not radically oppose. He did not want the trouble of a war, nor the risk of losing prestige, popularity, and ultimately power through a military engagement where clear-cut victory could not be guaranteed.

The purely military problems probably acted as a constraint upon British policy. With its immensely superior military and economic resources, Britain could eventually have forced Rhodesia into submission; but the vital questions were how long, with what difficulties and at what cost. Rhodesia would not be an easy enemy: it possesses a well-trained, well-equipped army and a formidable modern air force; its troops, while defending Rhodesia against Britain, would have the advantage of knowing the terrain. Some Rhodesian soldiers might have scruples at fighting Britons, but most of them would be fired by passionate loyalty to Rhodesia. P. K. van der Byl, a Rhodesian Minister, put it this way in January 1966: 'Does Harold Wilson believe that we in this country, whose forefathers fought at Agincourt, Dunkirk and Vechtkop, are endowed with any less resolution than the Russians displayed when in retreat from the Germans? If he were to prevail in this country, he would take over a smoking ruin and a desert.'[35]

Rhodesia also has long borders with South Africa and the Portuguese territory of Mozambique; if Rhodesia were at war with Britain, these countries would probably not help Rhodesia directly, but they would give valuable indirect support, as they have in combating sanctions.

Britain's problems in mounting an attack against Rhodesia would be serious. In order to raise sufficient troops to cope successfully with the Rhodesian forces, Britain would have to call on troops from other parts of the world where they might be needed. The logistics of the operation would be formidable, as these soldiers would have to be flown to bases in Zambia and then maintained by air for as long as the operation lasted. The organization required for this vast airlift would be immense and the demands on air transport severe, so that the British government would have to meet a big challenge, even before the attack on Rhodesia started. Then the army would have the hard task of crossing the Zambesi.[36]

Even if these considerations were not sufficient, along with the non-military arguments, to deter Britain from using force, the cost of a military expedition with Britain already in economic difficulties surely would. Finally, the problems of first administering a conquered Rhodesia and then creating a new political system with new political leaders would provide a further motive for seeking other than violent means to end the Rhodesian rebellion.

Throughout the Rhodesian affair, the British government has received vociferous advice from Commonwealth States, especially those in black Africa. Rhodesian ministers often felt that Britain succumbed to their influence, but the British government's conduct over Rhodesia is distinguished more by its resistance to the emotional pressures of the Third World. At the United Nations and at the conferences of Commonwealth heads of State, Britain was under strong pressure to insist on majority rule in Rhodesia and to use force once Rhodesia had seized independence. Although the British government shared the fundamental moral principles of the black African states and their allies, it differed from them about the practical implementation of these principles in the case of Rhodesia.

Although Britain chose its own methods of handling the Rhodesian situation in defiance of the bellicose indignation of the new States, it did not carry out its policies without any concern for 'world opinion'. There was a danger that an unpopular Rhodesian policy would strengthen Russian and Chinese influence in Africa. Wilson, too, had no wish to split the Commonwealth over Rhodesia. The extent to which Britain would compromise with the Rhodesian government was limited principally by the British government's unwillingness to depart too far from its principles, but also by fear of poisoning Britain's relations within the Commonwealth. During the negotiations with Smith, Wilson did not forget Commonwealth interest in Rhodesia;[37] the barrage of criticism from Commonwealth African States, particularly at the conferences of Commonwealth heads of State, probably helped the British government to resist temptations to offer more concessions to the Smith régime than they did.

Nevertheless, the general lines of Britain's policy over Rhodesia were remarkable for their independence of Commonwealth opinion. Before Rhodesian independence became an issue, Britain had become experienced in resisting demands in the United Nations for radical change in Rhodesia; it took, and steadfastly maintained, the position that Rhodesia was Britain's sole responsibility. At successive conferences of Commonwealth heads of State, Wilson insisted on this, and argued against the clamorous demands for stronger action by Britain. Even Tanzania's and Ghana's breaking of diplomatic relations with Britain in 1965 did not affect Britain's Rhodesia policy. Britain no longer ruled an Empire, but she could defy the Commonwealth.

Other constraints on British policy in Rhodesia were distinctly stronger than fear of Commonwealth disapproval, although none deprived the government of choice. However, the combined effect of several constraints was to provide a powerful deterrent to the use of force. The government was held back from such a policy by its own moral scruples, by the tradition of non-intervention in colonies desiring independence, by fears that military success might not be easily achieved, by calculation of the costs, by the wish to exclude hostile States from Central Africa, and by the desire to preserve political power at home.

Yet the whole of British policy to Rhodesia cannot be interpreted as the consequence of constraints. The refusal to recognize the régime after UDI and the attempts to negotiate a compromise constitution stemmed partly from positive adherence to moral principles and the desire to preserve prestige. Also, the exaggerated faith in sanctions and talks sprang from misjudgements of the strength of the Rhodesian nationalists' passionate determination for independence, of Smith's relation with his cabinet and of the effects of sanctions. Finally, the British government was interested in projecting a statesmanlike image by continuing talks even when they offered little hope of a satisfactory solution.

Postscript

After this chapter was completed, the Conservative government that was elected in June 1970 reopened negotiations with the Rhodesian government. In November 1971 a delegation led by the Foreign and Commonwealth Secretary, Sir Alec Douglas-Home, flew out to Salisbury and reached agreement with representatives of the Rhodesian government on proposals for a settlement. Both sides undertook to implement these proposals when the British government had satisfied itself through a commission that they would be acceptable to the people of Rhodesia as a whole. The proposed constitution makes African majority rule a possibility in the distant future, whereas it cannot be achieved under the 1969 constitution. However, according to the calculations of Dr Claire Palley,[38] under the proposed constitution the earliest date for majority rule is 2035, whereas under the constitution proposed on *Fearless* in 1968 it might have come by 1999. Ian Smith is abandoning some of the ground that he took in the 1969 constitution, but the British government is offering more than it did in 1968. The proposed constitution of 1971 is distinctly less favourable to the Africans than the 1961 constitution, which before UDI the British government insisted should be slightly modified to the Africans' advantage before independence could be granted.

[Ed. note. A commission led by Lord Pearce visited Rhodesia early in 1972 and found that the proposed settlement was not acceptable to the Rhodesian people as a whole.]

NOTES

1 *Southern Rhodesia: Documents relating to the Negotiations between the United Kingdom and Southern Rhodesian Governments, November 1963–November 1965* (Cmnd 2807), pp. 68, 72–3; *Relations between the Rhodesian Government and the United Kingdom Government, November 1965–December 1966* (Salisbury, 1966), p. 58.

2 Claire Palley, 'No Majority Rule before 1999', *The Guardian*, 14 November 1968; Leo S. Baron, 'Africans Can Never Have a Majority in Twelve Years', a letter in the *Bulawayo Chronicle*, 13 July 1964. During the pre-UDI talks, a Rhodesian minister said that majority rule might come in 1972, even 1970, but he had a strong motive for suggesting an early date, as Wilson had just asked how he could justify the grant of independence if African political advance was slow (*Southern Rhodesia: Documents*, p. 129). After UDI in September 1966 Smith said that he had recently received figures from the Ministry of Education which indicated that Africans could on educational qualifications alone obtain enough votes for a majority in five to six years (*Relations*, p. 58).

3 *Southern Rhodesia: Documents*, p. 15. See also p. 13, and *Southern Rhodesia: Correspondence between Her Majesty's Government and the Government of Southern Rhodesia, April–June 1963* (Cmnd 2073), p. 9.

4 *Southern Rhodesia: Documents*, p. 7.

5 Ibid., p. 59.

6 Ibid., p. 66.

7 Ibid., p. 67–8.

8 Ibid., pp. 90–3.
9 Ibid, pp. 112–13.
10 Ibid., pp. 129–30.
11 Ibid., p. 124.
12 K. Young, *Rhodesia and Independence*, 2nd edn (London, 1969), p. 633.
13 *Relations*, p. 14.
14 Ibid, p. 4; see also p. 135.
15 Ibid., p. 128.
16 *Rhodesia: Report on the Discussions held on board H.M.S. Fearless, October 1968* (Cmnd 3793), p. 3.
17 *Relations*, p. 135.
18 *Statement on Anglo-Rhodesian Relations, December 1966–May 1969* (Salisbury, 1969).
19 *Southern Rhodesia: Documents*, p. 113.
20 Ibid., p. 83.
21 Ibid., p. 115.
22 *Relations*, p. 14.
23 *Rhodesia: Documents Relating to Proposals for a Settlement 1966* (Cmnd 3171), p. 24; *Relations*, p. 127.
24 *Relations*, p. 128; *Rhodesia: Documents*, pp. 55, 101.
25 Young, op. cit., p. 100. Smith said this in February 1966 in conversation with Young.
26 Ibid., p. 633 (this is from the transcript of the telephone conversation); *House of Commons Debates*, vol. 720, cols 352–3.
27 *House of Commons Debates*, vol. 720, col. 525.
28 Ibid., p. 473.
29 *Relations*, p. 117.
30 *House of Commons Debates*, vol. 711, col. 639.
31 R. Hall, *The High Price of Principles* (London 1969), pp. 116–17; R. B. Sutcliffe, 'The Political Economy of Rhodesian Sanctions', *Journal of Commonwealth Political Studies*, vol. 7, no. 2 (July 1969), p. 114. See also Dudley Seers, 'The Structure of Power', in Hugh Thomas (ed.), *Crisis in the Civil Service* (London 1968), pp. 97–8.
32 *La Revue française de l'élite européene* (English edition), no. 209 bis (November 1968), p. 6.
33 *Rhodesia: Documents*, p. 101.
34 Young, op. cit., pp. 384–6, 441–2, 516; *House of Commons Debates*, vol. 756, cols 239–40; Sutcliffe (op. cit., pp. 115–17) argues strongly that the cost of sanctions to the British balance of payments in 1966 was probably considerably less than £40 million, and that the role of Rhodesia in the balance of payments deficit of £404 million in 1967 was 'quite trivial'.
35 Young, op. cit., p. 379.
36 On the military aspects of the Rhodesian crisis, see Neville Brown, 'Military Sanctions against Rhodesia', *Venture*, vol. 17, no. 12 (January 1966), pp. 9–12; William Gutteridge, 'Rhodesia: the Use of Military Force', *The World Today*, vol. 21, no. 12 (December 1965), pp. 499–503; Young, op. cit., pp. 328–31.
37 *Southern Rhodesia: Documents*, pp. 61, 71; *Rhodesia: Documents*, pp. 51–2; *Relations*, p. 125.
38 *The Sunday Times*, 28 November 1971, and *The Guardian*, 14 November 1968.

IX Constraints on Economic Sovereignty

JOHN WILLIAMSON

An obvious feature of the present international economic system is that it severely circumscribes the freedom of action of its constituent States; the economic sovereignty of individual States is very far from absolute, and this is particularly true for those Western industrial nations that form the core of the international economy. One aim of the present essay is to offer an explanation of why nations have accepted these considerable constraints; such an explanation would seem an essential prerequisite of any attempt to assess the desirability of these constraints and the possibility of easing them, which are subjects taken up later in the chapter.

Typically, the constraints take the form of obligations accepted on joining an international organization. A clear-cut example is provided by the General Agreement on Tariffs and Trade (GATT), membership of which denies a country the right to raise its tariffs unilaterally. Membership of the European Free Trade Association (EFTA) has a similar condition, except that tariffs against other members are zero. The loss of sovereignty is a good deal more ambiguous in most other cases. Participation in the International Monetary Fund (IMF) involves a nominal loss of freedom over exchange-rate policy, but the Fund never objects to countries doing much as they please in this connection. The obligation to maintain external convertibility is more real, while the major source of power the Fund can exert over its members arises from the 'consultations' it has with a country that is borrowing from it. A country refusing to amend its policies to accord with the wishes of the Fund might well be denied borrowing privileges in the higher echelons. The loss of sovereignty involved in membership of the Organization for Economic Co-operation and Development (OECD) is even more tenuous, for the Organization has no sanctions comparable to the Fund's power to refuse credit. Its committees include the Economic Policy Committee, which is concerned with co-ordinating economic policies (and especially payments policies, dealt with in the subcommittee known as Working Party No. 3), the Invisibles Committee, which has been concerned to liberalize restrictions on invisible trade and capital flows parallel to the work of GATT on commodity trade, and the Development Assistance Committee, the function of which is to promote the flow of aid. Although these committees pursue their ends through moral suasion, it would be quite wrong to conclude that they lack influence. The diplomatic rating of a country is affected by its standing in the OECD, and consequently an unco-operative stance can help to undermine the general effectiveness of a country's foreign policy. There is also the personal element: those attending are influential people in their own governments, and they are naturally sensitive to the opinions of their foreign counterparts.

Not all international organizations involve a sacrifice of sovereignty. Membership of the World Bank and the International Development Association (IDA) simply involves the contribution of funds. Conversely, constraints on sovereignty may also be accepted by signing bilateral or multilateral treaties: examples include double-taxation treaties, patent agreements, and limitations on whale fishing. Nevertheless, the major objects of interest are the obligations imposed by membership of international organizations; and Britain seems likely to accept substantial additional constraints, as a result of accession to the Common Market, in the not-too-distant future. The first task is to clarify the reasons why countries accept such constraints.

Homo economicus is an abstraction, but he has proved to be a useful one. A parallel assumption in the present context is that each country is interested in furthering its own national interest, interpreted as its real gross national product (GNP), with little concern for events beyond its own borders unless these threaten to undermine its security. It is well known that such a country can gain by imposing an 'optimal tariff', provided its partners do not react; but if all countries try to impose optimal tariffs, there is a strong presumption that each of them will end up worse off than under free trade. Hence there is scope for mutual gain by reciprocal reduction of tariffs, which is precisely what GATT is designed to accomplish. It is not hard to think of other examples which are analytically identical; they include double-taxation treaties and limitations on whale fishing.

Superficially it might seem that British participation in such bodies as the World Bank, IDA, Food and Agriculture Organization (FAO) or the Development Assistance Committee (DAC) of the OECD cannot be explained in the same way, because the purpose of these organizations is to provide benefits to less-developed countries, and not to developed countries like the UK. Yet it does not follow that membership is an act of pure altruism, and it is difficult to interpret the behaviour of the advanced countries in these organizations in that light; for example, an altruist would surely react to a threatened cut in aid by another country by increasing, or at least by not reducing, its own aid programme, whereas in fact both IDA and DAC operate by persuading countries to match each others' efforts. In contrast, it is easy to rationalize this pattern if one accepts the statements of the leaders of the advanced countries to the effect that economic development will contribute to the evolution of a more stable world, for this implies that development will be of joint benefit to the advanced countries, irrespective of which of them contributes the necessary funds; while unilateral action by any one of them would impose costs greater than the anticipated benefits, an all-round increase can be mutually advantageous. On examination, therefore, these agreements are in some respects similar to those mentioned in the previous paragraph.

It also seems possible to interpret many of the agreements in the monetary field as the products of a search for mutual gain through reciprocal forbearance. The limitations on exchange-rate policy embodied in the IMF articles originated from the need to avert the threat of competitive devaluation as practised in the 1930s. The additional reserves, that is special drawing rights (SDRs), and reserve-borrowing facilities provided by the Fund enable liquidity to be expanded without the waste entailed in using the traditional reserve asset, gold; all countries, except those with a vested interest in gold, benefit from agreement to create a synthetic substitute. Reserve borrowing is accompanied by precautions to ensure that loans are repaid; it is these restrictions which were previously argued to be the principal channel through which the Fund curtails sovereignty. The logic of the 'multilateral surveillance' practised by the Economic Policy Committee of the OECD is that a country's policies with regard to demand management, competitiveness, interest rates, and hence the balance of payments have spill-over effects beyond its own borders, for the obvious reason that one country's surplus is another's deficit. One of the principal preoccupations of Working Party No. 3 has been the attempt to ensure consistency of payments objectives, which means that the sum of all balance of payments targets should be equal to the expected growth in reserves.

Any economist who reads the foregoing explanations of why countries agree to sacrifice sovereignty will no doubt be struck by the similarity with that area of economic theory that goes under the inelegant label of 'externalities' – that is, acceptance of such constraints can be rationalized in terms of the possibility of mutual gain by reciprocal action. The provision of aid is a 'public good' to the advanced countries; the imposition of tariffs involves a divergence between national and world welfare; monetary policies have spill-over effects. In each case, an efficient solution requires that the total benefits and costs accruing to the whole world – and not merely those that come to rest in one country – should be taken into account in the decision-making process. Faced with such divergences between social and private costs and benefits within a nation, economists have traditionally conceded that there is a *prima facie* case for government intervention. In recent years, however, many of the more *laissez-faire* economists have contested this implication by arguing that the interested parties will have an incentive to bargain away any inefficiencies that would arise through individual maximizing.[1] One may doubt whether the costs of bargaining are sufficiently minor to be brushed aside as in this theory; but the fascinating fact is that at the international level there is no alternative to bargaining, because there is no central world authority able to impose a solution on the parties.

There are at least three distinct ways of persuading a decision-maker to take account of the spill-over effects of his actions: he can be subjected to a series of rules and regulations designed to curb the costs he imposes on others; or he can be faced with *ad hoc* pressures from those affected, in which case the parties are likely to end up bargaining; or the terms on which he chooses between the available alternatives can be altered to reflect the effects that his actions have on others. The first remedy is that customarily used to control (for example) smoke emission at the national level, and also to restrain tariff changes at the international level; the second expedient seems to be little adopted at the national level, presumably because of the number of parties involved, but is of dominant importance at the international level; the third alternative is applied at the national level by imposing taxes on objects that yield external dis-economies, such as motor cars, but it seems to be virtually absent in the international context. Economists tend to have a preference for this third remedy, when practicable, on the grounds that it reconciles decentralized decision-making with a situation in which decisions are reached in the light of their total consequences.

It has been argued above that sacrifices of economic sovereignty generally arise because nations believe there is scope for mutual gain through mutual restraint. If this is true, it surely suggests that any blanket attempt to restore national sovereignty would be undesirable; it would seem more probable that there are additional gains that could be tapped by limiting sovereignty further. Nevertheless, there remain two circumstances under which one could profitably increase sovereignty: the first occurs where the spill-over effects are in fact absent or insufficiently important to justify the resulting loss of national autonomy; the second arises where a reform of the international economic system would be capable of altering the incentives facing national governments, in such a way as to persuade them to take appropriate account of the interests of other countries without the need for conscious intervention or pressure from international sources.

These principles provide a frame of reference within which one may hope to judge whether economic sovereignty in particular areas is excessively great, about right, or unreasonably limited. Consider first the problem of tariffs. It is absolutely clear that countries need to be restrained from the pursuit of individual national interests in this area, because the cheapest way of curing a payments deficit normally involves the imposition of tariffs, and thereby throwing a substantial part of the burden on to other countries. GATT seems well designed to achieve this objective, and has achieved a surprising measure of success in actually reducing tariffs over the years. Customs unions and free trade areas, such as the EEC and EFTA, have of course achieved even more in this direction on a regional basis. At one time there were serious fears that such blocs might be a new and more subtle way for a group of countries to exploit the rest of the world by obtaining more favourable terms of trade, but the evidence now suggests that 'trade diversion' is minor compared to the 'trade creation' that results.[2] There does not, therefore, seem to be any pressing need for institutional changes in the tariff field.

The provision of aid is a field in which, judged by any reasonable world-wide welfare function, the sums provided are still grossly inadequate. This is hardly surprising in view of the fact that aid is a 'public good'. How many towns would have an adequate sewage system if the service were financially dependent on voluntary contributions? There seems little hope of remedying this state of affairs without further curtailing national sovereignty; since the sacrifice of sovereignty involved in allowing a world authority to tax directly the rich for the benefit of the poor would be too great for the present generation to accept, progress is likely to depend upon placing new sources of finance at the disposal of the aid-giving agencies. One potential source, the high seas, has probably been lost already by the recent extensions of territorial rights to cover Continental shelves; with more imagination the mineral and fishing rights in these areas might have been inter-nationalized, and then yielded income to the international community. A second source would be provided by 'the Link', which is the term given to the proposal that the profits involved in creating international money (SDRs) be transferred to the less-developed countries by issuing new SDRs to those countries, and so requiring the advanced countries to earn their reserve increases;[3] in the absence of a new source of finance, increased aid will be dependent on the uncertain process of trying to shame countries into giving more. The prospects of increasing the real value of aid may be slightly brighter, in so far as there might well be scope for mutual benefits from a multilateral agreement to untie aid, that would again involve a minor encroachment on sovereignty.

The other area in which there is a strong technical case for curtailing sovereignty is in relation to the environment. The blue whale is threatened with extinction, and the Atlantic salmon has declined precipitately, as a result of over-fishing by nations which seem to argue that restraint on their part would simply result in the greed of others being more fully satisfied. It is surely time for this sort of irresponsibility to be outlawed, and the only reasonably certain way of accomplishing that is to curtail the right of individual nations to contract out of international agreements, limiting fishing to levels that will conserve stocks.

The main hope of easing constraints on sovereignty would seem to lie in the monetary sphere. The most vexatious constraints are those which curtail the freedom to pursue economic policies judged to be domestically desirable because of their payments implications; these constraints are as liable to distort policy in countries like Germany and the Netherlands, that are more inflation-proof than the world average, as in countries like the UK, that are excessively inflation-prone; one avoids the constraint by being average, not by being virtuous, and it is not at all obvious that these sacrifices are well conceived. In fact, many economists doubt whether fixed exchange rates are on balance advantageous; if they were to be abandoned in favour of floating rates, one could dispense with much of the apparatus of multilateral surveillance and borrowing from the IMF, because multilateral surveillance is primarily intended to prevent countries imposing unacceptable payments outcomes on each other, and reserve borrowing is undertaken to defend a fixed exchange rate. The latter would, in turn, mean the end of Letters of Intent, which have been known to impose terms of sufficient stringency to cripple a country's freedom to react to unexpected developments. That is, in fact, their purpose: they are intended to ensure that, if the unexpected happens, priority is given to external rather than domestic objectives.

Suppose, however, that it is really true that floating exchange rates cause a great disruption of foreign trade, so that in the long run it really is in the national interest to maintain a régime of fixed rates (perhaps with the possibility of occasional changes). It is still worth asking the question whether it would be possible to devise a system that could safely dispense with the current surveillance of economic policy carried out by the OECD and the IMF. To answer the question it is necessary to analyse the motives for multilateral surveillance in rather more detail. One could distinguish four potential conflicts of national

M

interest that the system might resolve: there is the danger of competitive devaluation as practised in the 1930s, there is the possibility of a global shortage of reserves, with countries competing with one another to lay their hands on a larger proportion of a fixed supply; thirdly, there is the question of the way in which the burden of adjustment should be shared between the surplus and deficit countries; and, finally, there is the interest that the creditor countries have in ensuring that the debtor countries repay their debts. These factors are of uneven importance: competitive devaluation ceased to be a sensible policy on the day that active demand management became feasible, which explains its conspicuous absence from the post-war world; likewise, the fear of countries engaging in a self-defeating scramble for a fixed stock of reserves has been stilled by the successful introduction of SDRs. The important question is that centred on the distribution of adjustment burdens because, if the deficit countries move into surplus, one can be confident that the debts will be repaid.

In a two-country world, a deficit in Country A would be a surplus for Country B. The payments balances of both countries could be corrected either by A deflating or by B inflating. If both were initially close to the demand pressure that they prefer for internal reasons, it would be natural for A to prefer that B inflate and for B to prefer that A deflate. If there were no possibility of borrowing reserves, B need only sterilize its inflow of reserves and wait for A to adjust, which it would be compelled to do in due course because its initial stock of reserves is inevitably limited. This has led many observers to complain of the inadequate pressure placed on surplus countries to contribute to the adjustment process. What they overlook is that, in reality, surplus nations do not stand by and watch deficit countries forced into precipitate adjustment; they lend reserves instead. One suspects that they do this because of the fear that precipitate adjustment could lead to social disruption, and even overthrow, of the political system. So long as such fears exist, deficit countries can rest assured that their partners will not let them go under. This alters the strategic balance between creditor and debtor nations. It means that, to ensure repayment, the creditor nations must either shoulder the adjustment burden themselves or else must develop sanctions other than the threat of bankruptcy to persuade the deficit nations to adjust. This is the major purpose of multi-lateral surveillance by the OECD and consultations with (and Letters of Intent to) the IMF.

If the above analysis of the rationale for international supervision of countries' economic policies is correct, it follows that one requires an alternative type of adjustment incentive. This might be created by varying the interest rates paid on reserves in such a way as to encourage countries to adjust, and to penalize those that fail to do so. This would be in strong contrast to the present system, under which virtually all reserves carry low interest rates, so that reserve lending results in a transfer of real income from the lender to the borrower. An ideal system would involve the pooling of all reserves into a 'conversion account' at the IMF, so that a country's reserves would simply consist of its balance in the account.[4] This would yield interest at a rate which decreased with its size, and interest would be charged on the country's indebtedness to the Fund at a rate that increased with the extent of the borrowing. (How rapidly the interest rate changed would have to depend upon the country's target level of reserves, which would need to be agreed between the Fund and each member individually.) In this way countries would have a much stronger incentive to try and ensure that their reserves did not stray far from their target level, but one would not obstruct the exercise of their own judgement in determining in what way and how fast the return to the target reserve level was secured. In practice, of course, creating a conversion account with an optimal interest-rate structure may be so difficult that one will have to think of approximating the same effect, for example, by raising the charges on Fund lending. Unfortunately, the decision to attach the unrealistically low interest rate of $1\frac{1}{2}$ per cent to SDRs is contrary to this objective. To the extent that it proved possible to create an interest-rate structure that provided an incentive to adjust, it should be possible to reduce the effort currently devoted to supervising the policies of individual countries.

The conclusions to which the above argument leads are that constraints on economic sovereignty are generally accepted for rational reasons, to compensate for spill-over effects; that the absence of a central world authority able to impose solutions means that there remain unexploited opportunities for gain from further curtailing sovereignty in certain directions; but that nevertheless there may be scope for reducing the interference in economic policy practised by such organizations as the IMF and OECD, provided that the system is reformed in appropriate ways. It may seem that the analysis refers only to those cases where sovereignty is partially surrendered in the search for specific gains, rather than to the formation of institutions (such as the EEC), where the ultimate objective is a merging of sovereignty. But the latter would seem to rest on a judgement that nation States are too small to retain ultimate sovereignty in the late twentieth century. If economics were the only question at issue – which clearly it is not – the notion of nations being 'too small' would be one of spill-over effects being so ubiquitous and so difficult to take fully into account through bargaining as to promise great rewards to the creation of supra-national institutions. Even the major loss of sovereignty that may ultimately be involved in membership of the Common Market can therefore be rationalized in the framework developed in this chapter.

NOTES

[1] R. H. Coase, 'The Problem of Social Cost', *Journal of Law and Economics* (October 1961).
[2] J. H. Williamson and A. Bottrill, *The Impact of Customs Unions on Trade in Manufactures* (Warwick Economic Research Paper no. 13, 1971).
[3] R. Triffin, 'The Use of SDR Finance for Collectively Agreed Purposes', *Banca Nazionale del Lavoro Quarterly Review* (March 1971).
[4] See for example, *Next Steps in International Monetary Reform*, Hearing before the Subcommittee on International Exchange and Payments, Joint Economic Committee, US Congress, 19 September 1968.

X Multi-national Companies and the British Economy

LOUIS TURNER

Although some of the outcry about the 'multi-national company' should be taken with a pinch of salt, it is perfectly reasonable to be worried about some of its aspects. The ways in which the British economy is managed will certainly change as a consequence of its intrusion and growth; policy areas in which our economic managers once thought they had absolute power will be affected by new complex forces. However, the day is not yet in sight when the Treasury knights will find themselves powerless in the face of a handful of foreign company presidents. The rise of the multi-nationals merely imposes new pressures on the economic policy-making function; they will not necessarily dominate it. For a full discussion, the reader can consult books like Charles Kindleberger's symposium *The International Corporation* (1970), or my own *Invisible Empires* (1970); a more limited consideration is required for the purposes of this chapter.

When we talk about 'multi-nationals', we are using the word loosely to describe a tendency whereby companies are increasingly treating whole continents, or the globe itself, as single units of operation. The more a company does this, the better it deserves the title. IBM, the US-owned computer firm, is probably the archetypal multi-national. Its non-American operations (which provide just over 50 per cent of the firm's world-wide sales) are co-ordinated closely with its American operations. Within Europe, its research laboratories in different nations are given specific types of research; for example, the UK handles the computer needs of insurance and banking; and Sweden handles medical computing. When a new range of computer models is introduced, their final assembly is carried out in different countries; thus the System 370 range announced in 1970 is produced in Britain (model 165 – the largest), France (model 155), and Germany (model 145). However, the components for any one of these models will have come from IBM plants all over Europe as well, so that someone buying an IBM computer in, say, Britain, is buying the product of IBM in a number of countries; to give this computer a 'national' identity is to make little manufacturing sense.

Other companies follow policies which are not so comprehensive, but which tend to move in the same direction. Thus Ford has had a policy of common car and van designs within Europe since the early 1960s (engines excluded), even though its plants in Germany and Britain have been kept independent; however, its latest venture, an automatic transmission plant in Bordeaux, is designed to provide transmissions for Ford cars throughout Europe. Other companies co-ordinate a flow of products, rather than components, across Europe, like Philips, whose washing machines and refrigerators increasingly come from Italy, and tape recorders from Austria.

What this has created is the interpenetration of economies, not so much by traditional imports and exports, but more by the flow of capital which leads to individuals in one country owning a growing proportion of the industrial activity of another country. Thus Dunning[1] shows that in 1965 American and Anglo-American financed subsidiaries employed 6 per cent of the labour force in British manufacturing industry, supplied 10 per cent of the total goods coming from British factories, and accounted for $17\frac{1}{2}$ per cent of British visible exports. Some predictions hold that the proportion of UK industrial assets controlled by foreign investment should increase to between 20 and 25 per cent by 1975. This is not, of course, a particularly high proportion by some standards; even in 1963 foreign ownership of Canadian manufacturing industry was some 54 per cent.

Even in the traditional export–import sector, the multi-nationals have been taking over. Around 50 per cent of US exports in 1967 were the product of arrangements whereby a US firm exported to an affiliate or subsidiary – a 'within-the-family' deal, which just happened to cross an international border and therefore become an export.[2] Similarly, a Board of Trade survey in 1968 showed that in 1966 exports to related concerns in foreign countries represented 22 per cent of total exports from Britain.

On the whole the opposition to the spread of multi-nationals has not been led by economists. The studies by Dunning in the UK,[3] Safarian in Canada,[4] and Brash in Australia[5] have, on balance, found the activities of foreign corporations within their separate economies neutral or beneficial. The objections have been on more strictly political grounds; are they justified? Can an economy be kept relatively independent in an age in which the interpenetration of the world's economies via multi-national companies seems inevitable? Does interpenetration of economies lead to standardization of domestic economic (and other) policies?

We should at this point distinguish two types of power that a multi-national can exercise. The more obvious type I call 'direct' power, in which a corporation, or a foreign government working through such corporations, puts pressure on the host government (that is the government receiving the investment) by the use of force, subversion, or threats; in the case of Britain, we shall see that this kind of pressure is relatively unimportant. The less obvious kind of power I call 'indirect', in which the host government modifies its behaviour because it is in competition with surrounding governments for the investment of multi-national companies. In this case, no threats may ever be uttered by the company, whose ultimate power lies in a refusal to invest in a country whose policies are not satisfactory. In consequence, governments are responding less to individual companies than to the policies of their neighbours in the light of factors which allegedly motivate companies to invest in one country rather than another.

There is very little evidence that foreign multi-nationals in Britain have ever resorted to the cruder forms of political pressure; there is not even, for instance, a single foreign company on the list of contributors to the Tory party – legend, in fact, has it that one local managing director who proposed making such a donation nearly lost his job. There are not many lobbies representing foreign business interests, though they are more active in Brussels.

Where the UK government is obviously still vulnerable is to pressures from foreign governmental legislation – the US government in particular. In fact, Britain has probably not suffered particularly badly from this, and the potential for such interference is slowly being removed. The US government's trading-with-the-enemy provisions have caused most trouble to the Canadian and French governments in the past; however, with the change in US relations with China, trade by US subsidiaries to China is now permitted, providing the goods are not of strategic importance. Despite this change, it is still not clear whether US parent companies will feel entirely free to negotiate major deals – both Ford and IBM recently turned down business with Russia at least in part because of pressures within the US. At one remove, therefore, the British economy can arguably be said to have suffered since their British subsidiaries would have had part of the business which the parent turned away.

British firms involved in Eastern Europe would also claim that their US-owned competitors, uneasy about getting too heavily involved in this market, but frustrated when British firms (amongst others) capitalize on their absence, use their influence with the US government to delay deals which need permission from the NATO committee which controls the sales of strategic goods to Warsaw Pact countries.

The other major charge laid against the US authorities, in particular, is that their anti-trust policies can hinder the freedom of other governments to restructure their industry as they see fit. In practice, this is a bit far-fetched: certainly there are disputes over the degree of extra-territoriality an anti-trust judgement may have, but there is little evidence that any government's policies have really been impeded in this way. The Ciba–Geigy merger was admittedly delayed while complications in the US were ironed out with the anti-trust authorities, and British firms like BP felt for a while that anti-trust policies were being used to bar their entry to the North American market; but a dispassionate look at these cases does not really support an alarmist line. As it happens, one can argue that, so far from regretting the influence of the US anti-trust authorities, we should welcome the extension of their principles to Europe, which has been less active in this field than some might like.

One further consideration worth bearing in mind at this point is that, as well as being a recipient of the investment of multi-nationals, Britain is the parent country of some of the world's largest companies outside the US. This, in itself, imposes obligations: until the early 1960s, this could mean heavy diplomatic involvement; the 1938 Mexican and 1951 Iranian oil expropriations both led to intense British diplomatic activity. Similarly, Britain's involvement with oil companies has complicated British reactions to the various Middle East crises and to the Biafran secession attempt. During the 1960s, however, there was obviously a growing awareness that developing nations had a right to impose control on their own economies, even if some of the firms involved were British-owned. Diplomatic efforts, therefore, switched away from trying to avoid any interference in such companies to trying to get the best possible compensation if governments were to go ahead with expropriations.

Critics have also made the point that Britain's treatment of the oil industry may have been influenced by the fact that Britain has interests in Shell and BP. They point out that Britain was slow to pressure oil companies to refine crude oil in Britain instead of importing the refined product from abroad. Similar allegations have been made about the British authorities' relative lack of concern about the low declared profits made by oil companies in Britain. The argument is that an investigation of the oil industry's transfer pricing policies could prove embarrassing to the British companies if other countries used the investigation as a precedent. It is virtually impossible to prove or disprove such charges. There is certainly no published material to support them, though the facts are suggestive.

So far, I have not been too impressed by the arguments considered above, but we now come to an analysis of the more indirect pressures government policy-makers may face, and here I think there is more reason for concern. To have control over the management of one's economy, one needs to be able to pursue monetary and fiscal policies without interference, and one would hope – perhaps wrongly – that one's industrialists would respond to incentives and exhortations to follow reasonable policies on exports, priority of research, and location of plants in development areas. One would also hope that the government should feel free to nationalize, should there be a domestic political mandate, and to rationalize industries where it is felt that enforced mergers, for instance, may lead to a more efficient final unit. Above all, policy decisions should be taken after purely domestic debate, and should not be forced on the government by any external agency. The emergence of the multi-national corporation has tended to erode this autonomy.

Ironically, in one area in particular, the arrival of multi-nationals has actually led to an increase in the effectiveness of government policies. British regional policies have benefited heavily from the fact that incoming US firms have been located in development areas; Layton[6] shows that just over half the US firms coming to Britain since 1945 have done so, and Scotland's diversification into electronics would have been impossible without US companies. The willingness of such companies to respond to regional incentives is quite simple to explain: coming into Britain for the first time, they will obviously have no existing plant which has to be considered as a factor affecting location decisions. Even where the company has existing British plants, foreign managers are less likely to be swayed by traditional loyalties to one British locality.

However, there are dangers. The more cynical would argue that the US companies are motivated mainly by the financial incentives offered by the British government as part of its development area policies. There is, therefore, the danger that the British government finds itself having to set the level of such incentives, not in relation to the relative appeal of other parts of Britain, but in relation to the incentives offered by other governments elsewhere in Europe. European governments could find themselves in competition, offering increasingly generous incentives to foreign companies in competition with their own. The EEC has been sufficiently worried about this to start thinking of limiting the amounts which a government can offer in its regional incentives, and of specifying the kind of factor (age of industrial structure, unemployment, and general infrastructure) which should be taken into account when deciding what levels of incentives should be offered.

At the moment, this is not really a problem which affects Britain very greatly. Lind and Flockton[7] show that Britain's incentives are somewhat higher than those offered in most of the rest of Europe, so that it is the rest of Europe which will tend to move, if at all, toward

Britain, rather than the other way round. Also the countries which have been most aggressively bidding for multi-national investment in the recent past – Belgium and the Netherlands – have just started learning about the problems of congestion and pollution which go with over-industrialization. In the longer run, however, the situation is less clear; if by the late 1970s the drift toward the Mediterranean is confirmed, then our more northerly and westerly regions, like Scotland and Ulster, may well be in serious trouble unless the British government can offer incentives which do more than match the best incentives offered in areas like southern Italy.

Both the major tools of economic management, fiscal and monetary manipulation, show signs of becoming more difficult to use. In part, this is because of the activities of multi-nationals. One of the brutal facts of contemporary political life is that manipulation of interest rates can actually have results diametrically opposed to those they are supposed to have. Thus a country with a sluggish economy may decide to reflate, lower its interest rates in order to spur investment, only for there to be a switch of funds into currencies offering higher rates of interest. This is, for instance, what happened in April and May 1971 when the lowering of US interest rates built up into a full-scale speculative assault on the Deutschemark. This was hard on the Germans, who had relatively high interest rates, because they were trying to damp down the inflation within their economy. They were faced with a choice between savagely cutting their interest rates or else revaluing; they chose the latter course.

The 1971 financial crisis was similar in nature to the crises which have attended the US dollar, English pound, French franc and Deutschemark since the early 1960s. Throughout the decade, the flow of 'hot money' has been increasing, so that it has now become commonplace for the flows at the height of a speculative period to be enough to clear a country's official reserves in three or four days, unless drastic recycling devices are used. Until the mid-1960s reluctant governments could avoid changes in their currency rates of exchange in situations where their economies were very uncompetitive; today speculation can force changes, because 'confidence' is somehow lost. The best example is the French economy, which, up to the unrest in May 1968, was considered one of the world's strongest (probably mistakenly). The passing of de Gaulle and the 'May troubles' suddenly raised doubts about the economy, which was really no stronger or weaker than it always had been. In August 1969, the franc was forced to devalue.

The growth of multi-national business activity is one of the factors which have led to this situation. However, it is not absolutely clear exactly how much responsibility should be laid to this source. One feels intuitively that it should be considerable, but there is little or no evidence that proves anything either way.

Certainly the rise of the Eurocurrency market has been a major factor. This pool of floating money is now over the $50 billion mark, starting from a base of $1 billion in 1959. Partly it has been created by purely structural factors, like the continuing weakness of the US economy during the 1960s; partly it has grown specifically to meet the needs of multi-national companies, which can arrange their activities to take advantage of any pools of unused currency all round the world. To service this need, the banking system has been spreading round the world as well, and has been generating new services, like the relatively new global cash management services, whereby a bank or a consortium of banks takes a multi-national's total cashflow, manipulating it so that the firm's transactions are fulfilled with the minimum cost (exchanging currencies can add $500,000 per annum at least to the cost of running a large multi-national). These schemes are well suited to take advantage of differences in interest rates round the world. There is evidence that international interest rates are in fact converging[8] as a result, so that this is one weapon which the economic manager will find increasingly difficult to use; an alternative will have to be found for manipulating interest rates. This trend is probably inevitable, given the degree to which national economies have become interpenetrated through the activities of the multi-nationals.

It is interesting to note that the yen, which was the most grossly under-valued currency at the time of writing, had managed to escape revaluation, despite the almost unanimous feeling of economists that it should. The Japanese government sought to take its time over such a move, and play with alternatives such as encouraging Japanese firms to speed up their investment outside Japan. This is because the Japanese economy is fairly independent of multi-nationals. Its own firms are basically exporters who are under sufficient government surveillance to find it difficult to speculate against the yen. Few foreign firms are heavily enough involved for their transactions to carry weight.

The second major weapon of the economic managers is the manipulation of tax rates. Again, this is a power which is being eroded, though this is not a trend which is too easy to document. Corporation taxes seem to be stabilizing themselves in Europe around the 45–50 per cent mark, and it is hard to see that any European country could continue levying total corporate taxes of much over this level; if it did, it would be hampering its own companies and would be discouraging investment from multi-nationals. The general level of taxation may not be the only factor at work. In 1970, the British government switched its investment incentive scheme from an investment grant system to one of depreciation allowance (basically, this means companies get their refunds on capital outlays at a later date). This promptly changed the economics of a number of capital-intensive schemes which were on the drawing board; it led to Shell, amongst other companies, cancelling some major investment plans in the north-west of England, with the attendant fear that planned expansion would be based elsewhere in Europe. A further restriction on British control on the national economy is that it would now be virtually meaningless for a left-wing government to try nationalizing the assets of major corporations; ICI's activities in Britain are so integrated with its refineries on the continent of Europe that a nationalization could be sabotaged effectively if European countries decided to retaliate against the subsidiaries. This is even more so where the firm is foreign-owned; nationalizing the British end of IBM would be worthless, since its products are designed solely for processing in other IBM plants round the world; certainly the British computer firm, ICL, would find the IBM plant pretty useless. Similarly Ford's operations in Britain would be of marginal use without the European assembly plants, the North American distribution system, and the North American models for some of its components. Besides this, any hostile act to an American subsidiary could be countered by American retaliation against the US subsidiaries of firms like ICI or BP.

Yet another problem facing the economic manager is that wage demands may become increasingly aimed at 'European' rather than purely British goals.[9] To some extent this will come about because trade union members will no longer be concerned with getting parity of earnings within England in certain industries, but will start demanding parity with Continental workers in the same firm. This is most likely to happen first within the car industry, but this could be a potent conveyor-belt to ensure that inflation in the major economies is transferred to the others. Even without conscious internationally-oriented union action, the same phenomenon could occur because the overall profitability of a company may depend on key operations in Britain which may affect highly profitable operations in other markets. Thus Chrysler was attacked by the Tory government in early 1971 because it made a highly inflationary wage settlement with its British employees; and yet, from a Chrysler viewpoint, the concessions made sense. A model from their British plants was to be sold under their banner in the United States as their answer to the small cars manufactured by GM and Ford. To have fought the British unions would have meant a strike, just at the time when they were planning to get the cars to their American dealers; therefore an inflationary settlement in Britain made perfectly good sense in the short run for the company. This type of pressure should get worse; as these industries move further toward oligopolistic entities, companies with flows of products and components across the world will be increasingly vulnerable to union action.

What, therefore, is happening is that the British economy, like that of most of its competitors, is becoming very vulnerable to the actions of a few key decision-makers, a number of them owing no national loyalty to the UK. However, the nationality of the owners of the multi-nationals should not be over-stressed. British Leyland, the surviving British auto firm, has been busy rationalizing its activities in the southern hemisphere, with the aim of making its Australian and South African operations totally independent of components and models from England. There was even talk at one time of using Australian-based models for exporting to the US market rather than European-made models. All of these are decisions which affect the British economy. On balance, they will probably lead to a decrease in exports to these areas which should be compensated by higher dividend and royalty payments; but whether the UK economy will benefit is a moot point.

In particular, the economy is becoming vulnerable in those marginal situations where a multi-national has a 'green field' plant which it could locate anywhere in a number of locations within Europe. There are some obvious strictly economic factors which will make certain countries more attractive than others (wage rates, taxation levels, investment incentives, etc.). However, given the planning time needed to put up a major plant and the length of life during which the plant will be running, it is fairly obvious that a mathematical calculation that in, say, August 1971 company X will get its best rate of return by an investment in country Y would be a pretty arbitrary way of making the decision. Economic management may well become a tactical question of providing the right psychological climate to attract the potential investor.

There is not a great deal of hard evidence about exactly what factors actually influence management when making major investment decisions.[10] At one extreme, the international headquarters of one company were moved allegedly so that the relevant managing director could be near his mistress; at the other, you find the manager who is perfectly happy to sit down with government officials to discuss his company's investment plans, and is open to persuasion. Companies like IBM have a policy of not affecting a country's balance of payments too much one way or another; if they are running a large trade deficit with one country, they will aim to establish manufacturing or servicing operations of a magnitude sufficient to balance the negative flow.

Intuitively one feels – though again one cannot demonstrate statistically – that the policy increasingly followed by the Labour government's Ministry of Technology was the right one; Wedgwood Benn, the ex-Minister, had put it that the Labour government was the first in the world to establish full diplomatic relations with the multi-national corporations operating in Britain. In one series of meetings, the Ministry and the company concerned spent two months talking about the agenda for a weekend meeting between Benn and his top civil servants and the top international management of the company concerned; in the course of such meetings, the company's past record and future intentions regarding export policies, research policies, and investment plans would be discussed, and the company could raise such issues as government purchasing policies and likely developments in the government's policy towards research. More graphically, the recent travels of Henry Ford II resemble the voyages of a royal personage more than anything else; thus, during the search for the site for the Ford transmission plant which was established eventually in France, Mr and Mrs Ford were fêted at the presidential palace. (One should note that the somewhat mysterious way in which the location of this plant suddenly shifted from north-east France to Bordeaux at the time of a particularly crucial by-election affecting the French Prime Minister is evidence of the political element in the location of such plants.) Again, during the 1971 Ford strike Henry Ford arrived in England on a routine visit, to be swept to 10 Downing Street for a working lunch which was attended by the Prime Minister and the three leading economics ministers; many a head of government would like to have this amount of time with these ministers! But then, few heads of government control investment decisions which can affect the British balance of payments by at least £10 millions annually.

Obviously, it would still be possible to reject all foreign investment and to survive. There would be obvious dis-economies. For instance, even with increasingly close links to French and American computer firms, it is by no means certain that ICL, the remaining British computer company, can in fact survive in a world where IBM controls 65 per cent of the non-Communist world market. In a closed economy, a government could keep the company going; but it would obviously produce computers which were more expensive or less advanced than those on the world market. The car industry and a number of others would be similarly affected. Economically, it would not make much sense.

However, a wave of economic nationalism is growing round the world which would challenge such strictly economic conclusions; how fast this movement grows in Britain would obviously depend on the relative success of our remaining independent firms. To some extent, one can argue that we are about to go through the phase which areas like the southern USA went through earlier this century, as regional economies became integrated into the national economy; local firms were bought up, and economic decision-making was moved to the darkest crannies of Wall Street, Detroit or elsewhere. The South did not like the idea of losing control either; but, within limits, it has transferred its allegiance to the national economy over the years, and the days when local businessmen who fought the process were local heroes (and ultimately became bankrupt) have been forgotten.[11]

For nations like Canada, the transitional approach is obviously going to be extremely painful, since her only logical approach is to come to an understanding with the US. Countries like Britain do at least have the politically acceptable option of encouraging links like the Dunlop–Pirelli merger, where the necessary integration is between partners of roughly equal standing. Again, a solution for ICL which involves co-operation and perhaps eventual mergers with a French company as well as one of the smaller American ones is psychologically less threatening than disappearing into IBM's maw.

The last constraint on the British economic planners is the nationalistic one. Irrespective of entry into the EEC, it is likely that an increasing proportion of the British economy will fall under foreign ownership. Economically, there is no particular reason why this process should be slowed down; however, we have yet to find out under which circumstances a burst of popular economic nationalism may force the government to slow down the process. The British government has been one of the most tolerant in Europe to the incoming multi-nationals; it cannot be assumed that it will remain so in all circumstances.

NOTES

[1] John H. Dunning, *The Role of American Investment in the British Economy* (London, 1970).

[2] Marie T. Bradshaw, 'US Exports to Foreign Affiliates of US Firms', *Survey of Current Business* (May 1969).

[3] See note 1 above.

[4] A. E. Safarian, *Foreign Ownership of Canadian Industry* (New York, 1966).

[5] D. T. Brash, *American Investment in Australian Industry* (Canberra, 1966).

[6] C. Layton, *Transatlantic Investment* (Paris, 1967).

[7] H. Lind and C. Flockton, *Regional Policy in Britain and the Six: Community Regional Policy* (London, 1970).

[8] See R. H. Cooper, 'Towards an International Capital Market', Paper presented to the International Economic Association (Algarve, August–September 1969).

[9] For a fuller description of the trade union developments see Louis Turner, *Invisible Empires* (London, 1970), ch. 6.

[10] Yair Aharoni, *The Foreign Investment Decision Process* (Harvard, 1966), provides some information on this aspect.

[11] For a highly readable account of one such incident, see John Brooks *Business Adventures* (London, 1969), in which he describes the attempt by the Memphis owner of Piggly Wiggly Stores (*sic*) to destroy Wall Street.

XI Britain's Place in the Changing World

F. S. NORTHEDGE

In the affluent society, nearly all but millionaires regard themselves as middle-class. Similarly, in international relations the millionaire States, or super-powers, are easily distinguished – especially two of them, the United States and the Soviet Union – while most other States, except the obvious dwarfs like the Gambia and Fiji, tend to place themselves about in the middle rank. Some writers have written learned papers, the conclusion of which is that a super-power simply disposes of more power than the average State. We can go further than this, and say that the United States and the Soviet Union are about the only States today capable of fighting a full-scale war, involving the most up-to-date of modern weapons, with some chance of surviving – though no doubt with a decimated population – which also have the means for waging such a war. Perhaps we should also demand of the super-power a certain universality of interests in the sense of a claim to be consulted about problems in any part of the globe, together with some capability of enforcing that claim.

By the former criterion, Communist China is still potentially, rather than actually, a super-power. While her ability to survive a thermo-nuclear conflict, in however crippled a condition, is perhaps equal to, if not greater than, that of America or Russia, she seems as yet not to possess the full complement of the most monstrous armaments of the present day. As to the second qualification – capability to affect events in any part of the globe – the Peking régime undoubtedly aspires in that direction, but is still far from reaching its goal; even the United States and the Soviet Union have limited capability to influence events in each other's sphere of interest.

However that may be, by either test there can be no question that Britain – like France and Federal Germany, or even such comparative newcomers to the middle rank of States as Canada and Australia – cannot claim to stand alongside the acknowledged giants, even though their spokesmen sometimes speak as though they could. It has been credibly estimated that six hydrogen bombs of the greatest destructive capacity now available, if dropped in the seas surrounding Britain, would suffice to extinguish all life in these islands, provided the winds were blowing off the water into land, as they normally are in the eastern Atlantic; and a similar drop from the bucket of nuclear power now commanded by the super-powers would do the same for almost any other country. It is true that Britain has her own nuclear capability and, with her Polaris submarines, now disposes of second-strike capability like that of the giant powers, at least in token form; but no one pretends that this could protect the British people if war à l'outrance were to break out. The British so-called 'independent' nuclear deterrent exists, partly as a nominal contribution to the total nuclear deterrent force of the North Atlantic collective defence system, and partly to make the conquest of these islands not worth while if the aggressor has to suffer even Britain's minor retaliatory nuclear force, supposing that we are truly alone (as in 1940), and our allies, especially the United States, are standing aside with arms folded – as indeed America was in 1940.

None the less, it is not quite so clear that British ministers in the years since the Second World War have even yet abandoned their claim to the second attribute of the really heavyweight class of State – namely, the claim to have a say in the settlement of international questions in any part of the globe. Most British administrations since 1945, Conservative and Labour alike, have claimed the right to be consulted, to encourage and to warn – if we may use Asquith's famous phrase (borrowed from Bagehot's *The English Constitution*) about the prerogatives of the Crown – in almost any international problem in almost any part of the world.

Formally, this right to be consulted is symbolized by Britain's permanent membership of the United Nations Security Council, by her now almost obsolete participation in four-power occupation rights in Germany and Berlin, and by her prominent role in almost all the collective defence arrangements which have been constructed, largely under United States leadership, to contain the Communist heartland of Euro-Asia since 1949: the North Atlantic Pact of April 1949, the South-East Asia Treaty Organization (SEATO), formed in 1954, and the Central Treaty Organization (CENTO), formerly the Baghdad Pact, which was created in 1955. Though Britain was never admitted into the Anzus Treaty of 1951, which links together the United States, Australia and New Zealand in a regional collective defence system for Australasia, and the United States–Canadian defence arrangements covering North America, she is associated with both by her membership of the Commonwealth and the overlapping NATO and SEATO defence systems. The Conservative government formed in June 1970, in establishing a five-power Commonwealth defence force based on Malaysia and

Singapore involving Australia and New Zealand, has sustained the link with the Anzus system. It is true that the north-western Pacific is now even formally beyond the reach of British interests, and that Britain has no part in the US–Japanese mutual security system, but Britain's long-standing support for the admission of Communist China into the United Nations shows that even this region is not yet entirely outside the range of British concern. Britain still has her Far Eastern colony, Hong Kong, but makes no pretence of being able to defend it if Communist China attacked it with all her forces. Moreover, almost as though to match the seemingly exclusive character of US–Japanese mutual defence arrangements in the north-western Pacific, the Heath government's apparent determination to join energetically with South Africa in defence of the sea routes round the Cape of Good Hope – even though, so far, the security of these routes has created no great anxiety in Washington – shows the continuing will of the British government to have their say in relatively distant affairs.

But, even more than these purely formal residues of the world-wide extent of British interests as the government defines them, albeit with the country's shrunken status of the present day, is the apparent determination of British ministers to have their voice heard in the highest councils of the greatest powers in whatever region of the world; this has been as true of Labour ministers, who might have been expected to renounce a continuing world-wide role for Britain as an obsolete relic of imperialism, as it has of Conservative leaders, who might be suspected of sustaining Victorian imperial dreams in the new guise of a world-wide concern for peace and stability. When Mr Attlee (as he was then) flew to Washington in November 1950 to caution President Truman against the use of nuclear weapons in the Korean war; when ministers in the two Labour governments of 1945–51 rejected the role offered to them of leadership in the early stages of integration in Western Europe, in preference to their assumed function as partners with the United States in the conduct of global politics with the Communist world; when Mr Harold Wilson, as the British Prime Minister from 1964 to 1970, grasped with both hands at every opportunity to act as a go-between in the Vietnam war, and Mr George Brown, when Foreign Secretary, issued formula after formula for settling the Middle East imbroglio – it was evident that to be Labour was by no means to be a 'little Englander'. In the election campaign in the autumn of 1964 which gave the Labour party power after thirteen years of Conservative rule, Mr Wilson accused the then Prime Minister, Sir Alec Douglas-Home, of indulging in illusions of grandeur about British power in the world, questioned the worthwhileness of the British nuclear deterrent, and advised the country to concentrate on the 'white-hot' technological revolution at home. But, exactly one month after winning that election, Mr Wilson said at the Lord Mayor's banquet in Guildhall in November: 'We are a world power, and a world influence, or we are nothing.'¹ Was this whistling in the dark to keep up courage? Only compassionately could it be so described.

If Labour ministers since 1945 have been under the spell of the continuing notion of Britain as a world power with a right to be consulted on world problems, Conservative spokesmen have held the same conviction. Sir Winston Churchill, Conservative Prime Minister from 1951 until 1955, was hardly the man to be satisfied with a back seat for Britain in world affairs. He energetically pressed for the unification of Western Europe, with its own army and integrated command structure, but left no doubt that Britain, with all its extra-European concerns, would not make any contribution to it other than moral encouragement. Sir Winston tended to see the supreme issues of world affairs as still determined by the Big Three of Yalta and Potsdam, though perhaps with Britain as the counsellor of the new American giant rather than as a world power in her own right. Churchill's Foreign Secretary, and later his successor as Prime Minister, Sir Anthony Eden, said quite bluntly in a speech at Columbia University, New York, in January 1952, that 'the American and British peoples should each understand the strong points in the other's national character'.

> 'You will realize [he went on] that I am speaking of the frequent suggestions that the United Kingdom should join a federation on the continent of Europe. . . . We know that if we were to attempt it we should relax the springs of our action in the Western democratic cause, and in the Atlantic association which is the expression of that cause'.²

Mr Harold Macmillan, on the other hand, entered office as Prime Minister in January 1957 at a time when West European integration was proving itself to be more than the abstract dream many British politicians and Foreign Office officials took it to be, and was realistic enough to appreciate that, if the six States of Western Europe did succeed in forging a full-blown political combination on supra-national lines, Britain would then run the risk of being excluded from the new channels of diplomatic communication, running between Washington, Europe and Moscow, which would come into existence. Hence, with the declaration that Britain 'must be at the centre of power', Mr Macmillan reached the momentous decision in 1961 to reverse British policy towards Europe, which had been followed since the French took the initiative with a proposal to pool the coal and steel industries of Western Europe in June 1950 and to apply to join the Six. At the

N*

same time – and evidently without fully realizing that President de Gaulle wanted to see Britain enter Europe as a European power, and not as a junior partner of the United States – Mr Macmillan elected to continue the larger oceanic role for Britain by reaching the Nassau agreement on Polaris submarines for Britain with President Kennedy in December 1962.

After Mr Macmillan's retirement as Prime Minister in 1963, his successor, Sir Alec Douglas-Home, emerged as a distinctly 'greater Britain' man, though with no small disdain for the new Afro-Asian countries, a majority in the General Assembly of the United Nations, with which Britain must remain on good terms if she wished to be taken seriously in the world outside Europe. Sir Alec's claim in the General Election campaign in 1964 was that Britain's status as an independent nuclear power gave her, if not quite total, at least an appreciable degree of parity with the United States and the Soviet Union; the combination of the three nuclear powers in negotiating and concluding the partial nuclear test ban treaty in August 1963 as good as restored Britain, in Sir Alec's own words, to the status of 'one of the opening batsmen in the world cricket team' – or, if preferred, to the place once hers in the great days of Yalta and Postdam. All this, as we have seen, was stuff and nonsense to the Leader of the Opposition, Mr Harold Wilson; but no sooner had the two men changed places than practically the same tune was sounded on the government bench, modulated by some cat-calls from the seats behind.

It is curious to observe the reversals of attitudes between the Conservative and Labour parties on the subject of the Commonwealth. Labour leaders have emerged as Commonwealth men since 1945, partly because the post-war Commonwealth, with its increasing Afro-Asian members, was to some extent a Labour creation; India and Pakistan, granted independence by the Attlee government in 1947, were the foundation stones of the new Commonwealth of the post-war period. At the same time, Labour leaders sided with the struggle of the coloured Commonwealth countries for economic development and equality; it echoed and extended their own struggle on behalf of the underprivileged at home. Yet it is also hard to acquit the Labour party of regarding the Commonwealth as a new and more altruistic source of long-suppressed national pride, a new reason why the world should continue to regard Britain as a leader in world affairs – but now for its social ideals and achievements rather than for its military and imperial power of the past.

Returning to the theme of Conservative opinion on Britain's international status, Mr Heath, then Leader of the Opposition, supported the Labour government's decision in May 1967 to make a second application to join the European communities, but tended to see an enlarged Western Europe rather as a community potentially equal in power to the United States and the Soviet Union, than as a contrivance to enable Britain to deal successfully with her chronic economic problems. Much in the manner of Franz-Jozef Strauss, the CSU leader in Federal Germany, he advocated the formation of a single European nuclear deterrent, to be based on the existing British and French nuclear forces, and to be held 'in trust' by Britain and France for the rest of Western Europe. This notion was immediately repudiated by Prime Minister Wilson and his colleagues.

Immediately after his surprising victory in the General Election of June 1970, Mr Heath lost no time in asserting that the British voice would be heard loud and clear in the world and speaking with strictly British accents on behalf of strictly British interests.

'I speak today [Mr Heath said in his address to the twenty-fifth session of the UN General Assembly] for a newly elected British government committed to vigorous policies in the interests of the security and prosperity of the British people. I make no apology for defining so plainly our objectives before this assembly.'[3]

Mr Heath confidently begged to differ from African Commonwealth statesmen such as Dr Kenneth Kaunda of Zambia, who visited London to talk to the new British ministers about African affairs in October 1970, and on the effects of a resumption of the sale of British arms to South Africa. In an interview given to *The Times* on 26 October 1970, Mr Heath seemed to set little store by the Commonwealth and insisted that Britain was quite capable of pursuing her own interests in the world, which she had every right to do, without, if need be, Commonwealth support.

'In the talks I have been having recently with so many leaders of the Commonwealth countries, I found there is now a growing realization that Britain cannot be taken any longer for granted and that there are British interests and British concerns, as well as their own, of which they must take account.[4]

Throughout these statements Mr Heath minced no words in insisting, first, that Britain meant to pursue her own national interests and, secondly, to continue making her contribution to international peace on a world-wide scale.

These ideas were further underlined by the Conservative government's Defence Policy Statement for 1970, published a week after the Prime Minister's United Nations speech. In this the new Defence Minister, Lord Carrington, proposed, while claiming to prune the military budget, to reverse the previous Labour government's decision substantially to bring an end to the British military presence east of Suez by the close of 1971. While the statement was cautious about the future role of British forces in the Persian Gulf, it outlined quite unequivocally the government's intention to join with Australia, Malaysia, New Zealand and Singapore in the formation of a force to promote stability in the vast region of South-East Asia. The British contribution was to be modest indeed: five frigates or destroyers on station; a British battalion group, including an air platoon and an artillery battery; a detachment of Nimrod long-range maritime recon-naissance aircraft; and a number of helicopters.[5] But the force was supposed to symbolize a British determination to contribute to peace-keeping forces far removed from Europe and the Mediterranean, to which the former Labour government had proposed normally to limit the British military effort overseas. In much the same way, Mr Heath's apparent resolve to breathe new life into the Simonstown Agreement with South African naval defence, notwithstanding moral protests against the policy at home and abroad, symbolized – or seemed intended to symbolize – a British intention independently to assess threats to the peace in distant parts of the world, and to make an independent contribution towards suppressing them.

The grounds on which British ministers have claimed a 'seat at the top table' are worth examining, before we consider whether this claim is still supportable. In the first place, there is the long British experience of international affairs, and Britain's former status as *primus inter pares* in the old European international system before the giant powers of today emerged. It is not much more than half a century ago that a British Foreign Secretary could say, with truth, that 'it is in the hands of the British Empire; and if they will that there shall be no war, there will be no war'.[6] There are good reasons, too, for thinking that Adolf Hitler in the late 1930s considered Britain, not Soviet Russia, as the country with which he must finally make peace if his régime was to survive. It is true that Britain committed many major errors of foreign policy in those inter-war years, and has committed more since, notably the under-estimation of Western Europe's capacity to create viable forms of integration, and the over-estimation of British power to wage war from a sound economic base during the Suez crisis in 1956. Nevertheless, when compared with that of the United States – the acknowledged leader of the democratic States since 1945 – British insight into international realities, especially those affecting the allied Western democracies as a whole, has been good.

British ministers, notably of course Winston Churchill, were quicker than the Americans to grasp the implications of the expansion of

Soviet power in Europe at the end of the Second World War. Yet, once the Atlantic Alliance had been forged in 1949 – again in no small measure owing to British initiative and resourcefulness – Britain acted as a salutary restraint upon the United States during the crisis-ridden 1950s. Afterwards, following the death of Marshal Stalin in March 1953, Britain realized the necessity for peaceful coexistence between the Communist and non-Communist worlds long before President Kennedy delivered his famous address on the same subject at the American university in Washington in June 1963. Britain, too, has shown greater grasp of the importance of normalizing relations with Communist China than the United States, while never committing the folly of believing that the Peking government could be displaced by Generalissimo Chiang Kai-shek's ageing régime on Formosa. Above all, British policy on the principal world issues, especially relations with the Communist world, has never suffered from the alarming *bouleversements* of United States policy, the swings of the pendulum from crusading anti-Communism to a close community of interest with the Soviet Union, exemplified in President Kennedy's undertakings in his inaugural address to shrink from no sacrifice or burden in order to liberate men everywhere from oppression and wrong, and the cautious tone of President Nixon's statement of 18 February 1970 entitled 'American foreign policy in the 1970s; a new strategy for peace'. Britain may have made grievous mistakes about policies for the defence of her own interests, but, as far as alliance policy is concerned, her record compares favourably with that of the United States.

The second ground on which British governments have claimed a right of representation wherever issues affecting the international community as a whole are under consideration is the widespread character of British interests, even with the diminished economic resources of the country during the post-1945 period. These interests are of two kinds, the general and the particular. No country has a greater stake than Britain in stability in international relations on a global scale; a small, densely populated island, depending for half its food supplies and raw materials on imports from almost every part of the globe, and despatching to almost every part of the globe exports equivalent in total value to one-fifth of its gross national product, cannot but be hideously vulnerable in the event of full-scale conventional or nuclear war, or even prolonged unrest abroad which interferes with the world's channels of communications or its economic prosperity. Britain's policy, because of her economic character and interests and her geographical situation, must continue to be, as Lord Avon (then Mr Anthony Eden) described it in the 1930s, as one of peace 'at *almost* any price'. Secondly, and in a more particular sense, British economic interests, the markets in which she sells, the suppliers by whom she is provisioned, and the investments from which she draws valuable invisible earnings, are all scattered, like hostages to fortune, throughout the world. The super-powers may on occasion be impatient with British verbal interventions designed to alleviate tense situations from the Middle East to South-East Asia, but British ministers are in duty bound to do what they can, however little, so vital to a world-wide trading nation are the Suez Canal, the Straits of Malacca, the Cape of Good Hope, and other avenues of world commerce.

But there is yet a third reason, lying perhaps more in the sub-conscious of British ministers than in their verbal utterances, why Britain claims, and no doubt with some justification, a certain say in the deliberations of the mighty. This is the essentially unfanatical character of the British political style, the rejection of ideological extremes, the refusal to believe that points of view – no matter how outwardly irreconcilable and bitterly pressed home – cannot be harmonized provided that the talking goes on long enough. Connected with these assumptions is the characteristic, and possibly sometimes unfortunate, British belief that in the long run compromises can be effected between, and bridges thrown across, opposing positions which will at least remain durable for the foreseeable future: politics, in other words, is in British eyes often a matter of living from day to day – 'Give us peace in our time, O Lord'. That may be called a recipe for improvidence, for patched-up solutions which fail to stand the test of time. On the other hand, pretensions to solve the dilemmas of the human predicament once and for all can be, not merely erroneous, but capable of dragging down into destruction all which stand in their path.

This long-standing British style in foreign affairs derives partly from the prominence in the minds of British ministers of commercial and business considerations. 'Nothing', said Mr Heath in his United Nations speech on 23 October 1970, which we have already quoted, 'contributes more effectively to development than expanding trade'. Trade, business, commerce – all assume the existence of a middle term – a price, in short – which makes settlements practicable between buyers and sellers, employers and workers, borrowers and lenders. In precisely the same way, the middle term is obtainable in politics, always provided that the bargaining is sustained long enough; in fact, what is politics – especially international politics, British ministers for two centuries or more seem to have asked themselves, except building a framework in the midst of which the true work of society – business – can be carried on successfully? Lloyd George in his dealings with Lenin in the early 1920s, Neville Chamberlain in his with Adolf Hitler in the late 1930s,

Harold Macmillan in his with Nikita Khrushchev in the 1950s – all refused to believe that dictators could throw away opportunities for trade relations profitable to both sides in the interests of a fanatical ideology.

After the unspeakable horrors of the First World War, Neville Chamberlain and his followers could not bring themselves to believe that the head of a great European State, Germany, could, with eyes open, plunge his people into war for the second time, all for the sake of such a mystical and barely intelligible ideal of establishing a world-wide hegemony of the *Herrenvolk*, whatever that might be. They were proved wrong, but not altogether discreditably so; as Professor A. J. Toynbee wrote, the British of the 1930s were 'prematurely humanized'.[7] In much the same way, Mr Macmillan seems to have considered that Mr Khrushchev surely could not persist in sinning against the light by pressing forwards with the inflexible Marxist belief in the inevitability of violent conflict between Communist and bourgeois worlds. It could be argued that the failure of the Paris 'summit' conference in May 1960, for which Mr Macmillan had worked so hard, was as much the nemesis of the business man's illusions as was the entry of German troops into Bohemia in March 1939 in defiance of the Munich Agreement. But – who can tell? – perhaps even the Russians have also learned that the unromantic British philosophy of 'trade and let trade' is at least one convincing formula which could save the world from destruction at its own hands.

The other source of this essentially unfanatical spirit of British policy is the almost instinctive assumption of Britain's rulers, to be traced back at least as far as the Tudors, that quarrels with other nations – and alliances, too – should not be based upon ideological persuasions, or religous convictions, or beliefs concerning the better ordering of society. Since the Second World War, many people in Britain and other countries have condemned the Chamberlain government of the late 1930s for not waging war earlier than they did against Hitler, on grounds of his ideological tenets and the horrors which flowed from them, and even perhaps for sympathizing with the Nazi régime out of a feeling of ideological affinity with any anti-Communist force; and for not taking sides in, say, the Spanish civil war, which, the critics say, was merely the rehearsal on Spanish soil of the European war which broke out in September 1939, thereafter quickly to transcend its European limits. But, looking back from today, it is not hard to see that Chamberlain's instinct was the correct one. It is an unfortunate reality that no country is strong enough, or in the last resort prepared to pay the price, to take issue with every other nation in which man's inhumanity to man is practised. In the last resort, a government can only command the resources – and their people will usually only allow them to command the resources – to defend the State's own interests, narrowly conceived: survival, security, territorial integrity, independence, economic well-being, and so on. Once a government commits the country on an ideological issue in foreign relations, it runs the risk of jeopardizing perhaps the most powerful resource the country has: the cohesion and solidarity of its own people.

Generally speaking, a national people can be relied upon to make sacrifices on behalf of their national existence when patently threatened from abroad; but most people most of the time will not fight for abstract ideals, which may in any case be highly controversial among them. 'I simply ask you one thing: please be careful', the British Foreign Secretary, Anthony Eden, warned Leon Blum in July 1936, when the French Prime Minister told him that he intended to meet the Spanish Republic's request for arms against Franco.[8] No doubt Eden meant that Blum might find himself involved in a civil war in his own country, especially after the Paris riots of February 1934. The same words might well have been spoken to the Americans in 1954 when they committed themselves to the defence of the South Vietnamese régime on behalf of the principle of protecting a free people against aggression or subversion from outside. Fourteen years later President Johnson said that he could no longer continue to lead a nation fundamentally divided over the ideological issues of the war in Vietnam.

In this age, with its nightmarish potentialities for mutual destruction – the United States alone is said to possess nuclear capability sufficient to destroy the world six hundred times over – the British assumption that somehow, by patient bargaining and give-and-take, even the most intransigent opponents can somehow learn to rub along together, is one too vital to lose from sight; the weaker Britain is in world affairs, the weaker is the voice of moderation, toleration, restraint. Sometimes these virtues mean blindness – or what seems like it – to the most sickening inhumanities inflicted upon others, like the Soviet suppression of the Hungarian revolution in 1956 and of the liberalization programme in Czechoslovakia in 1968; but politics must always represent the weighing of greater evils against lesser evils. The British acceptance of the inescapability of evil in one form or another is ultimately more humane and civilized than the simplistic view that, by wiping out our present opponents, we can enjoy an unalloyed freedom from evil for evermore.

Claims to be heard in the highest councils of the nations, however, no matter how well justified in theory, cannot usually be upheld in international affairs unless there are resources behind them, and in this respect Britain has fallen from the highest rank since 1945. What is more, the most fundamental axiom of foreign policy, that commitments must never be allowed to exceed the means to fulfil them, though obvious enough, has rarely if ever sunk into the minds of the British people in the twentieth century. It is commonly acknowledged that Britain is at the present time a middle-range power, but scarcely anywhere in this country is thought being given to the question of what this implies in terms of national behaviour within the international system. The result is that British foreign policy since 1945 has been repeatedly overtaken by events, decisions have been imposed on governments after years of struggling in the contrary direction, and policy has swung wildly from the over-estimation of British power in the Suez crisis of 1956 to what now looks like an under-estimation when the Wilson government not only declined to use force against the illegal declaration of independence by Rhodesia in November 1965, but loudly proclaimed its intention not to use force.

The insufficiency of resources has been primarily an economic one. In 1945, at the end of a world war which had consumed practically all the income-earning assets of Britain abroad, an expansion of British exports to a volume something like two-thirds greater than imports was required to fill the gap in payments from overseas represented by the wartime sale of foreign investments. At first it was thought that this economic problem was mainly due to the after-effects of the war until, at the time of Marshall Aid (1948–52), the balance of payments problem was recognized to be more deep-seated. Then followed the great re-armament drive following the outbreak of the Korean War in June 1950; the resulting pressure on Britain's trading accounts with the outside world drove the second post-war Labour government out of power, and there has followed up to the present the depressing, recurring cycle of boom followed by 'squeeze'. The basic difficulty appears to be that British industry cannot take full advantage of the continuous technological revolution which alone can make it competitive in world markets, without new investment; but this draws resources from current production into producing the means of increasing income in the future. The result is rising prices, which serve to depress the sale of exports and increase the demand for imports. Then investment has to be slowed down, with the resulting falling back of the efficiency and competitiveness of British goods sold abroad. And so the cycle goes on. Neither political party has yet discovered the solution to this self-generated pattern of one step forward, one step back.

In part, too, the problem is psychological. The British people as a whole, after their sacrifices in two World Wars and their active military service, ostensibly in the cause of peace, in different parts of the world in peacetime, have tended to feel since 1945 that they deserve a respite from international responsibilities, and a taste of its good things while they are enjoying life: some butter after so much margarine. Our modern world of commercial advertisement and televised invitations to possess the good things of life has also made the poorer people wonder why their standard of living should not approximate more to that of the well-paid or the slick profiteers who mushroom in present-day society. Mr Bonar Law, as he gazed round the room at a dinner party in the 1920s, when asked by his wealthy hostess what 'these tiresome strikers *really* want', could reply: 'Well, I suppose a little of all this, madam', and the answer would be even more pointed today, when almost all the old social deference of the ordinary man and women towards the rich has vanished.

Yet, if the British people are told that, if they want jam – or rather, caviare, today – on their bread, they must work for it, they tend to reply that other people – employers, civil servants or the politicians – must look into that. Or, if told that the British annual rate of increase in the gross national product (2½ per cent) is one of the lowest in the world among advanced countries, and that expectations of rising standards of living depend upon it increasing faster, the reply is that competition between countries to exceed each other's rate of increase in gross national product may be all right for the Germans and Japanese, but is too much of a rat race for a people like the British, who deserve a better deal out of life after saving the world from domination by the Germans or Japanese. It seems all too easy for the British to forget that, with Empire and the wealthy foreign possessions of the past gone, they have only their own native skill, ingenuity and effort to rely upon; and that the living standards they now demand as of right cannot be maintained or improved merely by blaming other people for acquiring too big a share of the national cake, while demanding a bigger slice of it themselves. The world no longer owes Britain a living, if it ever did; she must earn one by the sweat and tears of all her people. Few politicians, it seems, are willing to risk losing votes by reminding them of these unpalatable facts.

There are three circumstances in particular which have placed Britain in a situation since 1945 in which her governments have repeatedly been compelled to reduce her commitments to the level of available resources: the fact that, unlike the continental European States, Britain never lost her sovereignty during the Second World War, which left people in this country to conclude that they need make no radical change in their international position after the war; the intense competition between the Conservative and Labour parties for the goodwill of the electorate, which resulted in their both promising an improvement in the voter's standard of living if they were returned to office, without requiring anything extra from him by way of effort or sacrifice; and, finally, the slowness of the British people and their governments to realize that the comfortable old three-circle concept of British foreign policy – embracing the Atlantic community, the new, post-war Commonwealth, and Europe – had eroded as the years since the war passed by, so that the first two had lost much of their significance, leaving Europe as the sole convincing theatre of British diplomacy and the source of its future strength.

The point is worth developing. The three-circle concept of Atlantic community, Commonwealth and Europe was developed, especially, by Winston Churchill in the high noon of his prestige after the Second World War. It implied that Britain would try to ensure that developments in none of the three circles would ever force Britain to choose one and discard the others. The Atlantic community, to take the first, was in all essentials another name for the former 'special relationship' with the United States; British ministers never took seriously the call by certain British pressure groups for an Atlantic federation or confederation, based on the Atlantic Pact of April 1949. Without doubt the United Kingdom had a most vital role to play in moderating the intense anti-Communist feeling sweeping the United States during the Eisenhower–Dulles régime in the 1950s. By the time the United States came to understand the reason behind coexistence with the Communist world in the 1960s, they were grasping at what was to them a novel idea, but one which Britain had been preaching for years. Yet, no sooner had American administrators seen the necessity for living along with the Communist States, than they realized that the real dialogue was between themselves and Moscow. What further need was there for Britain to stand at America's side and whisper counsels of restraint or encouragement into the American ear? Add to this the extraordinary leap forward of Russia and the United States into space exploration, and the development of ever more formidable weapons in the shape of multiple missile systems, and it was clear that Britain could no longer claim the role of equal partnership with the United States, but only the role of perhaps the most important of America's allies.

The Commonwealth in its turn suffered a similar erosion but for different reasons. As we have seen, Labour politicians on various grounds acquired great affection for the Commonwealth; it appealed to the feelings of patriotism latent in all of us, but somewhat suppressed, for obvious reasons, in politicians of the Left. No doubt, too, the Commonwealth, in Labour eyes, represented a possible solution to one of the central problems of the twentieth century – that is, the problem of equality and justice as between white and coloured races. The

United Nations, while being legally committed to the cause of racial equality, seemed unable to achieve it in practice; perhaps the Commonwealth, with its unique history, could do better. The ending of this hope came with the withdrawal of South Africa from the Commonwealth in 1961 as a result of the campaign against apartheid by the black African member States of the Commonwealth.

The Commonwealth in the end proved not to be the formula for agreement between South Africa and the rest of the world. This was further underlined by the Rhodesian crisis of 1965, the acute phase of which began with the unilateral declaration of independence by the Smith régime in November of that year. Coloured member States of the Commonwealth regarded the British refusal to use force against the Smith régime as an indication of racial bias; on the other hand, many people in Britain wondered why they in particular should be singled out to fight for the ideal of the equal rights of men in southern Africa, while the independent African States themselves sat in the sidelines and hissed and booed the British performance. To add to the forces undermining Commonwealth unity, the British wish, from 1961 onwards, to join the European communities angered some Commonwealth countries, since it seemed to threaten their livelihood from trade with Britain. At the same time, the British people tended to be moved by these unhappy events to suspect that other countries only consented to remain in the Commonwealth for what they could get out of it in materialistic terms. Whatever truth there may be in these conflicting arguments, it is indeed hard to see how, if Britain were really swept into the integration process in Western Europe, she could continue to stand out as an independent country within the Commonwealth.

What all this seems to add up to is that Britain has hitched her wagon to the European *caravanserai* – not so much out of affection for the ideal of European unity *per se*, or belief in its feasibility, but because the other two theatres of British diplomacy, the Atlantic world and the Commonwealth, have lost much of their plausibility. It is interesting to recall the reaction almost of relief with which British people seem to have received the news that the late General de Gaulle had vetoed, in January 1963, British membership of the Common Market, and the somewhat one-sided estimates in a British White Paper published early in 1970 of the heavy cost, in terms of increases in the cost of living, which would result from British membership of the European Economic Community.

At the time of writing (July 1971) it seems almost as though the majority of the British people would welcome failure in the Conservative government's efforts to join the European Communities. The idea of European unification makes no heart beat faster in Britain, which is no doubt why the Government, in setting out the case for British membership of the European Communities in its White Paper of July 1971, referred only in the most cautious terms to political union as the ultimate goal of the Communities, and reiterated that no loss of sovereignty was involved in the proposed policy of going into Europe.[9] And yet this was despite the fact that almost every dispassionate economic and political consideration seems today to point in the direction of larger groupings of States. Indeed, one might wonder whether Britain had any real option in foreign policy other than that of entry into the European Communities. Mr Harold Wilson said, in proposing the second attempt to enter the European Communities in June 1967, that 'it is not a case of Europe or bust'; and yet the alternatives – as, for instance, joining an economic union with North America and hence becoming a small fragment of the American colossus – seem even less attractive.

Now, more than ever, is it vital for Europeans, including the British, to consider what they stand for, and what they mean to do in a rapidly changing world situation. Could the present Soviet–American *détente* ever develop in a manner detrimental to European interests? No European can be sure. With the gradual emergence of Communist China, shall we see, as prophesied in George Orwell's novel *1984*, a continuous pattern of hostilities between the three super-powers, America, China and Russia – first two against one, then a different two against a different one – with Europe left, perhaps, to suffer the nuclear fall-out? These are by no means dreamy possibilities; every day makes them seem more real. Europe, the ancient birthplace of modern diplomacy, and still the home of some of the most gifted people in the world, must think of where the major directions of its policy lie as these larger outlines of world politics shift and change. In this process, by reason of her experience and almost ingrained political sagacity, Britain has a role of the first importance to play; but she can only measure up to her immediate responsibilities by putting aside the illusion that she can 'go it alone' in a world in which even the medium-sized State's sovereignty is more of a myth than a reality, and the equally dangerous feeling of despair that, in dealing with foreign States at close quarters, we are always bound to come off worse than the rest.

NOTES

[1] *The Times*, 17 November 1964.
[2] *New York Times*, 12 January 1952.
[3] *The Times*, 24 October 1970.

[4] Ibid., 27 October 1970.
[5] *The Times*, 29 October 1970; Cmnd 4591, 1970.
[6] Sir Austen Chamberlain in the House of Commons, 24 March 1925 (*House of Commons Debates*, vol. 182, col. 322).
[7] The Royal Institute of International Affairs, *The World in March 1939* (London 1952), p. 34.
[8] *Les événements survenus en France de 1933 à 1945: rapport* (Paris, 1951), vol. 1, p. 216.
[9] *The United Kingdom and European Communities* (Cmnd 4715, 1971).

INDEX

Acheson, Dean, 100, 108
Adenauer, Konrad, 44, 47
Adlington, Lord, 136
Alphand, Hervé, 40
Anglo-French deterrent, 82–3, 115–16
Anglo-Malayan (Malaysian) Defence Agreement, 87–8, 92–3
Attlee, Clement, 194
Australia, 94, 98

Baghdad Pact (1955), 41
Beer, Samuel, 46
Bell, Coral, 40
Berlin Blockade, 38
Bevin, Ernest, 36, 37–8, 40, 42, 43
Blue Streak, 47
Blum, Leon, 202
Bottomley, Arthur, 162
Brandt, Willy, 77, 116
Briand, Aristide, 40
Britain, 122
  consequences of membership of EEC, 54–69
  decline as a world power, 35–50
  entry into EEC, 46–50, 65, 143
  'East of Suez' policy, 50, 71, 86–101, 198
  NATO and policy towards, 70–84
  relationship with United States, 40–5, 98, 103–19, 205
  Rhodesia and, 150–70
  ties with Commonwealth, 120–45
Brown, George, 48, 194
Brussels Pact (March 1948), 37
Burnham, Forbes, 135
Byl, P. K. van der, 167

Canada, 30, 72
Carrington, Lord, 91–4, 197
Castro, Fidel, 27
Chamberlain, Austen, 40
Chamberlain, Neville, 201
China, 96, 192
Churchill, Winston S., 39, 43, 195, 198, 205
Colombo Plan (1951), 42
COMECON, 17
Commonwealth, 41–2, 48, 196
  Rhodesia and, 168–9
  ties with Britain, 120–45, 197, 205–6
Commonwealth Strategic Reserve, 87
Council of Europe, 40

Crowe, Eyre, 144
Cuba, 27
Czechoslovakia, 17, 27, 38, 75

Dalton, Hugh, 37
de Gaulle, Charles, 16, 36, 46–7, 49, 72, 107, 113–14, 116
Diego Garcia, 100, 119
Douglas-Home, Sir Alec, 91, 129, 131–2, 170, 196
Dulles, John Foster, 41, 43–4, 110–11
Duncan Report, 35, 84
Dupont, C. W., 156

Eden, Anthony, 43–4, 195, 199, 202
European Defence Community (EDC), 29, 44
European Economic Community (EDC), 22, 23
  Power of institutions of, 54–69
  Sovereignty in, 30–3, 60–1, 67–9
European Free Trade Association (EFTA) (November 1959), 46, 48, 172

Field, Winston, 154
Ford, Henry II, 190
Foster, William, 76

General Agreement on Tariffs and Trade (GATT), 172, 176
Germany, 36–7
  Ostpolitik, 50, 77–8
Gordon-Walker, Patrick, 145
Gorton, John, 94

Hague Declaration (December 1969), 49
Halifax, Earl of, 35
Hancock, Sir Keith, 126
Harmel Report (December 1967), 75
Healey, Denis, 72, 90, 110, 144
Heath, Edward, 49, 50, 73, 74, 82, 84, 90–1, 114, 135, 139–40, 196–7, 200
Herz, J., 20

Iceland, 26–7
India, 42–3
Indian Ocean, 92, 99–100, 142
Indonesia, 88, 92, 93, 94
International Monetary Fund (IMF), 172

209